Śamatha and Vipaśyanā

Śamatha and Vipaśyanā

An Anthology of Pith Instructions

Composed and Translated by
B. Alan Wallace and Eva Natanya

Wisdom

Wisdom Publications
132 Perry Street
New York, NY 10014 USA
wisdom.org

Library of Congress Cataloging-in-Publication Data
Names: Wallace, B. Alan, author, translator. | Natanya, Eva, author, translator.
Title: Śamatha and vipaśyanā: an anthology of pith instructions / composed and translated by B. Alan Wallace and Eva Natanya.
Description: New York, NY, USA: Wisdom, [2025] | Includes bibliographical references and index. | Text in English. Translation from Tibetan.
Identifiers: LCCN 2024054620 (print) | LCCN 2024054621 (ebook) | ISBN 9781614299691 (hardcover) | ISBN 9781614299868 (ebook)
Subjects: LCSH: Vipaśyanā (Buddhism) | Śamatha (Buddhism)
Classification: LCC BQ5630.V5 W355 2025 (print) | LCC BQ5630.V5 (ebook) | DDC 294.34435—dc23/eng/20250304
LC record available at https://lccn.loc.gov/2024054620
LC ebook record available at https://lccn.loc.gov/2024054621

ISBN 978-1-61429-969-1 ebook ISBN 978-1-61429-986-8

29 28 27 26 25
5 4 3 2 1

Cover image: Arapachana Manjushri Kham Province, Eastern Tibet; 19th century Pigments on cloth Rubin Museum of Himalayan Art Gift of Shelley and Donald Rubin C2006.66.464 (HAR 925).

Cover design by Jess Morphew. Interior design by PerfecType.

Printed on acid-free paper that meets the guidelines for permanence and durability of the Production Guidelines for Book Longevity of the Council on Library Resources.

Printed in Canada.

Maitreya, know that all mundane and supramundane virtuous qualities, whether of śrāvakas, bodhisattvas, or tathāgatas, are the result of śamatha and vipaśyanā.

—*Saṃdhinirmocana Sūtra*

Contents

Preface xi

Part I.
Core Teachings in Translation by Buddhist Masters

Atiśa and the Kadam Tradition:
Bodhicitta and the Middle Way 3

1. Blaming Everything on a Single Culprit 19
   Atiśa (982–1054)
2. Cutting the Root of Suffering and Equalizing Excitation and Laxity 27
   Atiśa
3. A Guide to the Two Realities 41
   Atiśa
4. Commentary to Atiśa's *Pith Instructions on the Middle Way* 45
   Prajñāmokṣa (11th c.)
5. The Eight-Verse Mind Training 67
   Geshé Langri Thangpa (1054–1123)

The Words of Mañjuśrī: Sakya Pith Instructions to Transform One's Life 69

6. Practical Instructions on *Parting from the Four Types of Clinging* 75
   Sachen Kunga Nyingpo (1092–1158)

7. Unmistaken Practical Instructions on *Parting from the Four Types of Clinging* 77
   Sakya Paṇḍita (1182–1251)

8. Meditation Guidance on the Mahāyāna *Parting from the Four Types of Clinging* 79
   Khenchen Appey Rinpoché (1927–2010)

The Words of Mañjuśrī and Vajrapāṇi: View, Meditation, and Conduct as Taught to Tsongkhapa 83

9. Guidance in the View of the Middle Way 93
   Jé Tsongkhapa (1357–1419)

10. A Shower of Siddhis: Guidance in the View of the Middle Way as a Song of the Four Recollections 95
    The Seventh Dalai Lama (1708–1757)

11. The Synthesis of Practice 99
    Jé Tsongkhapa

12. On the Union of Śamatha and Vipaśyanā 103
    Jé Tsongkhapa

13. Garland of Supreme Medicinal Nectar: Questions and Answers 119
    Lhodrak Drupchen Namkha Gyaltsen (1326–1401)

The Words of Avalokiteśvara: Śamatha and Vipaśyanā in the Mahāmudrā Tradition of Mingyur Dorjé and Karma Chakmé 145

14. The Cultivation of Śamatha 149
Karma Chakmé (1613–1678)

15. The Analytical Cultivation of Vipaśyanā 173
Karma Chakmé

Śamatha, Vipaśyanā, and Guru Yoga in the Teachings of Düdjom Lingpa and Sera Khandro 201

16. Taking the Aspect of the Mind as the Path 213
Düdjom Lingpa (1835–1904)

17. How to Establish the Ground of Being by Way of the View 223
Düdjom Lingpa

18. Prerequisites for Practice of the Direct Crossing Over 233
Sera Khandro (1892–1940)

Contemporary Masters of Dzokchen and Mahāmudrā: Domang Yangthang Rinpoché 243

19. A Summary of the View, Meditation, and Conduct 247
Domang Yangthang Rinpoché (1930–2016)

Contemporary Masters of Dzokchen and Mahāmudrā: Drupön Lama Karma 257

20. Experiential Instructions on Śamatha 261
Drupön Lama Karma (b. 1953)

Part II.
Pith Instructions for Aspiring Contemplatives in the Twenty-First Century
B. Alan Wallace

1. A Lamp for Dispelling the Five Obscurations: Pith Instructions for Achieving Śamatha in the Dzokchen Tradition 285
2. The Crucial Point of Settling Mental Speech in Its Natural State of Silence by Settling the Respiration in Its Natural Rhythm 297
3. Taking Consciousness as the Path: A Synthesis of Pith Instructions from Our Lineage Gurus 313

List of Oral Commentaries 331

Bibliography 337

Index 343

About the Authors 359

Preface

On the afternoon of July 20, 2023, when I was meditating in my solitary retreat above our hermitage, Miyo Samten Ling, in Crestone, Colorado, just as dawn was breaking in India on the day commemorating the Buddha's first turning of the wheel of Dharma, it occurred to me that I had in my possession a number of unpublished translations that I had made over the past forty years, containing precious teachings by some of the greatest Buddhist masters in history. I had offered oral teachings on many of these texts, but since each one is relatively brief, I had not yet found the right context in which to publish each one of them. With a burst of inspiration, I spent several hours compiling those translations, like a garland of pearls, into a sequence of pith instructions on the core meditations of *śamatha*[1] and *vipaśyanā*[2] to share with others in the hope that they would cherish and benefit from them as I have. Over the course of many months, Eva Natanya and I have added to and embellished this garland to form the present anthology.

The garland begins with two conversations between Atiśa—who is often viewed as a speech emanation of Guru Rinpoché, or Padmasambhava, and

1. *Śamatha* (pronounced "shamata") can be explained briefly as follows: By focusing the attention continuously, without being diverted to other objects, the mind eventually rests naturally upon its chosen object. When the exceptional joy and bliss of pliancy in body and mind arises, then this concentration (or *samādhi*) becomes śamatha. This arises simply from maintaining concentration of the mind inwardly, without being distracted, but it does not rely upon fathoming the actual nature of any phenomenon.

2. *Vipaśyanā* (pronounced "vipashyana") can be defined as the wisdom imbued with the exceptional bliss of pliancy that arises in dependence upon śamatha and comes about by the power of discerningly investigating the phenomenon upon which it focuses.

also as a previous incarnation of the Paṇchen Lama—and his foremost disciple, Dromtönpa—recognized as an emanation of Avalokiteśvara and a previous incarnation of the Dalai Lama. When I first encountered these two conversations, I felt I had slipped into a time machine and was there with them in person, reveling in the profound wisdom and humor that this noble guru and his beloved disciple shared together.

In this anthology, I have then added Atiśa's seminal text on the nature of the two realities—obscurative and ultimate—followed by a commentary by his Indian disciple Prajñāmokṣa on Atiśa's *Pith Instructions on the Middle Way*.

The next jewel I plucked from my satchel of translations was *The Eight-Verse Mind Training* by Geshé Langri Thangpa, one of the great masters of the Kadam tradition founded by Atiśa and Dromtönpa. This was the text His Holiness the Dalai Lama chose for his first public teaching in the West, in the summer of 1979 in Mont Pèlerin, Switzerland, for which I had the tremendous honor of serving as his interpreter.

Earlier in my personal history, after studying the Tibetan language for one year at the University of Göttingen, I spent the summer of 1971 at the Tibet Institute in Rikon, Switzerland, in preparation to leave for Dharamsala that autumn. During that time I had the good fortune to come under the guidance of the Sakya lama Sherab Gyaltsen Amipa. It was he who taught me my first Tibetan Buddhist text, a commentary on the classic pith instruction *Parting from the Four Types of Clinging*, revealed in a divine vision by Mañjuśrī to Sachen Kunga Nyingpo, the son of the founder of the Sakya order. This essential Dharma is revered by masters of all schools of Tibetan Buddhism, and I have included here a translation of a concise commentary on this revelation by Sakya Paṇḍita Kunga Gyaltsen, Sachen Kunga Nyingpo's grandson (who is regarded by many as an incarnation of Atiśa), as well as translated excerpts from an eloquent twenty-first century oral commentary given by Khenchen Appey Rinpoché.

Then, shortly after His Holiness's teachings in Mont Pèlerin in 1979, I again had the privilege of interpreting for him in Zollikon, Switzerland, as he granted his oral commentary to the Seventh Dalai Lama's root text *A Shower of Siddhis: Guidance in the View of the Middle Way as a Song of the Four Recollections*, which summarizes four crucial themes of practice, beginning with guru yoga and finishing in the nonduality of appearances and emptiness.

To provide context for this composition by the Seventh Dalai Lama, it is preceded here by the "special, practical instructions that the noble Mañjuśrī directly bestowed upon the great Dharma king Tsongkhapa," upon which the Seventh Dalai Lama explicitly based his *Song of the Four Recollections*. It is well known that Jé Tsongkhapa, like Sachen Kunga Nyingpo before him, experienced visionary encounters with the embodiment of the wisdom of all the buddhas, appearing in the form of the youthful Mañjuśrī. Initially, these encounters took place through the mediation of Lama Umapa Pawo Dorjé, who had gained the extraordinary ability to converse directly with Mañjuśrī and was able to pose Tsongkhapa's questions to this divine being. The root verses of Tsongkhapa's longer text, *Guidance in the View of the Middle Way*, were revealed to Lama Umapa and Jé Tsongkhapa in 1392.

Following these parallel texts from Tsongkhapa and the Seventh Dalai Lama on *Guidance in the View of the Middle Way*, a second revelation to Tsongkhapa included here captures the essence of Mañjuśrī's pith instructions even more succinctly. This *Synthesis of Practice*, spoken directly to Lama Tsongkhapa himself, consists of core instructions for practice in solitary retreat and bears a distinctive resonance with the teachings of Mahāmudrā and Dzokchen. To show Tsongkhapa's mature understanding of how to meditate on emptiness on the basis of śamatha, and then how to unite this vipaśyanā with śamatha while following the scriptural traditions of India as well as the Kadam tradition of Atiśa, we have included the crucial sections on the union of śamatha and vipaśyanā from Tsongkhapa's *Concise Presentation of the Stages on the Path to Enlightenment*.

Moreover, we have chosen to include another important visionary text that appears in Tsongkhapa's collected works, the *Garland of Supreme Medicinal Nectar: Questions and Answers*, which was actually transmitted and written down by one of Tsongkhapa's beloved teachers, Lhodrak Drupchen Namkha Gyaltsen. This Kadampa teacher, also known as Khenchen Lhodrakpa, was renowned for his visionary encounters with Vajrapāṇi, the "Lord of Mysteries," who is revered as the great bodhisattva who heard and transmitted many of the Buddhist tantras to the human realm. According to its vocabulary and content, this text is unmistakably an instruction in core Dzokchen practice, though as far as we know, Tsongkhapa never studied with any Nyingma teachers directly and never commented directly on Dzokchen within his writings. Thus, the presence of this text is a critically important anomaly within Tsongkhapa's life story, about which more will be said in "The Words of Mañjuśrī and Vajrapāṇi," below. As Tsongkhapa himself was well known for his reverence for the Kadam tradition, which traces back to Atiśa and Dromtönpa, and also for his transmission of the Ganden Aural Lineage of instructions on Mahāmudrā stemming from his encounters with Mañjuśrī, these four texts from Tsongkhapa's corpus offer a sublime bridge between what became the Geluk tradition of Mahāmudrā transmitted by Tsongkhapa, and the Kagyü and Nyingma lineages of Mahāmudrā and Dzokchen, which are represented in the texts appearing later in this volume.

While His Holiness has been my root lama since I first met him in 1971, the lama for whom I am most deeply indebted for what little knowledge and understanding I have of the Mahāmudrā and Dzokchen traditions of Indo-Tibetan Buddhism is the Venerable Domang Gyatrul Rinpoché, an incarnation of the *mahāsiddha* Kunsang Sherab, the first throneholder of the Palyul lineage of Tibetan Buddhism, and whom His Holiness the Sixteenth Karmapa identified as an incarnation of the great Kagyü and Nyingma master Karma Chakmé Rinpoché. I requested him to be my lama in the spring of 1990, and that summer he asked me to interpret for him in a public teaching he gave at the Shambhala Meditation Center in Los Angeles, on "Śamatha and Vipaśyanā in the Mahāmudrā Tradition" as presented by Karma Chakmé. It was many years later that I was able to complete my translation of this masterpiece; namely, chapters fifteen and sixteen of

Karma Chakmé's *Great Commentary to Mingyur Dorjé's Buddhahood in the Palm of Your Hand*, which comprise the next two texts in this anthology.

Then in 1995, Gyatrul Rinpoché first introduced me to Düdjom Lingpa's magnum opus among the visionary Dzokchen teachings that he, Düdjom Lingpa, received from his root lama, the speech emanation of Padmasambhava appearing in the form of Saroruhavajra, or the Lake-Born Vajra: *The Vajra Essence*. Over the next two years, as Gyatrul Rinpoché granted me the oral transmission and his detailed oral commentary to this work, with the request that I translate it into English, I was deeply inspired, and I have devoted myself to the study and practice of these teachings ever since. I have thus included here two short commentarial works by Düdjom Lingpa, which present quintessential instructions on the practices of śamatha and vipaśyanā within the Dzokchen tradition. The first is his commentary on the visionary teachings he received on śamatha from Saroruhavajra; the second is a commentary on vipaśyanā inspired by the visionary teachings that Düdjom Lingpa received from Avalokiteśvara and Saroruhavajra, respectively.

Following these highly streamlined excerpts describing the core practices for attaining insight into the ultimate nature of existence, we have inserted an excerpt from an even more advanced commentary by Sera Khandro on the direct crossing over (*tögal*): the final set of practices undertaken to achieve the rainbow body, here described as "liberation as a body of light." This excerpt, however, is taken from the section on the preliminaries to the direct crossing over and includes a clear description of the level of realization required to engage in such a practice effectively, as well as a magnificent presentation of guru yoga in a Dzokchen context. Sera Khandro's moving description of the guru yoga associated with the tögal practice can be applied at any level of the Vajrayāna path and indeed such guru yoga is essential for an effective practice of śamatha and vipaśyanā in the Dzokchen context. Though the root text for Sera Khandro's commentary was revealed by Düdjom Lingpa himself, Sera Khandro received the teachings on it from her own guru and spiritual partner, the fifth son of Düdjom Lingpa, Tulku Drimé Öser.

Returning to my personal narrative, it was much later, in the fall of 2015, that I was invited to co-interpret with the Nepalese monk Sey Namkha Dorjé for Domang Yangthang Rinpoché—widely regarded as an emanation of the Indian Dzokchen master Vimalamitra, and a lifelong friend of Gyatrul Rinpoché—as he granted his oral commentary to his own root text on Dzokchen titled *A Summary of the View, Meditation, and Conduct*, which is the next work translated in this volume. His Holiness Penor Rinpoché, the eleventh throneholder of the Palyul lineage and the third holder of the title of Supreme Head of the Nyingma,[3] referred to Yangthang Rinpoché as the most highly realized of all living Nyingma lamas, so this was a most precious opportunity to receive direct teachings from him. Yangthang Rinpoché first commented on excerpts from Atiśa's teachings in the *Book of Kadam* (*Kadam Lekbam*),[4] and followed this with pith instructions on Dzokchen. All of this was given to a small group of students from around the world at his home, the Yuksum Residency in western Sikkim.

When I was studying in Dharamsala in the early 1970s, the lama whom His Holiness appointed to hold Dharma classes for foreigners in the Library of Tibetan Works and Archives was Geshé Ngawang Dhargyey, who combined enormous erudition in Buddhism together with a boundless flow of love for his students and enthusiasm for the Dharma. After I had studied under his guidance for more than a year, he gave an oral commentary on Maitreya's *Ornament of Clear Realizations* (*Abhisamayālaṃkāra*), in which the five sequential paths to buddhahood, beginning with the Mahāyāna path of accumulation, are presented in great depth and detail. In the midst of those teachings, he spoke with me privately and admonished me to make it my priority to reach the Mahāyāna path of accumulation in this lifetime. There was nothing more important for me to do, he emphasized, and if I didn't make it a priority in this lifetime, what else had I found that was more

3. Tib: *snga 'gyur rnying ma'i dbu 'dzin khri rabs*. Penor Rinpoché held this title from 1993 to 2001.

4. See Thupten Jinpa, trans., "The Sayings of Master Atiśa," in Jinpa, Thupten, *Wisdom of the Kadam Masters* (Somerville, MA: Wisdom Publications, 2012), 23–25, 31–36.

important to do? I understood from his teachings on this subject that he was primarily pointing to the medium stage of this path, which is imbued with what is known as *gold-like bodhicitta*, in which one's resolve to reach buddhahood will never decline until enlightenment. One gains the stability of such bodhicitta through a mind that has been made serviceable through śamatha and has begun to unite this śamatha with the wisdom of vipaśyanā. What impressed me so intensely from his teachings was that once one reaches this gold-like bodhicitta, one's insight into identitylessness is deep enough to protect one from ever losing one's resolve. For example, even if one sees someone doing such enormous evil that one might be tempted to give up on sentient beings, one realizes that such behavior is not an inherent quality of the sentient being, and one's determination to guide such a person to enlightenment becomes all the stronger. Thus, once one reaches the medium stage of this path of accumulation, one is assured of being a bodhisattva in all one's future lives until one achieves perfect enlightenment. One will never again be parted from the holy Dharma or the path to enlightenment, and one's resolve to reach enlightenment will be irreversible. Geshé Ngawang Dhargyey's words made a deep and lasting impression on me, and they have guided my practice ever since.

Returning to the more recent past, on November 29, 2017, I was granted a personal audience with His Holiness the Dalai Lama in Dharamsala, India, during which I told him about our plans for creating a Center for Contemplative Research in Tuscany, Italy, with an emphasis on guiding earnest practitioners to reach the Mahāyāna path of accumulation. He agreed to write an endorsement for this project and added that while the Buddha's second turning of the wheel focuses on emptiness as an object, the third turning, including the *Tathāgatagarbha Sūtra*, presents buddha nature, the ultimate nature of the mind, as a subject, which leads smoothly into the teachings of Mahāmudrā and Dzokchen. For many years prior to this audience, His Holiness had been emphasizing, during his public discourses in both the East and West, the crucial importance of achieving śamatha. When I commented that this would be a central practice to be emphasized in our Center for Contemplative Research, His Holiness was supportive, but he also replied that nowadays virtually no one has achieved śamatha.

A year later, it was to my enormous delight that I learned of a Bhutanese meditation master named Drupön Lama Karma, of whom it was said that he had become highly accomplished in the practice of śamatha, and through years of intensive meditation retreats progressed significantly along the path of Mahāmudrā and Dzokchen. Later, in the autumn of 2019, I had the honor of inviting him to teach in my hometown of Santa Barbara, California, where he graciously agreed to my request to narrate his own intensive experience of practicing and sustaining śamatha within the Mahāmudrā and Dzokchen tradition. This extraordinary account, including his guided meditation, was then meticulously translated into English by Khenpo Namchak Dorji, Khenpo Sonam, Eva Natanya, and me, and this is the next priceless entry in this volume, and the final translation.

All of the texts mentioned above were written by and for people who lived in traditional India and Tibet prior to the global domination of Western culture by way of European colonialism. When I read the extraordinary account *Stories from the Early Life of Gyatrul Rinpoche*, I was again struck by how profoundly different the world in which Gyatrul Rinpoché had grown up and been educated is from our world today, and the disparity appears all the greater when we read the biographies of great Indian masters such as Atiśa. While the Buddha predicted the gradual decline of the Dharma that he transmitted, the degree of degeneration we have witnessed over the past century has been and continues to be cataclysmic. Especially with the rampant, worldwide spread of European scientific materialism, hedonism, and consumerism since the mid-nineteenth century, the traditional worldviews, values, and ways of life promoted by the great spiritual traditions of Asia have been almost entirely eclipsed. While Buddhists take refuge in the Buddha, Dharma, and Sangha, the ultimate refuges, or ideals, of secular modernity are in general the pursuit of wealth, power, and status.

In the early 1970s, a young European man was granted an audience with

His Holiness the Dalai Lama, during which the young man bemoaned the drawbacks of our current degenerate age, commenting that perhaps the time was past when genuine realizations born of meditation could be gained. His Holiness, while acknowledging the reality of this decline in modern civilization, forcefully countered that even today, if one practices as Milarepa did, one will achieve realizations like those of Milarepa.

Out of deep humility and allegiance to Buddhist tradition, even highly accomplished Buddhist adepts commonly deny that they have any realizations, despite having spent, in some cases, many years in single-pointed meditative retreat. Yet when people today hear this, they may take such accounts literally and conclude that authentic, sustained meditative practice can no longer bring about any profound realizations or accomplishments—in other words, if there was ever a time of great siddhas with extraordinary meditative accomplishments, that time has passed.

It is for this reason, I believe, that in recent years, His Holiness has publicly acknowledged on repeated occasions that he has indeed reached and advanced along the Mahāyāna path of accumulation, with its requisite realizations of uncontrived bodhicitta and profound insight into the nature of emptiness. This is an epic accomplishment, for to reach and proceed to the medium stage of just the first of the five Mahāyāna paths is to achieve a state of irreversible spiritual transformation. As mentioned earlier, one has not only become a bodhisattva, but due to the protective power of one's understanding of emptiness, in all future lives—however many there may be—one will always be a bodhisattva until one achieves the perfect enlightenment of a buddha. Considering our countless previous lifetimes, when we have wandered in the darkness of ignorance from one rebirth to another among the six classes of existence, the prospect of setting out on a straight, irreversible path to enlightenment, without ever again being separated from the holy Dharma and our sublime gurus, is utterly breathtaking. What could be a more significant, unprecedented accomplishment in this lifetime than to effect such a radical departure from the beginningless pattern of wandering blindly in the miseries of saṃsāra?

I am certain that it was with the same motivation as His Holiness the Dalai Lama that Drupön Lama Karma accepted my audacious request to share his experience of practicing and gaining advanced experience of śamatha. He knew that the benefits of such disclosure would outweigh the tradition of concealing one's realizations from others. Buddhist practitioners in today's world are in great need of inspiration and the confidence that if we wholeheartedly devote ourselves to authentic meditative practice, we may achieve the results of the great adepts of the past. Drupön Lama Karma is indeed a great adept of the present, who has not only reached firm stability in śamatha but ascended along the path of the four yogas of Mahāmudrā. My gratitude for his generosity in sharing his experiences with us is boundless.

But can we, as Buddhists who have been heavily conditioned—physically and mentally—by the ravages of modernity possibly follow in his footsteps? The same teachings and practices that have been effectively transmitted over the centuries to traditional Buddhists may not yield the same results in today's world, where we have been to varying degrees caught in the vortex of materialism, overstimulation by the enticements of hedonism, and the mad pace of life in the pursuit of financial success, or at least financial security. This all takes an enormous toll on our bodies and minds, which need to be restored to balance before we can effectively devote ourselves to the profoundly transformative and liberating practices of traditional Buddhism.

The various practices of śamatha are precisely designed to refine and restore balance to our energetic nervous systems and to free our minds from the power of the five debilitating obscurations that obscure the natural clarity, eudaimonic well-being, and peaceful nonconceptuality of consciousness. These five obscurations were taught by the Buddha as (1) hedonism, or fixation on the allures of the desire realm; (2) malevolence, or ill will directed toward oneself or others; (3) laxity of attention and dullness of the mind; (4) excitation (which leads to distraction) and anxiety, or else rumination upon regrets about the past; and (5) afflictive uncertainty, or lingering doubts with respect to one's practice or the teachings.

The Buddha declared in the *Sāmaññaphala Sutta*, "So long as these five obscurations are not abandoned, one considers oneself as indebted, sick, in bonds, enslaved, and lost in a desert track." That is, as long as our interests are staked on what the objects of the senses can give to us, we are like a person in debt to the whole world. As long as there is even the slightest wish that someone not gain the happiness they desire, we are sick, like an insane person. As long as the mind has not been trained to overcome the tendencies for laxity or dullness, the mind is weighed down like someone bound in leg irons. As long as the mind is still drawn away by compulsive conceptualization—whether this involves uplifting thoughts that pleasantly agitate the mind, or depressing thoughts that lead to anxiety or guilt—we are enslaved by such conceptual disturbances that overpower the mind. As long as we are continually oscillating between possibilities of how we might or might not practice, about what might be true—or might not—and reminding ourselves that we still cannot be totally sure that this practice will lead to the goals it is supposed to lead to, and maybe we should try something else . . . we are lost in a vast desert with no trail, no compass, and no food.

The Buddha furthermore offered the following analogies for these five obscurations of the conditioned mind: While the nature of the mind is like a luminous, pure pool of water, when it is obscured by hedonism, it is like water mixed with dye. When obscured by malevolence, it is like boiling water. When obscured by laxity and dullness, the mind is like water covered over by moss. When obscured by excitation and anxiety, it is like agitated water whipped by the wind, and when obscured by afflictive uncertainty, it is like turbid, muddy water.

The intensive practice and achievement of śamatha, in which the mind is freed from these five obscurations and imbued with the five *dhyāna* factors,[5] plays a crucial role in reaching and progressing along the path, for an

5. These will be explained in "A Lamp for Dispelling the Five Obscurations" in part 2 of this

ordinary mind encumbered with these five obscurations is hardly a suitable vessel for the noble pursuit of achieving irreversible spiritual freedom. For one who aspires to the total enlightenment of a buddha, in order to have the capacity to lead all sentient beings beyond suffering and its causes, reaching this first entryway to the Mahāyāna path, the path of accumulation, entails developing a mind in which the firm resolve to achieve enlightenment for the benefit of all beings (or bodhicitta), arises spontaneously and continuously, without needing to generate it over and over again based on reasoning. This is known traditionally as "uncontrived bodhicitta." But for a mind to be stable enough to hold such a sublime intention and resolve continuously—and subliminally, even when not explicitly thinking about it—it needs to be a mind that has consistently overcome the debilitating diseases and limitations imposed by the five obscurations. Effectively, it is a mind that has achieved a level of meditative stability either very close to or equivalent to that of actual śamatha.

Practically speaking, to attain such stability, one requires both inner and outer prerequisites, including a suitable environment and spiritual maturity. As Atiśa wrote in his *Lamp for the Path to Enlightenment* (*Bodhipathapradīpa*): "As long as the conditions for śamatha are incomplete, *samādhi* will not be accomplished even if you meditate diligently for a thousand years."[6]

A suitable outer environment for the successful practice of śamatha is said to have the following qualities:

- Food, clothing, and so on are easily obtained.
- You are not disturbed by people, carnivorous animals, and so on.
- The location is pleasant; that is, it is not inhabited by enemies, and so on.
- The land is good; that is, it does not make you ill.

volume.

6. Unless otherwise cited, all translations are by the authors.

- You have good companions; that is, their ethical discipline and views are similar to your own.
- The location has few people around during the daytime and little noise at night.

And the necessary psychological, or inner, qualities to be cultivated in tandem with one's practice of śamatha are as follows:

- Having few desires
- Contentment
- Having few concerns and activities
- Pure ethical discipline
- Completely dispensing with conceptualization involving desire and so on

Based on my own experience over the past forty years, such a supportive outer environment, in which one is surrounded by spiritual friends who aid in one's cultivation of the inner, psychological prerequisites, is exceedingly difficult to find, both in the East and the West. For this reason, over the past several years, in collaboration with friends around the world, I have been developing two branches of the Center for Contemplative Research: Miyo Samten Ling Hermitage, or Hermitage of Unwavering Samādhi, in Crestone, Colorado, USA, and Drölkar Ling, or Sita Tara Hermitage, in Tuscany, Italy.

During this time, I have also been guiding about twenty to twenty-five meditators engaged in full-time retreat in these two retreat centers and elsewhere, who are devoted to achieving śamatha and reaching the Mahāyāna path—through realizing uncontrived bodhicitta—in this lifetime. In particular, since the beginning of 2023, I shared with them much earlier versions of the three sets of pith instructions included in part 2 of this volume. These were intended to help guide them in their practice and to overcome the obstacles, particularly manifestations of the five obscurations, which they have inevitably encountered along the way. Eva Natanya and I have since significantly revised and expanded these pith instructions for this volume. These are like three candles held up to the brilliant sunrays of the previous texts in this anthology, but we hope they may be of some service to aspiring contemplatives in our contemporary world who are setting out on this sacred path of śamatha and vipaśyanā.

We have included at the end of this volume a list of oral commentaries, which is composed of links to talks that directly or indirectly relate to each of the texts in this anthology. Some of these talks have historic value, such as His Holiness the Dalai Lama's teachings in Switzerland, given in 1979 during his first teaching tour in Europe, and Yangthang Rinpoché's commentary on "Sayings of Master Atiśa," given in Sikkim in 2015. If you would like to derive the greatest possible benefit from reading the texts translated here, then we encourage you to alternate between reading each text and listening to the corresponding oral commentaries for that particular text, where available.

Acknowledgments

Since I have remained in full-time retreat throughout the editorial process for this manuscript, I have relied on the assistance of two Dharma colleagues to bring this book into its current form. Eva Natanya, who had already begun editing many of these translations in previous years, has newly edited the translations for this volume, in many cases consulting several different Tibetan editions of each text. Eva also researched and composed the historical and thematic introductions to the chapters, and contributed several translations of her own. Virginia Craft contributed significantly to the biographical research and brought her sharp editorial eye to the manuscript as a whole.

We wish to extend our sincere thanks to the Buddhist Digital Resource Center, in collaboration with Internet Archive, for the treasure trove of

Tibetan texts that they offer online in the form of digital scans, from which most of the texts cited in this volume have been obtained. The full references for our Tibetan source texts and the alternative editions consulted are in the bibliography. We also wish to express our gratitude for the wealth of historical biographical material available at the Treasury of Lives, the reliable Tibetan texts and translations available at Lotsawa House, and the valuable resources regarding the Tibetan canons available at 84000: Translating the Words of the Buddha.

B. Alan Wallace
April 23, 2024, Dükhor Düchen,
the commemoration of the Buddha Śākyamuni's teaching
of the *Kālacakra Tantra*
Crestone, Colorado, USA

Part I

Core Teachings in Translation by Buddhist Masters

Atiśa and the Kadam Tradition

Bodhicitta and the Middle Way

Atiśa Dīpaṃkara Śrījñāna was born in the year 982 in Vikramapura, a major Buddhist center in what is present-day Bangladesh, and given the name Candragarbha as a prince of royal lineage. At the age of ten, disenchanted with palace life, he withdrew into the forest, where he met the brahmin Jitāri, who was a lay Buddhist scholar and tantric master. At eleven, he had his first vision of Tārā, the feminine embodiment of enlightened compassion, who became his personal deity (*yidam*),[7] and about a year later, Jitāri encouraged him to enroll in the monastic university of Nālandā for further study. There he met the realized monk Bodhibhadra, from whom he received novice vows, and he went on to study with many prominent masters, including Vidyākokila, a direct student of Candrakīrti who was also said to have realized ultimate reality, and the mahāsiddha Avadhūtipa, known as a fourth-stage *ārya* bodhisattva. The latter became Atiśa's root guru, under whom he studied for seven years (from the age of twelve through eighteen) and became an accomplished adept of Vajrayāna and particularly Mahāmudrā.[8]

At the age of twenty-nine, after dreaming that the Buddha encouraged

7. The Tibetan term *yidam* can be glossed as that which one never abandons with one's mind (*yid kyis mi btang ba*) and to which one holds firmly (*dam du bzung bya*). It refers primarily to a buddha or bodhisattva—appearing in the form of a divine being as set forth within any one of the Buddhist Vajrayāna systems—to whom one offers one's devotion in a unique or special way, hence the translation "personal deity." The Tibetan term translates the Sanskrit *iṣṭadevatā*, which literally means "chosen deity." In a Buddhist context, then, this is the manifestation of the Buddha with whom one most closely resonates or has a heart connection.

8. James B. Apple, *Jewels of the Middle Way: The Madhyamaka Legacy of Atiśa and His Early Tibetan Followers* (Somerville, MA: Wisdom Publications, 2018), 3–5, 200.

him to take ordination as a *bhikṣu*, Atiśa did so at a monastery in Bodh Gayā, where he was given the ordination name Dīpaṃkara Śrījñāna. Around the year 1014, Atiśa began his eleven years of mind training (*lojong*) in the cultivation of relative and ultimate bodhicitta under the guidance of Suvarṇadvīpa Dharmakīrti (known to Tibetans as Serlingpa), on the isle of Suvarṇadvīpa (possibly Muaro Jambi, Sumatra or else Kedah, Malaysia).

After returning to India in 1025, at about the age of forty-four, renowned now as one of the preeminent paṇḍitas in all of India, he soon accepted a teaching post at the monastic university of Vikramaśīla. In the 1030s, a king in western Tibet, Jangchup Ö, sent two successive delegations of Tibetan translators to invite Atiśa to come to Tibet to revive the Buddhadharma, which had fallen into deep decline. After much hesitation, but with the encouragement of Tārā (appearing to him first in a dream and then as three different *yoginīs*), Atiśa accepted, finally arriving in Tibet in 1042.

When the Indian mahāsiddha Padmasambhava had come to Tibet in the mid-eighth century, the Tibetan empire under the reign of King Trisong Detsen was at the height of its power. While the bodhisattva paṇḍita Śāntarakṣita ordained the first Tibetan Buddhist monks and taught the Sūtrayāna, Padmasambhava, using his powerful *siddhis*, overcame the malevolent forces in Tibet that obstructed the dissemination of the Buddhadharma and helped Śāntarakṣita to establish Samyé, the first Buddhist monastery in Tibet. Padmasambhava also took a seminal role in teaching Vajrayāna in general and Dzokchen in particular throughout the land.

But by the time Atiśa came to Tibet, the monastic tradition had degenerated, and many Tibetans believed the Sūtrayāna and Vajrayāna teachings were incompatible. As an impeccable bhikṣu, an eminent paṇḍita, a consummate bodhisattva, and an accomplished mahāsiddha, Atiśa revitalized and integrated the whole of the Buddhadharma at a time when the mighty Tibetan empire had splintered into many minor kingdoms. For these reasons he has been revered by all schools of Tibetan Buddhism to the present day.

In Tibet, Atiśa resided first in Ngari, western Tibet, for about three years, offering teachings to King Jangchup Ö, as well as to the great translator Rinchen Sangpo and to a delegation of scholars from central Tibet. At this point, Atiśa was supposed to return to Vikramaśīla; one of the translators who had originally come to India to study with Atiśa and invite him to Tibet—named Naktso Lotsāwa Tsultrim Gyalwa—had promised the abbot, the great master Ratnākaraśānti, that Atiśa would return after three years. However an ongoing war in Nepal at the time made passage unsafe, and Atiśa acknowledged that there was now no ethical fault if he did not return.[9] It was during his time in Purang, waiting near the border of Nepal, that Atiśa met a special layperson about whom Tārā had made a prophecy to Atiśa:[10] Dromtönpa Gyalwa Jungné, who would become his closest disciple. The two of them, spiritual father and son, journeyed throughout central Tibet and eventually settled in Nyethang, where Atiśa would pass away around the age of seventy-seven (ca. 1054). A year after Atiśa's passing, a temple dedicated to Tārā was built in Nyethang, and Atiśa's body was embalmed there. The following year, 1056, Dromtönpa established Radreng Monastery, from which the Kadam tradition was established.

The Dialogues

The texts we have chosen for this volume represent some of the most profound and important themes of Atiśa's teachings, though of course they cannot encompass the full array of all that he transmitted throughout his lifetime. The two dialogues here, excerpted from *The Jewel Garland of Dialogues*, draw us into the heart of a text long cherished by the Tibetan people, *The Book of Kadam*, which includes both the "Father Teachings" (of Atiśa), to which *The Jewel Garland of Dialogues* belongs, and the "Son Teachings"

9. James B. Apple, *Atiśa Dīpaṃkara: Illuminator of the Awakened Mind* (Boulder, CO: Shambhala Publications, 2019), 50.

10. Apple, 48.

(which focus on the past-life stories of Dromtönpa). Thupten Jinpa has thoroughly introduced this work in *The Book of Kadam: The Core Texts*, so here we will set the stage in the briefest way.

One of the well-educated monks who met Atiśa during his journey into central Tibet was Ngok Lekpé Sherab, who would become one of his devoted disciples and would facilitate and request many of Atiśa's teachings. A colophon placed at the end of the Father Teachings narrates that while Ngok Lekpé Sherab was immersed in study in the region of Sangphu, he had a vision of Mañjuśrī, who urged him to go at once to the region of Yerpa, where Atiśa and Dromtönpa were engaged day and night in a series of intensive dialogues on the Dharma, "resembling a golden rosary."[11] Setting off in haste, Ngok Lekpé Sherab arrived when the dialogues were nearly finished, but fortunately Atiśa helped him catch up by transmitting the Son Teachings. Ngok received a private transmission from Mañjuśrī for the main part of the Father Teachings, and then heard the final two chapters directly from Atiśa and Ḍrom themselves.[12] Other accounts say that Ngok had requested the entire set of teachings by offering a *maṇḍala* to Atiśa and Drom at Yerpa.[13]

An oral transmission of the teachings passed from Ngok Lekpé Sherab to select individuals continued in memorized teachings for about two hundred years, until the first full written form of the work was completed by Khenchen Nyima Gyaltsen (1223–1305) in the thirteenth century. Nevertheless, there was an earlier prototype of the sacred transmission written down by Phuchungwa Shönnu Gyaltsen (1031–1106), one of the three most famous disciples of Dromtönpa, sometime in the eleventh century.[14]

There is a dramatic quality to these dialogues that rings true to their legendary origins, evoking the sacred wit, spontaneity, and poignant depth

11. Thupten Jinpa, *The Book of Kadam: The Core Texts* (Somerville, MA: Wisdom Publications, 2008), 390.

12. Jinpa, 393.

13. Apple, *Atiśa Dīpaṃkara*, 63.

14. Jinpa, *The Book of Kadam*, 22–26.

that Atiśa and Dromtönpa must have shared in their close relationship of teacher and disciple, especially when one can view the individuals as emanations of Amitābha (or else Padmasambhava) and Avalokiteśvara, respectively. The identification of Dromtönpa with Avalokiteśvara (which would become crucially important for the Tibetan understanding of the Dalai Lamas as later incarnations of the same line) traces directly to *The Book of Kadam*, while the association of Atiśa with Padmasambhava, though lesser known, can be traced to respected sources within the treasure tradition of the Nyingmapas.[15] The verses that summarize each dialogue at its conclusion are actually verses from Atiśa's own written work, *Bodhisattva's Jewel Garland*, and these verses form the overarching structure of the Father Teachings.[16]

15. See, for example, Matthieu Ricard, *The Life of Shabkar: Autobiography of a Tibetan Yogin* (Boston: Shambhala Publications, 2001), 3, in one of Shabkar Tsogdruk Rangdrol's verses introducing his autobiography: "When the teachings degenerated due to changing times, Padmakara took birth again as Lord Atisha," and on page 584: "The third section [of Shabkar's *Emanated Scriptures of Orgyen*] describes how Lord Atisha Dipamkara and Tsongkhapa Lobzang Trakpa were both emanations of Padmasambhava. The second Dalai Lama, Gedun Gyatso, for instance, wrote,

> Awareness Holder, the Lord of Siddhas, Padmakara,
> Crest Ornament of five hundred [panditas], the glorious Dipamkara,
> Mighty Vajra Bearer, the exalted Lobzang Trakpa:
> I bow down to you who display the dance of various emanations."

See also the autobiography of Yeshé Tsogyal published in English as *Lady of the Lotus-Born: The Life and Enlightenment of Yeshe Tsogyal*, translated by the Padmakara Translation Group (Boston: Shambhala Publications, 2002), 189; cf. the Tibetan source text, *Bod kyi jo mo ye shes mtsho rgyal gyi mdzad tshul rnam par thar pa gab pa mngon byung rgyud mangs dri za'i glu phreng*, revealed by *Nus ldan rdo rje* (Kalimpong: Düdjom Rinpoché, 1972), 249, where Atiśa is clearly named as a speech emanation of Padmasambhava, and the Tibetan can be understood to point to Dromtön Gyalwé Jungné ("Jayākara") himself as a rebirth of Yeshé Tsogyal: "A speech emanation of Orgyen, the last rebirth of Śāntarakṣita, named Atiśa, will spread the teachings of sūtra and tantra, while I, Tsogyal, will emerge as his disciple, the translator from the family of Drom, known as Jayākara [Sanskrit for Gyalwé Jungné]." (*O rgyan gsung sprul zhi 'tsho skye mtha' zhig, a ti sha zhes mdo sngags rgya cher spel, mtsho rgyal bdag ni dza ya ka ra zhes, 'brom rigs lotsā nye gnas byed pa 'byung*). (Our translation.)

16. Jinpa, *The Book of Kadam*, 12. For a translation of *Bodhisattva's Jewel Garland*, see Jinpa, 61–64, and also Jinpa, *Essential Mind Training: Tibetan Wisdom for Daily Life* (Somerville, MA: Wisdom Publications, 2011), 25–30.

While these intimate, impromptu conversations between spiritual father and son may not seem to provide a formal teaching on how to reach the Mahāyāna path, if one takes time to allow them to penetrate one's heart, they can indeed convey the essential themes of bodhicitta—the unwavering resolve to achieve the state of buddhahood in order to fulfill the needs of all sentient beings—rooted in the four immeasurables (that is, immeasurable compassion, loving-kindness, empathetic joy, and impartiality). We find gentle prodding to realize the emptiness of all phenomena as a personal experience, as well as the tender but firm admonishment of the guru, showing us the nature of our own pride—at the fine edge between a harmful mental affliction and a wholesome state of mind that can take us forward on the path. We glimpse the heart-rending, limitless compassion of Tārā and Avalokiteśvara, and are also led to imagine the sublime perspective from which buddhas can guide all beings beyond suffering without ever sinking into the mire themselves. We learn how to eliminate conceptualization as soon as it arises, and how to transform every thought—whether useful or useless—into a deeper understanding of the ultimate nature of reality. We are shown, right here within these personal exchanges, the very qualities we need to develop within ourselves in order to actualize uncontrived, continuous, and spontaneous bodhicitta as the manifest nature of our stream of mental consciousness, which is the heart of what it means to enter the Mahāyāna path.

Middle Way Teachings

The two texts by Atiśa on the Middle Way that we include here, *A Guide to the Two Realities* and *Pith Instructions on the Middle Way* (which is embedded within its commentary by Prajñāmokṣa), appear to be texts that Atiśa taught specifically to his close disciples in Tibet, to those he felt were mature enough to receive the Madhyamaka view, or view of the Middle Way, that he himself had received from his teachers in India, especially from Bodhibhadra, Vidyākokila, and Avadhūtipa.[17]

The educated scholar-monks whom Atiśa encountered on his travels throughout Tibet, and especially near Lhasa, were familiar with the Madhyamaka teachings of Śāntarakṣita and Kamalaśīla that had been translated into the Tibetan language hundreds of years earlier,[18] but they had not yet encountered the writings of Candrakīrti, whose works would not be fully translated into Tibetan (by Atiśa's disciple Naktso Lotsāwa) until after Atiśa's death.[19] Thus Candrakīrti's interpretation of the classical works of Nāgārjuna was unfamiliar to the Tibetans whom Atiśa encountered, and at times they questioned Atiśa's explanations. It may be helpful for us to read these works of Atiśa with fresh eyes as well, perhaps as though we had never heard of the later Tibetan formulations of the distinctions between "Prāsaṅgika" and "Svātantrika," so that we can hear Atiśa's transmission of the views of the realized being Vidyākokila and the Vajrayāna *yogin* Avadhūtipa without categorizing his use of key terms according to later systematizations.[20]

At that time, even in India, interpretation of Nāgārjuna's teachings on Madhyamaka continued to be under heated debate, and Atiśa found himself in disagreement with some of his revered teachers on key points of the view. Atiśa's epic journey to the isle of Suvarṇadvīpa in order to receive from the famed Guru Serlingpa the lineage on developing bodhicitta is well known, but what may be less well known is that, according to early Kadampa com-

17. See Apple, *Jewels of the Middle Way*, 5, 17–18, 26–29. A much earlier version of our translation of the root text, *Pith Instructions on the Middle Way*, appeared in B. Alan Wallace, *The Art of Transforming the Mind: A Meditator's Guide to the Tibetan Practice of Lojong* (Boulder, CO: Shambhala Publications, 2022), Appendix Two.

18. Apple, 14.

19. Apple, 17.

20. For example, Atiśa is able to integrate some views of Bhāviveka (such as "authentic obscurative phenomena") seamlessly with the teachings of Candrakīrti (whereby not even consciousness can withstand ultimate investigation), while still rejecting the idea that emptiness can be realized as the result of inference—namely, hearing and understanding the conclusion of a formal logical syllogism. This will be discussed further on in this section.

mentaries, Atiśa composed *A Guide to the Two Realities* "in order to convert Serlingpa from a Yogācāra to a Madhyamaka view."[21] The abbot of Vikramaśīla, Ratnākaraśānti, held a sophisticated view known as Yogācāra-Madhyamaka, which Atiśa nonetheless recognized to be disparate with the view of Candrakīrti, and could not accept. Whether or not this philosophical tension with his abbot and teacher was a factor in leading Atiśa to accept the invitations he received to journey to Tibet,[22] it is significant to recognize that even at Vikramaśīla the "highest interpretation" of the teachings of Nāgārjuna and Asaṅga was still very much a matter of debate.

The fact that *A Guide to the Two Realities* was translated from Sanskrit into Tibetan by Gya Lotsāwa Tsöndrü Sengé (as indicated by its colophon) tells us that this text was translated before Atiśa came to Tibet, since we know that Gya Lotsāwa studied with Atiśa for several years at Vikramaśīla but died suddenly in Kathmandu, in the process of escorting Atiśa to Tibet. Thus, we can be confident that *A Guide to the Two Realities* was translated at Vikramaśīla, when Atiśa was working closely with both Gya Lotsāwa and Naktso Lotsāwa.[23]

We have seen that the transmission of *The Book of Kadam* is closely linked with the request from Ngok Lekpé Sherab, perhaps inspired by his vision of Mañjuśrī. It was the same Ngok Lekpé Sherab who, some time earlier, requested Atiśa to teach Madhyamaka when he arrived in Lhasa, to which Atiśa responded in part by composing and teaching his *Pith Instructions on the Middle Way* to a worthy disciple, Geshé Naljorpa.[24] Since this text's beautiful commentary by Prajñāmokṣa must also have been written while Atiśa was in Tibet, we can only surmise that Prajñāmokṣa was an Indian preceptor who had traveled with Atiśa all the way from Vikramaśīla and

21. Apple, *Jewels of the Middle Way*, 30.

22. Apple, 35.

23. See Apple, *Atiśa Dīpaṃkara*, 29.

24. See Apple, *Jewels of the Middle Way*, 15–16.

thus had spent years in his entourage.[25] For this reason, we can be confident that the commentary faithfully reflects Atiśa's own oral teaching on his root text; an Indian disciple still among Atiśa's retinue after years in Tibet would never have simply made up his own ideas about the master's root text!

The Two Realities

As we have seen, Atiśa composed *A Guide to the Two Realities* much earlier, before his journey to Tibet, for the sake of his beloved teacher in Suvarṇadvīpa. His highly distilled text assumes knowledge of the issues at stake in debate and discussion among Indian Buddhist masters in the early eleventh century, but it is also possible for us to derive immense benefit from his text by grappling simply with the meaning of the verses, without extensive commentary. We will address here only the most essential points that need to be understood as background for reading the text.

We have chosen the term "two realities" over the more common translation "two truths" because, in general, a statement such as "all composite phenomena are impermanent" is a *truth*, but the referents of that statement—namely impermanent, composite phenomena themselves—are *realities*, in that they exist and are perceived by particular observers. In the context of the Middle Way, the two realities are classically perceived at different levels by two different types of observers, respectively. That is, ultimate reality (Skt. *paramārthasatya*) is found by the primordial wisdom of an ārya (one who realizes emptiness directly) during meditative equipoise. This primordial wisdom is a distinct type of consciousness that emerges when one has first investigated with discernment how phenomena exist, in an ultimate way. Finding that any possible inherent characteristics that could exist ultimately are *not to be found*, then, from a state of meditative

25. See Apple, 279. Note that Prajñāmokṣa and Prajñāmukti refer to the same person (Tib. *Shes rab thar pa*); we have chosen the former Sanskrit rendering of his name because that is the way it appears in Tibetan transliteration within the verse colophon to his own commentary in all editions of the Tibetan Tengyur: *man ngag gsal por Pradznya mokṣas byas*.

equipoise, that primordial wisdom encounters phenomena *as they exist ultimately*, utterly free of characteristics and free of conceptual elaboration. This reality is emptiness (Skt. *śūnyatā*).

Obscurative, or deceptive, reality (Skt. *saṃvṛtisatya*) is that which is found by ordinary individuals, in whom the eye of the mind is completely covered by the cataracts of ignorance, so that what they perceive appears to be determined through characteristics of its own, while in actuality it is not something that could ever be determined with inherent characteristics or an essential nature of its own. Thus, according to the accurate and authentic seeing of those āryas who have realized ultimate reality—which is the epitome of what it means to be trustworthy—what is perceived by ordinary beings is proven to be false, or deceptive.

We have chosen to translate the Sanskrit term *saṃvṛtisatya* (Tib. *kun rdzob bden pa*) as "obscurative reality" because this utilizes the English words whose meaning is actually closest to the meaning of the Sanskrit words in this context, along with their Tibetan translations. That is, the Tibetans who worked in close collaboration with Indian scholars chose Tibetan words that would reflect the meaning of the Sanskrit word intended in a particular context, and while *saṃvṛti* is a multivalent term in Sanskrit, in Tibetan *kun rdzob* (pronounced *kün dzop*) simply means, "totally obscurative." Indeed, this is a kind of reality that totally obscures the actual nature of reality (Skt. *dharmatā*, Tib. *chos nyid*) from the perspective of those whose minds are still veiled by the obscurations of ignorance. The phenomena themselves are not "lying," or "deceiving"; it is the ignorance that veils our minds that causes us to misperceive the actual nature of obscurative realities. Obscurative realities themselves—that is, the whole range of phenomena that we perceive as our world and its sentient inhabitants—function consistently according to the laws of cause and effect, so they certainly must not be ignored!

Obscurative realities are determined by conventional valid cognitions, which are states of mind that are perceiving correctly at the level of cognitive frames of reference shared with other sentient beings, but that have not yet engaged in a penetrating investigation into *how* phenomena exist. Thus, obscurative realities are said to be a kind of reality, but they are real only from the perspective of a state of mind that mistakenly grasps to things as real, whereas ultimate reality is real in the sense that nothing higher or more profound than emptiness—freedom from conceptual elaboration—will ever be found. Neither of the two realities is established through any characteristics of its own, but ultimate reality is the only reality that is invariant across all conceptual frameworks.

People who are utterly lucid in a dream know that the phenomena appearing to them are illusory and not inherently real, but those dream phenomena still appear to them as if they were "really out there" and can even have causal efficacy. All appearances that seem to be separate from the observer, whether in the waking state or while dreaming, are called "dualistic appearances," and even arhats, who are free of *afflictive obscurations* and their seeds—including the seeds for the ignorance that is at the root of grasping to real existence—are still subject to dualistic appearances. Such appearances of duality derive from the lingering habitual propensities for ignorance and are called *cognitive obscurations*. Only buddhas are free of both kinds of obscurations. Moreover, only the ultimate reality of emptiness exists in accordance with the way it appears to those āryas who directly apprehend it, while the dualistic appearances of all other phenomena are obscurative in that they obscure and are not in accord with the way that such phenomena actually exist.

Atiśa affirms two types of obscurative realities: false obscuratives (such as illusions and the ideas of philosophical systems that can be proven wrong through logic) and authentic obscuratives (such as what we normally consider to be phenomena that function consistently with our understanding of them). According to later Tibetan understanding, this distinction was aligned with the so-called Svātantrika Madhyamaka position, associated with Indian philosophers such as Bhāviveka and Jñānagarbha. But we should not be confused here, for while Atiśa relied on Bhāviveka's presentation of the Middle Way in some respects, especially when teaching publicly, he also explicitly refutes here the idea that emptiness could be shown to another as the conclusion of syllogistic reasoning with an independent line of logic—that is, using inference. In Atiśa's time, there were no systematic distinctions between "schools" of Prāsaṅgika reasoning (utilizing an argument *ad absurdum*), versus those of Svātantrika reasoning (utilizing an independent line of logical argumentation, as Bhāviveka taught). But if we view Atiśa's overall thought, it is clearly in the mode of the Prāsaṅgika Madhyamaka, and we know that he represented a lineage of teaching and realization that could be traced directly to Candrakīrti (through Atiśa's teacher Vidyākokila).

Moreover, in refuting that ultimate reality could ever be "of two kinds," Atiśa refutes an idea expressed in Jñānagarbha's *Verses Distinguishing the Two Realities* (*Satyadvayavibhaṅgakārikā*)—namely, that there are referents of conceptual understandings of emptiness that can be "classified" as ultimate reality, versus the "unclassifiable" ultimate reality that is perceived directly. Atiśa also refutes here the idea that there are somehow many emptinesses associated with each and every entity that has its own emptiness, or "its" actual nature: while there can be logical classifications of the "sixteen kinds of emptiness" and so on, which have authentic scriptural sources, these simply refer to the particular bases, or portals within obscurative reality *through which* one realizes emptiness, but emptiness utterly transcends enumeration.

When Atiśa says that only "fools with a confined outlook" (that is, those who have not yet realized emptiness directly) say that emptiness is realized through both direct perception and inference, we must interpret that he is not here refuting *yogic* direct perception (Skt. *yogipratyakṣa*), a type of knowing achieved only from the meditative basis of śamatha, through which Mahāyāna sources agree that emptiness must be realized. Rather, it seems that what Atiśa is refuting here is the idea that emptiness could ever be realized by an ordinary nonconceptual mental perception such as that by which we nonconceptually perceive images in dreams, much less by any of the other five senses. He may also have been refuting ideas within the Yogācāra view held by Serlingpa that the realization of emptiness could be verified by a type of reflexive direct perception of awareness (Skt. *svasaṃvedana*) in which consciousness itself is held to exist inherently—which was asserted by some Mind-Only proponents but rejected by Candrakīrti.

While Atiśa certainly relies on reasoning to guide his disciples to realize emptiness, he knows that inference that grasps onto the conclusion of a syllogism *as real*, will, at a certain point, only become an obstacle to realizing directly that which is free of all conceptual elaboration. Thus, while we can use inferential reasoning to refute the extreme views even within our own minds, when it comes to actually realizing emptiness in meditation, we need to allow our reasoning *ad absurdum* to take us beyond the limitations of conditioned consciousness itself. This means transcending not only the conditioned consciousness that is explicitly conceptual, but also that which is relatively nonconceptual (in the sense that it perceives mental images nonconceptually, as in śamatha alone, but still experiences them as dualistic appearances).

Throughout his teachings, Atiśa repeatedly emphasized the extensive practice of meditation as being more important than excessive conceptual study and debate, but we must also keep in mind how thoroughly his own teachings arise from his deep and subtle mastery of reasoning. Even as his *Pith Instructions on the Middle Way* will eventually point to the illusory nature of all phenomena—whether they seemed to be false or authentic obscurative phenomena to begin with—we must recall how intensely Atiśa emphasizes the power of "obscurative cause and effect, virtue and vice, and so forth," in *A Guide to the Two Realities*. If we can plumb the depths of the perfect balance between the two realities—obscurative cause and effect and the ultimate meaning that will be revealed once we have relied properly upon the conventional—then we will have begun to understand the priceless legacy of Jowo Atiśa.

Geshé Langri Thangpa

Geshé Langri Thangpa Dorjé Sengé was born in 1054 in the area of Langtang, in the Phenpo region of Tibet. He became one of the main disciples of Dromtönpa and was an eminent figure in the Kadam tradition, eventually founding Langtang Monastery as a Kadampa monastery near his birthplace. As a prominent teacher, he had about two thousand disciples, one of whom was Geshé Chekawa, who first wrote down *The Seven-Point Mind Training*, the most renowned of all mind-training texts.

Geshé Langri Thangpa was known for having a sour or grumpy face; he rarely smiled. When this was mentioned to him by a disciple, he responded that when he thinks about the endless sufferings of saṃsāra, how could he even begin to smile? His great compassion, wisdom, and love permeated his entire being and influenced how he taught and helped others. We have included here his most famous work, *The Eight-Verse Mind Training*, as a quintessential example of the lineage of mind-training teachings that flowed through the early generations of the Kadam tradition.

Translators' Note

We are deeply grateful to Thupten Jinpa for his translation of the same dialogues from *The Jewel Garland of Dialogues* in *The Book of Kadam*, which inspired us first to revise his translations, and then to begin working on our own new translations of these texts. For our source texts, we have relied primarily on *The Collected Works of the Glorious Lord Atisha*, compiled and edited by the Paltsek Research Institute for Ancient Tibetan Manuscripts; later we had the opportunity to consult the Tibetan edition that was compiled especially for Thupten Jinpa's translation. Any faults in translation or misunderstandings of the old Tibetan colloquial language used here are our own.

While *The Book of Kadam* has been well known in Tibet for centuries, Atiśa's teachings on Madhyamaka were rarely mentioned after the Kadam school was effectively absorbed into other lineages (by the end of the sixteenth century),[26] even though Atiśa himself continued to be revered by the luminaries of all schools of Tibetan Buddhism. Indeed, Tsongkhapa cites both of these Middle Way texts by Atiśa in his own writings: see *On the Union of Śamatha and Vipaśyanā* in this volume. Nevertheless, it is our privilege to discover these texts, which were hidden in plain sight within the Tengyur (the canonical collection of Tibetan translations of Indian treatises) all along. Our immense thanks goes to James B. Apple for his scholarship in bringing these texts to light, both in their Tengyur editions and also as included in collections of Kadam works only recently rediscovered and published in Tibet.[27] Our own translations of the Middle Way texts rely on the Tengyur, especially in the form of a critical edition of *A Guide to the Two Realities* produced by the Central Institute of Higher Tibetan Studies in Varanasi, India, and editions of the *Pith Instructions on the Middle Way* and its commentary included in the Pé Durma (*dpe bsdur ma*), a modern Tibetan critical edition of the Tengyur. We are also grateful to James Apple for his identification of many of the source texts from which Prajñāmokṣa drew his quotations, which we have simply rendered here in brackets as a guideline, without including detailed footnotes. We have also not attempted to be exhaustive in providing these sources, both because some are not readily available and also in order not to break the flow of the commentary for the English reader.

26. See Jinpa, *The Book of Kadam*, 10.

27. See Apple, *Jewels of the Middle Way*, ix–xv.

1. Blaming Everything on a Single Culprit

FROM *THE JEWEL GARLAND OF DIALOGUES*, CHAPTER 6

Atiśa Dīpaṃkara Śrījñāna

[28] Once, when Father Atiśa and his son were staying at their residence at Nyethang Or, Drom made three prostrations to Atiśa and, recollecting his mind's way of apprehending phenomena, and so on, stated,

"Sentient beings are brought about through these causes: ignorance, craving, and appropriation. Mental formations and becoming serve as their conditions, while their effects are consciousness, name and form, the six sense bases, contact, feeling, birth, and aging and death. So it is these three alone—causes, conditions, and effects—that turn the wheel of impurity throughout the circumference of space. Covering all our own defects with our palms, we point out all the faults of others with our fingers. Disciples do not implement the guru's words, and sons do not listen to what their fathers tell them. O great master, such an evil era has dawned and remains present. Although the impure cycle of the twelve links of dependent origination is the experience common to all sentient beings, the beings of this degenerate era are each participating individually in this common error [by which they fall into the impure cycle], so they remain in it. Since it could potentially benefit one or two seekers in future generations, please give a brief explanation of the twelve links of dependent origination."

The master replied, "I will explain this now as we lift our robes above the mire."

"Well then, what is the root of bondage?" asked Drom.

Atiśa replied, "It is grasping to a self."

"What is this grasping to a self?" inquired Drom.

"It is wanting all good qualities for oneself alone and wanting others alone [29] to take on all bad things."

Drom requested: "Then please explain it in such a manner that we can say, 'This is self-grasping.'"

Atiśa: "Regarding the superimposition of self-grasping, where could one find anything of which it could be said, 'This is it'?"

Drom: "In that case, please explain how it wants all kinds of things for itself and shifts all unjust blame onto others."

Atiśa: "Upāsaka, why do you need to ask me? It pervades sentient beings. You know this, so why do you need to ask? Still, I'll say that both attachment and hatred are sometimes labeled as self-grasping."

"Master, is there anyone who has such grasping?"

Atiśa countered, "Where would that one be?"

"It must be that this is within one's own mental continuum," suggested Drom.

"Upāsaka, but what is one's own mental continuum?"

"It must be that which has the grasping of wanting all kinds of things," replied Drom.

Atiśa: "I agree."

"Well then, where is this self-grasping located?" inquired Drom.

Atiśa: "I have never seen anything that doesn't have parts. I don't know of any spatially located thing that is not located anywhere. Nor do I know the color or shape of something that is without any essential nature."

Drom then asked, "If this is so, how can something so feeble exist?"

Atiśa: "Can't one perceive the water in a mirage, a double moon, horses and elephants in a dream, and so on?"

"Master, but those must be delusive appearances."

Atiśa: "I accept that. But if self-grasping is present, doesn't it create attachment and hatred? Dogs bark at an empty bowl in a deserted place, and one's mindstream becomes totally deluded without any basis in reality."

"Master, in light of such analogies, it seems as if self-grasping itself has never existed," said Drom.

Atiśa: "Why do you say, 'it seems as if'? That must be the case."

"Master, well then, do the pitfalls of the three miserable realms of existence, the positive qualities of the fortunate realms, and the ethical norms of what is to be accepted and to be rejected exist?"

Atiśa: "Does the dreamer of dreams exist?"

"Master, that's different. I don't create my dreams. They occur as lies. Birth in the fortunate realms and the miserable realms, and the ethical norms of acceptance and rejection are created."

Atiśa: "Who creates them?"

Drom: "They must be created by the mind."

Atiśa: "That's what I say, too. But dreams are also created by the mind. Upāsaka, if they weren't created by the mind, who would create them? Would they be created by someone else? If they weren't created by anyone else, and if they aren't created by the mind, Upāsaka, then you have lied about a lie itself. The objects in dreams are deceptions that are entirely empty of self and other. Likewise, everything that is to be accepted or rejected, such as the miserable realms, must be emanated by the mind itself, which then engages in accepting and rejecting."

Drom: "Well then, self-grasping is the root of attachment and hatred, so please tell me, is that one's own mind?"

Atiśa: "What is the color of the mind?"

Drom: "I've never seen it."

Atiśa: "Then what kind of shape does it have?"

"Master, I've never seen it."

Atiśa: "Well then, since neither its color nor shape is determined, [30] and also since it's never been seen with the eyes, that indicates that it does not exist as a form. So set it aside as being empty of form. Upāsaka, does the mind have a sound that is pleasant or unpleasant, loud or soft?"

"Master, I've never heard it."

Atiśa: "Well then, since it in no way appears as a pleasant or unpleasant sound, loud or soft, and so on, it is not heard by the ears. If it had a sound, it should be audible to the ears, but it isn't. Now since the mind is also devoid of sound, set that aside. Upāsaka, do you find that the mind has any odor, whether fragrant or foul?"

"Master, I've never detected any smell of the mind or odor coming from it."

"Drom, if it had an odor, there's no doubt it would have been smelled with the nose. Now since it is not detected with the nose, that indicates that the mind is devoid of smell. So set aside this emptiness that is the absence of smell. Drom, is there some kind of taste to your mind, be it savory or unsavory?"

Drom: "Whatever may reach me from the master's speech, how could I ever have a metric by which to judge whether it tastes good or bad when eating mind?"

"Drom, so are you saying there is none?"

"Master, how can the mind ever be eaten, and how can its taste ever be experienced?"

"Drom, this indicates that your mind is not a taste. If it were, the tongue would experience it. Since it is not experienced with the tongue, this indicates that it is not a taste. So set aside its absence of taste as well. Drom, what kind of tactile quality does your mind have: smooth or rough?"

"Master, I have never experienced anything like a tactile quality of the mind."

"Drom, why is this so?"

"What sort of metric could there be for assessing the tactile quality of the mind?"

Atiśa: "With incorrigible sentient beings there are many cases of there being no rules.[28] The fact that the mind is not an object of tactile experience

28. Tib. *khrims*. This is the same Tibetan word translated just above as "metric," so there is a pun here.

indicates that it is devoid of tactile qualities. So set aside the mind that is not a tactile sensation, either. Well then, Drom, if it were an object of mentation, of what sort would it be?"

"Master, for there to be an object of mentation, there must be an immediately preceding condition for its faculty. Without there first being an object of its faculty as an immediately preceding condition, it could not be an object of mentation."

Atiśa: "It could also come about from a conceptual fabrication."

"Master, even a fabrication must be preceded by a habitual propensity. Furthermore, isn't it going too far to say that because [the mind] isn't an object of any of the five sense faculties, the five objects don't exist?"

"Upāsaka, what are you saying? I have not given an account for all objects within those [five]. Rather, I have only counted your mind as something in addition to them. For if the mind is among them, then when you observe it, it should exist as a form, be heard as a sound, and so on. Since it doesn't appear as any of those things, where is the mind located? Upāsaka, ordinary people would all give up and say with a dismissive wave of the hand, 'I've never seen such a thing with my eyes, heard it with my ears, smelled its odor, or tasted its flavor, nor does it exist anywhere within the domain of mentation.' You, on the other hand, are someone who has been ripened by the practical instructions of sublime gurus, received siddhis from your personal deity, and who practices the three baskets of scripture in one sitting. So you should not impute branches and leaves where there is no basis [of a tree].

"Since I am a son of Avadhūti, I know that in this way all things are the mind, and I know that the nature of existence of the mind is just like that. [31] Now even if one's faults are exposed, they are the mind. Even if one is praised, that is the mind. Whether you are happy or miserable, it is the mind. Given that all of these are equally the mind, whatever faults are revealed in your mindstream—which appears to be a self even though no self exists—crush them and proclaim it. There's no point in concealing faults that are not determined to exist inside a cave that is not determined to exist. There's no point in letting them become poisons that will cause illness. There is no point in fixing the number of illnesses at five. You would only sever the life force of liberation that way. There is no point in casting yourself into the three miserable realms. Even though dreams are deceptive, there's no need to dream of suffering.

"Drom, expel all these deceitful defects. If the trace of having purified these faults is positive, that's fine, but if not, that's not good. Insofar as they are equal in being the appearances of a deceptive mind, if everyone else is pleased when praised, then offer praise and let it go. You, in whom there is no one who seeks, should not seek out the mistakes of someone else. Insofar as they are equal in being concealed, conceal your own fine qualities, too. When the time comes for it to be necessary, it will come. Insofar as they are equal in being proclaimed, proclaim the fine qualities of others. Others will be pleased, so they won't accumulate negative karma on your account. This also has the benefit of toppling the cornerstones of the mental afflictions of attachment and hatred. Once you have established individually whatever fine qualities others may have, then praise them. Upāsaka, do you understand everything to be the mind?"

Drom: "Yes, I do."

"Well then, do you understand the nature of existence of the mind?"

Drom: "I do."

Atiśa: "So why have desires for this mind? Be content. Many sentient beings appear, yet it is true that they are none other than your mothers and fathers who have cleaned your runny nose with their mouths and your excrement with their hands; they have given you kingdoms and nurtured you with delightful gifts. At times, they have abandoned you, but then they have cared for you again. They have all, without exception, been your fathers and mothers who have rejoiced when you are freed from difficulties and when you find good fortune.

"The fact that you display such fine qualities is due to the kindness of your guru. In general, it is your guru who continuously shows you the kindness of fulfilling your eternal longing, and it is your parents who have shown you the kindness of granting you joy and happiness in this life. So, you should recognize their kindness and try to repay it.

"For this, serve your guru with reverence, offerings, your spiritual practice, and so on. In order to repay the kindness of your parents, cultivate immeasurable loving-kindness, immeasurable compassion, immeasurable joy when they are happy, and immeasurable impartiality, free of bias toward those who are close or distant. For the benefit of all beings who have been your mothers, do everything you can to attain buddhahood, and, casting off uncertainty, intently focus on your spiritual practice. Ridding yourself of all obstacles such as sleepiness and dullness, strive with enthusiasm.

"Drom, when we speak of 'recognizing the kindness of others and repaying it,' it all comes down to cultivating the four immeasurables from loving-kindness and compassion onward, stabilizing your bodhicitta and increasing it to ever higher levels, and steering your parents' course with the oars of aspiring and engaging bodhicitta. So, once you have abandoned your selfish desires pertaining to this life, this facsimile of desire, the thought of longing to guide your parents, is the intention that desires to repay their kindness. This is what we call 'recognizing the kindness of others and repaying it.'"

[32] Drom: "Though the master has expressed many fine points, they can be summarized as follows:

> "Acknowledge your own faults,
> but do not seek out others' mistakes.
> Conceal your own fine qualities,
> but proclaim those of others.
>
> Forsake the gifts and veneration of others,
> and always relinquish arrogance and renown.
> Have few desires, be content,
> and repay the kindness of others.

Cultivate loving-kindness and compassion,
and stabilize your bodhicitta.
There is nothing more than this."

Atiśa: "So it is. When well summarized, everything is included there."

This concludes the sixth chapter from *The Jewel Garland of Dialogues*, "Blaming Everything on a Single Culprit."

Translated by B. Alan Wallace and Eva Natanya

2. Cutting the Root of Suffering and Equalizing Excitation and Laxity

FROM *THE JEWEL GARLAND OF DIALOGUES*, CHAPTER 14

Atiśa Dīpaṃkara Śrījñāna

[94] Once again, at that very same place and in the presence of the guru endowed with such sublime qualities, our guru, [Dromtön] Gyalwé Jungné, said [to Atiśa]:

"Please listen, O, wise one. We sentient beings of Tibet need to be tamed. Now, in that regard, Tibet's own language is a very foolish language for leading one to the path. So the time has come for me to appeal to you to use words whose meanings are comprehended the moment one hears them. What is the root of all suffering?"

Atiśa replied, "Drom, it is misconduct."

"Master, what is the root of misconduct?"

"Drom, it is the aggregates, the 'I,' or self."

"Master, now how does the 'I,' or self, act as the root of misconduct?"

"Drom, because it wants everything."

"Master, how does it want everything?"

Atiśa replied, "It wants oneself to be above and others to be beneath."

"Master, what is that called?"

"Drom, it's called 'that which is imbued with selfish attachment and hatred.'"

"Master, in whom is this most prevalent?"

"Drom, it is most prevalent in those with little spiritual practice but with great pride."

"Master, isn't pride due to having something?"

"Drom, fireflies think that there are no lights other than their own."

"Master, aren't they proud because they have even a speck of light?"

"Drom, none of the suns or moons is proud."

"In that case, Master, might pride lead one to the path or not?"

"Drom, if one has the pride of thinking, 'If I act for the sake of others, I shall certainly succeed in bringing about their welfare,' this will lead to the path. Drom, if one has the pride of thinking, 'If I engage in spiritual training, I shall certainly come to knowledge,' this will lead to the path. If one has the pride of thinking, 'By having strong remedies, if I observe ethical discipline, I shall certainly prevail,' this will lead to the path."

"Master, I wonder if all of those are definitive pride."

"Drom, I didn't say they are."

"Master, I wonder if there is a kind of pride that does not bear all its defining characteristics."

"Drom, what sort of characteristics would it need to have?"

"Master, I'm looking for the ones that indicate the defined object upon its basis of definition."

"Be quiet, Drom. Thinking that way will not lead you to the path. What leads to the path are facsimiles of pride."

"Master, are you saying that facsimiles lead to the path?!"

"Well then, Drom, does a facsimile *not* lead to the path?"

"Master, what facsimile could there be that leads to the path?"

"Drom, every time there is the recognition while dreaming that 'all phenomena are just like this dream.'"

"Master, if you want to call that *definitive*, so it is called. But nowhere does knowing that heat is the defining characteristic of fire lead to the path!"

"Drom, well then, but isn't heat the defining characteristic of fire?"

"Master, then are all phenomena permanent and truly existent?"

"Drom, it is not like that. There is no basis for anything being permanent and truly existent."

"Master, so the truth of heat being the defining characteristic of fire *does* have such a basis?"

"Drom, your words are hot."

"Master, does that mean they are fire?"

"Why, Drom?"

"Master, because you affirm that the defining characteristic of fire is heat, and so it is."

"Drom, with this you identify something that seems to be really true." [95]

"Master, for something that has never been real, there is no choice but for it to be a semblance."

"Drom, are you proud of yourself?"

"Master, if an imputation can lead to the path, then pride may be okay."

"Drom, is that a sense of superiority or not?"

"Master, is a sense of superiority something to be rejected or not?"

"Drom, if it entails clinging, it is to be rejected."

"Master, if it doesn't entail clinging, is it not to be rejected?"

"Drom, a sense of superiority free of clinging is a facsimile."

"Master, what should one do in response to a sense of superiority that entails clinging?"

"Drom, seek to crush that pride."

"Master, with what methods?"

"Drom, seek to bear in mind the practical instructions of gurus who have put the teachings into practice."

"Master, what are those gurus' practical instructions?"

"Drom, you have been taught from the time mundane existence came into being up to the present, and *now* you are asking your guru for practical instructions?!"

"Master, we have indeed had a relationship ever since mundane existence came into being, and we are still together, aren't we?"

"Drom, I was teasing you."

"Master, I was simply offering a good comeback to your chiding."

"Drom, your answer was red hot."

"Master, if it is timely, it is a comeback."

"Drom, in your case, is there such a thing as being timely?"

"Master, I'm not a sky flower."

"Drom, well then, who are you?"

"Master, who is white in color?"

"Drom, you know how to wait for the right moment."

"Master, if one waits for the right moment, one is wise."

"Drom, every wise person is on the go."

"Master, why is this so?"

"Drom, because they need to hasten after all the right moments."

"Master, whether or not it is fitting, one who hastens is on the go."

The master laughed and said, "Like you Tibetans."

"Master, or like Indian mendicants."

"Drom, they chew each grain of rice."

"Master, that results in the right degree of granularity."

As Drom spoke these words, a green lady carrying a vase filled with the nectar of primordial consciousness poured it into two crystal ladles—one white and the other yellow—and offered them to the master and his spiritual son. She said, "Swapping jokes makes you very thirsty. I, too, have heard the uproar about your humor, and it seems to be true. So I have come to listen."

Drom replied, "Lady, are you a mendicant as well?

"Hé! Hé! In the company of a white youth, I've had to go in all directions," she replied.

Atiśa asked, "Why was the white youth in such a hurry?"

"Master, because of having so many mothers, sometimes he was carried away by joy and happiness because they were so happy, and at other times he had to look after them because they were so sad."

"How many of them were there?" asked Atiśa.

"Master, it would be good if there were numbers and limits, but there aren't."

"Lady, isn't space their limit?" asked Atiśa.

"Master, then you measure space," she countered.

Atiśa replied, "I don't know how. Ask Drom, for he gets around a lot, and he likes to perform emanations and withdrawals. There should be some limit even to space."

"Master, how many acts of emanation and withdrawal do I perform?" asked Drom.

"Drom, your emanations are as extensive as space."

"Master, I beg you, then reveal the dimensions of space."

"Drom, what are you saying? [96] I've never measured the extent of space."

"Master, you have suddenly told a lie. Having said that I, Drom, perform emanations as extensive as space, you now admit that you have not measured space."

"Drom, I said your emanations are as extensive as space, but not that space has limits."

"Master, if you say that Drom performs emanations to the extent of space, when you relate this analogy to its referent, you should understand both the analogy and its referent. But you, a learned man, have related them without such understanding, haven't you?"

"Drom, for now, I'll grant you that. However, if, to say that something is as extensive as space, one had to comprehend space itself, no one could use space as an analogy."

"Master, is this not a case of acting out of ignorance? It is difficult for the mind to fathom the extent of space."

"Drom, well then, regarding the statement that the nature of existence of all phenomena is like space, who can measure this?"

"Master, that is taken as an analogy for what is measureless. If space had limits, it wouldn't be a suitable analogy."

"Drom, I rejoice! What a delight it would be if I were surrounded only by people like you who have no pride and are learned in the Dharma."

"Master, that would be of no benefit. Instead, it would be a far greater delight if all sentient beings became like me and were here in your presence to partake exclusively of the Mahāyāna Dharma. However, this seems to be as rare as it is difficult to attain enlightenment as a woman."

Just as he spoke those words, the blue-green lady appeared in the brilliantly luminous form of a [male] tathāgatha. Master Atiśa laughed and exclaimed, "What you have directly manifested to us is an excellent form indeed!"

Drom replied, "One who has already become enlightened can display any kind of form, both excellent and poor. I was referring to women who are bound by the fetters of mental afflictions."

Then the lady returned to her own form and asked, "Great Compassionate One, whose afflictions are greater, mine or those of a woman bound by the fetters of the afflictions? I carry the afflictions of all sentient beings, while a woman who is fettered by them carries only her own share. Without relinquishing the afflictions, one does not become enlightened, but the afflictions are so vast."

Drom replied, "In that case, I, too, am greatly afflicted, for I carry the burden of space."

She replied, "Drom, in space there is no burden to carry."

"Tārā, in you there is no one to carry that burden either, so release everything into equality."

Drom asked Atiśa, "Who is it that carries the burden of mental afflictions?"

"Drom, anyone who has self-grasping."

"In that case, Tārā has no self-grasping, so she is free. For those of us who have self-grasping, how can we relinquish it?"

"Drom, how many thoughts occur in a single day?"

"Master, an inconceivable number occur."

"Drom, how often does the absolute space of phenomena[29] arise?"

"Master, being overshadowed by thoughts, it does not appear to arise."

"Drom, for this, you need the approach of my teacher Avadhūtipa."

"Master, please reveal the practical instruction of your guru."

"Drom, however many thoughts arise, transform them into the actual nature of reality."

"Master, if all logs were to turn into gold, all the needs of people who want anything would be fulfilled. [97] But how can such a transformation occur?"

"Drom, by applying a gold-transforming elixir in reliance upon pith instructions, iron is transformed into gold. For that, one must know the essential point."

"Master, please reveal the essential point."

"Drom, to defeat the enemy, first you must recognize the enemy."

"Master, what is the enemy?"

"Drom, it is conceptualization."

"Master, how does one destroy it?"

"Drom, destroy it the moment it surfaces."

"Master, how should one proceed to destroy it?"

"Drom, observe where its basis lies; analyze its shape, color, and so on, and examine the thoughts that came before, the thoughts that come after, and so on. Seek where they go to and where they come from. At that time, they will not be found."

"Master, why is this so?"

29. Tib. *chos kyi dbying*, Skt. *dharmadhātu*. When translated as the "absolute space of phenomena," *dharmadhātu* refers to the ultimate ground of all phenomena in saṃsāra and nirvāṇa, which is also known as *emptiness*, *suchness*, and *the actual nature of reality*. As all phenomena are primordially free of arising, ceasing, and so on, they dwell in the manner of an absolute space that transcends all conceptual elaboration, and they are of "a single taste" in the sense of not being separate or divided into dualities. It is ultimate in the sense that it is that which is experienced by the primordial wisdom of an ārya, which perceives reality as it actually exists. It is through focusing upon this absolute space that all sublime qualities of the path are developed, so it is also known as the cause or domain of all sublime qualities possessed by the āryas.

"Drom, they cannot be found because they never existed."

"Master, when they are not found, what should one do then?"

"Drom, this is called 'transforming thoughts into the absolute space of phenomena.' If they cannot be found when searched for, this is a sign that they are the absolute space of phenomena. So place your mind at rest upon this."

"Master, what if they occur again?"

"Drom, then vanquish them again."

"Master, can that be done gradually with skillful means?"

"Drom, that wouldn't work, so strike them down with antidotes."

"Master, is there anything else to get rid of?"

"Drom, don't have a lot on your mind. Concentrate all your aspirations entirely into one."

"Master, are there other paths or not?"

"Drom, a two-forked road will not take you to your destination, so choose one and head straight down that path."

"Master, is there anything else to aspire to or not?"

"Drom, if you have too many aspirations, you will be diverted from your present purpose. Do not start too many tasks; choose one and be single pointed in your decision."

"Master, though this is true, nevertheless when adverse conditions happen, such as sickness, it is difficult."

"Drom, what are you saying? There is no better spiritual mentor than these."

"Master, what sort of spiritual mentor could they be? They are sent by an evil spirit!"

"Drom, why do you say this? Where can one find more excellent buddhas than these?"

"Master, a buddha? But they bring such acute pain!"

"You did not understand, Drom. Sickness is a great broom for misconduct and obscurations."

"Master, I do not know whether or not it is a broom for misconduct and obscurations. What it does do is to bring great suffering."

"Drom, in this regard, when you do not find it as you search for it repeatedly, then the great effulgence of the absolute space of phenomena comes forth."

"Master, in that case, should I be glad when suffering befalls me?"

"Drom, if you are to undertake a genuine Dharma practice, try to put a lid on your desires for happiness."

"Master, a cycle of suffering is bound to come."

"Drom, by enduring great hardships, seek to connect suffering with suffering."

"Master, I seek to do this to its end."

"Drom, when you connect them, they are severed. This is a crucial point."

"Master, why?"

"Drom, because suffering comes from constantly desiring only happiness."

"Master, to summarize all the points, how should one conduct oneself?"

"Drom, since self is the root of all evil deeds, discard it entirely, like the corpse of one's dead father."

"Master, what is to be embraced?"

"Drom, since helping others is the source of enlightenment, like finding a wish-fulfilling jewel, uphold and embrace it."

"Master, aren't there things that should be left neutral in equanimity?"

"Drom, since both self and others are unborn, [98] relax and release them in the equanimity of non-arising."

"Master, so you affirm that. What is the root of the mental afflictions that is to be relinquished?"

"Drom, it is this great conceptualization."

"Master, what is the method of destroying this?"

"Drom, none other than vanquishing it as soon as it arises."

"Master, how is it relinquished by means of its antidote?"

"Drom, by means of striking it down with no hesitation whatsoever. All paths, moreover, are traversed by means of this single path and all aspirations are concentrated into this single one as well. Since sickness and so on motivate one to perform virtue, you come to the point where there is no choice but to practice Dharma. Therefore, they are excellent spiritual mentors. They reveal the dangers of adverse conditions, such as malevolent beings, so you are able to regard those who teach you the means of protection as buddhas. Drom, it is difficult for ordinary beings to see all the buddhas.

"All of this is like a mother who disciplines her children and establishes them in goodness. True renunciation will arise within, and one bears in mind the excellent Dharma. One will be closer to the buddhas in heart, so it is said that this is excellent.

"Drom, if one takes on the sickness of all sentient beings every time one is ill, there is no opportunity for misconduct and obscurations to defeat a great hero.

"Drom, every time suffering arises, blame it on self-grasping, and when you search for it, you don't find it.

"Drom, if one hundred thoughts of suffering and the like occur, then, because one searches for them one hundred times, there will be one hundred times of not finding. Finding that truth of not finding is the absolute space of phenomena. In this respect, my teacher Avadhūtipa stated,

> The essential nature of thoughts is the absolute space of
>   phenomena;
> when they arise, rejoice, for they are an excellent incentive.
> Of what use are they, since they cannot be found?
> They culminate in the effulgence of the nature of existence.

"Drom, he holds the view of all the buddhas of the three times.

"Drom, I have also said,

> Even in a single day, within self-grasping
> hundreds of thoughts occur, useful and useless;
> the instant one arises, I seek it out with the antidote.

And thus, since I do not find it, it turns out to be the absolute
space of phenomena alone.
For if a thought did exist, insofar as there are so very many
thoughts,
could there be a rule that not even one of them is to be
found?"

Then, Drom said, "Today our conversation has been most enjoyable. The appearance of the goddess has also warmed the guru's heart, and his instructions were most profound."

This completes the teaching on how to bear in mind the guru's instructions when pride and a sense of superiority arise.

Again, Drom asked: "If this mind becomes too depressed, O guru, how should one dispel that?"

"Drom, set it astride the cool blowing breeze."

"Master, what should one do once one has mounted it thus on the wind?"

"Drom, given how very many animals there are, take joy that you have attained a human body."

"Master, after bringing this to mind, how should one meditate?"

"Drom, it is not enough to have found a human body, for it is easily destroyed."

"Master, what can be done about that?"

"Drom, gather the golden flowers of ethical discipline."

"Master, where should one seek shelter?"

"Drom, seek it in the ocean of stainless Dharma."

"Master, how does one live in such an ocean?"

"Drom, one partakes of the golden streams of Jambudvīpa."

"Master, I am not inquiring about my diet."

"Drom, how can one live without sustenance?" [99]

"Master, by consuming the food of samādhi."

"Drom, there is no greater food than this."

"Master, how does this help against depression?"

"Drom, think, 'How joyful it is to have this!'"

"Master, what is joyful about this?"

"Drom, it is so because your eternal longing will be fulfilled."

"Master, on what basis does depression arise?"

"Drom, it comes about due to the misconduct of others."

"Master, how can the influence of misconduct be dispelled?"

"Drom, think, 'It can catalyze forbearance.'"

"Master, what benefit is there in cultivating forbearance?"

"Drom, if one aspires for an attractive form, it is indispensable."

"Master, how does one acquire an attractive form by means of forbearance?"

"Drom, one acquires the bodily signs and symbols of a buddha."

"Master, is nothing else acquired apart from those?"

"Drom, one acquires the sixty qualities of the melodious speech of a buddha."

"Master, that is a wonderful method for dispelling depression! Master, but then will both excitation and laxity come?"

"Drom, they are in abundance in those who are incorrigible."

"Master, what methods are there to dispel them?"

"Drom, there is nothing better than impartiality."

"Master, what happens if one cultivates compassion?"

"Drom, even as it arises, one may feel depressed."

"Master, should one cultivate loving-kindness alone?"

"Drom, here, too, depression may arise."

"Master, should one cultivate empathetic joy alone?"

"Drom, here, then, it is possible that excitation may arise."

"Master, in that case, should one turn to impartiality?"

"Drom, here, moreover, it is possible that delusion may arise."

"Master, then there is nothing to be done."

"Drom, if one realizes inactivity, this is equality."

"Master, that may be so, but is it of any benefit?"

"Drom, it is not that there is no benefit; there is no one who acts."

"Master, isn't this because there is nothing to do?"

"Drom, now you have understood."

"Master, so how should one cultivate the immeasurables?"

"Drom, intensely and carefully, cultivate all four."

"Master, won't excitation and laxity occur?"

"Drom, that's why one cultivates all four of them."

"Master, aren't all four more difficult than just one?"

"Drom, but each one is the antidote for the other."

"Master, but won't all four cancel each other out?"

"Drom, what sort of reason do you have?"

"Master, what happens when clay pots attack each other?"

"Drom, what are you saying? How is that similar?"

"Master, even though that may not be similar, there is still a problem."

"Drom, when laxity raises its head, excitation will pin it down."

"Master, then won't one be left with excitation alone?"

"Drom, then excitation can also be overcome by laxity."

"Master, in that case, won't one be kept busy with these two?"

"No, Drom. They equalize each other."

"Master, how does such equalization occur?"

"Drom, it is like the absence of illness that occurs when the four elements are balanced."

"Master, is it okay to cultivate any one of them?"

"Drom, cultivate what you can."

"Master, I am worried that excitation and laxity might occur."

"Drom, have little concern in this regard."

"Master, should one meditate for as long as they don't arise?"

"Drom, if you meditate again and again, that will suffice."

"Master, if there is laxity, will that lead to the path?"

"Drom, can you meditate when laxity is at its strongest?"

"Master, this will not bring an end to conditioned existence."
"Drom, that is what I would say, too."
"Master, so how does one lay the defects of laxity to rest?"
"Drom, when the faults of laxity are recognized, it is dispelled." [100]
"Master, today's conversation has benefited my mind."
"Drom, I have never indulged in mere idle chatter."
"Master, then this is the teaching on how to dispel laxity."
"Drom, this is also the teaching on how to dispel both laxity and excitation."
"Master:

> Many teachings are included in three collections.
> Though there were many exchanges,
> with queries and responses,
> to summarize them well,
> the point is simply this:
>
> By never taking pleasure in misconduct,
> whenever a sense of superiority occurs,
> at that instant deflate your pride,
> and bear in mind your guru's practical instructions.
> When depression occurs,
> uplift your mind
> and meditate on the emptiness of both.

"There is nothing other than this."

This concludes the fourteenth chapter from *The Jewel Garland of Dialogues*, "Cutting the Root of Suffering and Equalizing Excitation and Laxity."

Translated by B. Alan Wallace and Eva Natanya

3. A Guide to the Two Realities

(*Satyadvayāvatāra*)

Atiśa Dīpaṃkara Śrījñāna

Homage to the Great Compassionate One.

1. The Dharma taught by the buddhas relies perfectly upon two realities: mundane, obscurative reality and likewise the reality that is ultimate.
2. We assert that what is obscurative is of two kinds: that which is false and that which is authentic. The first is twofold: a moon in the water and the concepts of detrimental philosophical systems.
3. A phenomenon that satisfies only as long as it is not examined, which arises and passes, and which is causally efficacious, is held to be an authentic obscurative[30] [phenomenon].
4. There is but one ultimate meaning, though others say it is of two kinds. How could the actual nature of reality, which is not determined as anything, ever become two, or three, and so on?
5. By applying explanatory terms, [the ultimate] is characterized as non-arising, unceasing, and so on. According to the way in which the ultimate is undifferentiated, it is neither an entity (*dharmin*) nor its actual nature (*dharmatā*).

30. Tib. *yang dag kun rdzob*.

6. In emptiness not even the slightest differentiations exist. When it is realized nonconceptually, it is said conventionally that "one sees emptiness."
7. In the ever-so-profound sūtras it is said that not-seeing itself is seeing. In that regard there is neither seeing nor a seer. With no beginning or end, there is peace.
8. It is devoid of being and nonbeing. Nonconceptual and nonreferential, without location or duration, without going or coming, it is without analogy.
9. It is ineffable, invisible, immutable, and uncompounded. When a yogin realizes this, afflictive and cognitive obscurations are eliminated.
10. Buddhists accept both direct perception and inference. Fools with a confined outlook[31] say that emptiness is realized in both those ways.
11. But this would imply that philosophical extremists (*tīrthika*) and śrāvakas also realize the actual nature of reality, not to mention philosophical idealists (*vijñaptika*).[32] Then no one would be incompatible with the proponents of the Middle Way (*mādhyamika*).
12. In that case, all philosophical systems would be in agreement, for they would comprehend it with valid cognition. But since all their lines of reasoning are incompatible, wouldn't the actual nature of reality comprehended by each of their valid cognitions have to become manifold?
13. Direct perception and inference are useless. Those who are wise use them to refute philosophical extremists in debate.
14. It is clearly stated in scripture, and the wise Ācārya Bhavya (Bhāvaviveka) also stated, that neither conceptual nor nonconceptual consciousness realizes [emptiness].

31. That is, non-āryas.

32. Tib. *rnam rig pa*. This term refers to proponents of the Cittamātra, or "Mind-Only," viewpoints.

15. Who has realized emptiness? Nāgārjuna, prophesied by the Tathāgata, and his disciple, Candrakīrti, who both saw the actual nature of reality.
16. By means of the lineage of pith instructions received from them, you can realize the actual nature of reality. Everything that is said in the 84,000 collections of Dharma leads to and lands upon this actual nature of reality.
17. One is liberated by realizing emptiness. All other meditations are for this purpose.
18. But if one familiarizes oneself with emptiness while disregarding authentic obscurative [phenomena], then in the world beyond, one will find one had been deceived with regard to obscurative cause and effect, virtue and vice, and so forth.
19. Those who rely on hearing just a few [teachings], without knowing the meaning of total isolation and without creating merit, are crude people who will be lost. If they view emptiness in the wrong way, those of little intelligence will be ruined.
20. Ācārya Candrakīrti declared,

> Obscurative reality functions as the means, and ultimate
> reality is its end.
> Those who do not know the difference between the two
> proceed to miserable states of rebirth due to their
> misconceptions.

21. Without relying on the conventional, you will never realize the ultimate meaning.
22. One who tries to ascend to the top of the palace of authentic reality without the stairway of authentic obscurative [phenomena] should not be counted among the wise.
23. If the way obscurative [phenomena] appear is investigated with reason, nothing whatsoever is found. That very not-finding is

the ultimate meaning, the primordially present, actual nature of reality.

24. Insofar as they are produced by causes and conditions, obscurative [phenomena] are determined just as they appear. If they could not be so determined, by whom would the moon in water, and so on, be produced?
25. Thus, all appearances are determined insofar as they are produced by various causes and conditions. If the continuum of the conditions is cut, they do not occur, even obscuratively.
26. Therefore, if one is not deluded by views and one's conduct is very pure, one will not go astray on a mistaken path, but will go to the realm of Akaniṣṭha.
27. Life is short, and there are many things to know. But since the exact length of your lifespan is something you cannot know, take up what you long for with gusto, like the swan that extracts milk from water.
28. Though I, a fool with a confined outlook, am incapable of establishing the two realities, this is a presentation of the two realities in the tradition of Nāgārjuna, based on the speech of my gurus.
29. Even should people today adopt this presentation, composed for the sovereign of Suvarṇadvīpa, they should examine it well and then take it up, but not merely out of faith and reverence.
30. After the sovereign of Suvarṇadvīpa, the Gurupāla, sent the monk Devamati to me, I composed this *Guide to the Two Realities* for his sake. It would be worthwhile for the wise of the present day to examine it.

This concludes *A Guide to the Two Realities*, composed by the ācārya and mahāpaṇḍita Dīpaṃkara Śrījñāna. That paṇḍita and the translator Gya Tsöndrü Sengé translated, edited, and finalized it.

Translated by B. Alan Wallace and Eva Natanya

4. Commentary to Atiśa's *Pith Instructions on the Middle Way*

(*Madhyamopadeśavṛtti*)

Prajñāmokṣa

Homage to Ārya Lokeśvara![33]

[233] Having paid homage to bodhicitta,
which dispels the miseries of sentient beings
and is the cause of ever-increasing virtue,
now I shall elucidate the *Pith Instructions on the Middle Way*.

So that those who, due to misconceptions,
have become mired in the swamp of saṃsāra,
may rely fully on the path of the pith instructions
and thereby achieve perfect enlightenment,
I shall explain just the meaning of the pith instructions.

> **I bow to supreme, holy beings**
> **whose light rays of speech**
> **open the lotuses of the hearts**
> **of all deluded beings without exception, including myself.**

33. Words appearing in bold font are from Atiśa's root text, *Pith Instructions on the Middle Way*.

The text begins by paying homage to one who is endowed with excellent qualities. The intention behind this is for the Ācārya himself to come to know those beings as the most excellent, holy beings, to pacify obstructive forces, and to commit to presenting the explanation. This verse reveals two points synthesized as one: devotion by praising excellent qualities and devotion by paying homage. Regarding excellent qualities, know that these can be included within the bounty of excellent qualities for the sake of others' interests and for the sake of one's own interests. Regarding excellent qualities for the sake of others, there are causes and results. In that respect, **whose light rays of speech** refers to the excellent cause. **Open the lotuses of the hearts of all deluded beings without exception, including myself** refers to the excellent result. **Supreme, holy beings** refers to the fulfillment of one's own interests; the plural of "beings" refers to there being many.[34] **I bow to** are words of paying homage.

Now I shall explain the meaning of each element of the homage. **Whose** is the word for the agent, and though it is a generic term, it clearly applies only to buddhas and not to any other beings. This is the occasion for devotion by praising the excellent qualities of the buddhas and by paying them homage. It is like saying, "Call the piebald!"; even though "piebald" is a generic term [for multicolored], it applies to a piebald cow when one wants milk. The expression **light rays of speech** refers, moreover, to the light rays of the enlightened body, speech, and mind. They are like white, red, and blue light and like the light of the sun and moon. With the rising of the sun, its light dispels great darkness, causes flowers [234] and so on to open up, causes various medicinal herbs and fruits to ripen, eases discomfort inflicted by the cold of frost and so forth, comforts sentient beings with the feeling of warmth, illuminates what is and is not the path and sheds light on things that are unclear, and it outshines other lights such as those from the

34. Though the plural marker does not appear in this line in Atiśa's root text in any extant editions of the Tengyur (*dam pa'i skyes mchog de la 'dud*), this explanation indicates that the Tibetan plural marker *rnams*, or more likely, its Sanskrit equivalent, appeared in the version of the root text on which Prajñāmokṣa was commenting.

stars. Likewise, the light rays that reveal the Dharma of the inconceivable life story of the Bhagavān by way of his enlightened body, speech, and mind dispel the darkness of the ignorance of beings; cause the lotuses of their minds to open up and all their unripened mindstreams to ripen; pacify harm from beings such as *māras*; soothe the suffering of all sentient beings; bring them to unsurpassable bliss; dispel and eliminate harmful views; and outshine the light of gods and so forth, which comes from karmic maturation. This is also taught in the phrase [from the *Abhisamayālaṃkāra* of Maitreya], "Their light is eclipsed."

Light rays indicate the acts of the agent, and **open** refers to the action that is performed. The words **including myself** refer to the Ācārya himself and so on, so that is easy to understand. **Deluded beings** refer to those who have not made manifest the reality of suchness. **Without exception** suggests that the compassion of the Bhagavān is not trifling but is all-pervasive and serves the needs of everyone. **Open the lotuses of the hearts** refers to the heart, which is the basis of the mind, so the name for the basis is applied to that which depends on it. Hence, it means "to open the lotuses of the minds." Moreover, they are like lotuses, for the sight of a lotus arouses pleasure, and it is the source of various fragrances and colors, as well as being the source of honey, and so on. Although it grows from mud, it is untainted by the mud and is far superior to it. Likewise, the mind, too, is the locus of various joys and sorrows, it can experience the taste of coemergent ambrosia, [235] and it can be the source of precious bodhicitta. Although it has adventitious stains, it is by nature clear light and utterly pure. Moreover, this is indicated by the scriptural sayings, "We assert it to be pure, as the element of water, gold, and space are pure," and "The nature of the mind is the Buddha; do not seek the Buddha elsewhere."

Open is to open like a lotus, for the [light rays of speech] expand the mind regarding the five fields of knowledge.[35] As it is said, "The mind

35. The five major fields of knowledge (Skt. *pañcavidyā-sthāna*; Tib. *rig pa'i gnas lnga*): the science of sound (*śabda-vidyā, sgra'i rig pa*), logic (*hetu-vidyā, gtan tshigs kyi rig pa*), inner knowledge of the mind (*adhyātma-vidyā, nang gi rig pa*), medicine (*cikitsā-vidyā, gso ba rig

of one who memorizes, recites, and practices, who inquires of others, listens, and remembers is like a lotus that opens due to the light rays from the sun." Moreover, this is indicated by the admonition [in the *Mahāyānasūtrālaṃkāra* of Maitreya]:

> If he has not become learned in the five fields of knowledge,
> even a supreme ārya will not achieve omniscience.
> Therefore, in order to defeat others in debate
> and to take them under your care,
> as well as for the sake of your own familiarization,
> strive in [the five fields of knowledge].

The phrase **supreme, holy beings** refers to beings who have perfectly abandoned all that is to be abandoned and have attained the perfect bounty of knowledge: that is, whose essential nature is that of the three *kāyas*. **I bow** indicates paying homage to them with virtuous deeds of the body, speech, and mind.

> **These are the pith instructions on the Mahāyāna's Middle Way: Obscuratively, with regard to all phenomena, from the perspective of those with a confined outlook, all presentations, including those of cause and effect, are real in terms of how they appear. Ultimately, or authentically, if whatever appears obscuratively—and just that—is deconstructed and negated with compelling reasonings, one must comprehend with certainty that the dimensions of something split even down to one-hundredth the size of the tip of a hair cannot be apprehended.**

pa), and fine arts and architecture (*śilpakarmasthāna-vidyā, bzo gnas kyi rig pa*). The five minor fields of knowledge: astronomy and mathematics (*jyotiṣa-vidyā, skar rtsis*), poetry (*kāvya-vidyā, snyan ngag*), rhetoric (*abhilāpa-vidyā, mngon brjod*), composition in meter (*chandas-vidyā, sdeb sbyor*), and performing arts (*nāṭaka-vidyā, zlos gar*).

Now, here is the actual presentation of the pith instructions. **These are the pith instructions on the Mahāyāna's Middle Way**, along with what follows, indicates a concise presentation by way of the cause: knowledge that comes from hearing, reflection, and meditation. In that regard, as for ***yāna***, there is the causal yāna and fruitional yāna. The causal [yāna] is the path of the bodhisattvas, for one proceeds from where one is. This, moreover, is in accord with the explanations found elsewhere, regarding how to proceed within the Mantrayāna and how to proceed within the Pāramitāyāna. The fruitional yāna is of the nature of the three kāyas, for that is the destination to which one proceeds. It is **mahā** because of its greatness in wisdom, compassion, and so on, as indicated by the phrase [in the *Prajñāpāramitāsaṃcayagāthā*], "great generosity, great intelligence, and great power." With great wisdom one knows all phenomena to be like illusions and [236] one is not attached to anything. With great compassion it is said that skillful means and wisdom are continuously integrated for the welfare of sentient beings. Such is the path of the bodhisattvas.

Those with little wisdom, compassion, and so on are called Hīnayānist, as it is said, "When there is no skillful means and there is a lack of wisdom, one falls to the state of a śrāvaka." Thus, a śrāvaka falls to the extreme of nirvāṇa. By manifesting nirvāṇa with the residual aggregates and then without the aggregates, one forsakes the welfare of sentient beings. Ordinary beings fall to the extreme of saṃsāra and experience all manner of sufferings. Bodhisattvas reject those extremes: with great wisdom they do not abide in the extreme of saṃsāra, and with great compassion they do not abide in the extreme of nirvāṇa, so theirs is called "the nirvāṇa that does not abide in either of the two extremes." This is explained by references to "non-abiding nirvāṇa" and the following verse:

> Indivisible emptiness and compassion:
> when a mindstream relies upon them fully,

> this is the means for becoming a Protector of the World.[36]
> This is the explanation given by all the buddhas.

Therefore, the Mahāyāna is wisdom and compassion. The Middle Way is that which is free from all extremes, and that is the essential, actual Middle Way. Moreover, there is the name and the actuality. The actual Middle Way consists of the two realities, which will be explained below. The nominal Middle Way is the sound that expresses "Middle Way," and that is the mere designation of the words for avoiding the two extremes.

Its **pith instructions** refer to something that is to be revered, for they are so called because with little hardship one realizes great meaning. The addition of "meditation upon them" will be explained below. "Since without beginning" refers to the lack of a beginning or end to saṃsāra. "Reification" means clinging to true existence, as in dualistic grasping and so forth. "Presented as two realities" indicates that in actuality they are neither one nor different.[37] If they were one, then in the process of abandoning obscurative reality, ultimate reality would be abandoned; just as there are different obscurative realities, there would have to be different ultimate [237] realities; and just as obscurative reality is tainted, ultimate reality would also have to be tainted. If they were different, there could not be both an entity and its actual nature; [the ultimate] would not supersede the characteristics of composite phenomena; and there would also be no point to following the path. Therefore, they cannot be said to be either one-and-the-same or different from one another. This is in accord with the more elaborate discus-

36. The Tibetan term for "the means for becoming" here (*sgrub thabs*) is a translation of the Sanskrit term *sādhana*. The "Protector of the World," Lokanātha, is the form of Avalokiteśvara to whom Atiśa pays homage at the beginning of the root text.

37. The phrases "meditation upon them," "since without beginning," "reification," and "presented as two realities," referred to here are not found in the extant versions of Atiśa's root text. "And meditation upon them," may have been added to Atiśa's opening reference to the "pith instructions on the Mahāyāna's Middle Way [and meditation upon them]," and the subsequent missing line may have meant something like "That which has been reified without beginning is presented here as being two realities."

sions of this point found elsewhere. In brief, it is stated [in the *Saṃdhinirmocana Sūtra*]:

> The domain of conditioned phenomena and the ultimate
> defining characteristic
> are utterly free from being one or different.
> Whoever thinks they are one or different is in error and
> misguided.

This also teaches that, just as it is with the whiteness of a conch shell and the like, [the ultimate defining characteristic] is free of being the same or other [than that which it defines]. This was the concise meaning.

To give an expanded explanation of the elements of the text: **Obscuratively, with regard to all phenomena,** along with what follows, indicates that "with the understanding derived from hearing and thinking, one trains in seeing all phenomena in terms of the two realities." Here, **obscurative** refers to a deluded consciousness that obscures the reality of suchness, as explained elsewhere. The phrase **all phenomena** means "all without exception" and is easy to understand. **Those with a confined outlook** are those who do not see reality. **From the perspective of** refers to their fixated attitude. **[All presentations,] including those of cause and effect** refers to the [presentations of the] aggregates, elements, sense bases, and so forth. **In terms of how they appear** refers to [what appears] when one is quite happy not to investigate further, suggesting that these phenomena appear but have no inherent nature. This is also the meaning of [Nāgārjuna's] verse [from the *Yuktiṣaṣṭikā*], "Things that are dependent, like the moon in water, are neither authentic nor false. Do not be carried away by views that assert them." **Real** means real in the sense of being capable of performing a function. They are real merely as appearances, but if they are investigated and examined, they are not determined to be real. Moreover, [Jñānagarbha's *Satyadvayavibhaṅgavṛtti*] states,

> If something is investigated with reasoning, it is not real.
> But apart from that, it is real.
> Thus, how could there be any contradiction
> between real and unreal regarding one single thing?

Ultimately refers to [238] authentic wisdom, which is *sublime* because it is not misleading with regard to authentic *reality*—or because it yields the *sublime* result—and so it is the *sublime goal* toward which one has earnestly striven.[38] If one investigates with this [authentic wisdom], nothing at all is determined to exist. **Whatever appears obscuratively** refers to external and internal entities. The term **compelling reasonings** refers to reasonings that are not misleading in terms of proving that which is to be proven; it also indicates [the logical concept] that "if there is a natural connection derived from conventional valid cognition, then it will be implicitly understood." **Compelling** [in general] means that [such reasonings] are compelling because they rely on conventional reasonings such as [inferring fire on the basis of] smoke and so on; but in that case, they are not misleading with regard to conventional objects. In this context, however, [such reasonings] are said to be compelling because they are not misleading with respect to authentic reality, they vanquish all categories of reified entities, subdue all demons of false views, and refute all extremes of conceptual elaboration. Thus it is said [in Nāgārjuna's *Mūlamadhyamakakārikā*], "This emptiness [taught by] all the *jinas*[39] definitively clears away all views." The plural [of "reasonings"] refers to four kinds:[40]

38. Note that the Tibetan word *dam pa*, which appears in the word for "ultimate reality," also means "sublime," and the word *don*, which is the term used here for "reality," can also mean a "goal," as in the phrase *don du gnyer ba*, "to earnestly strive toward."

39. Tib. *rgyal ba*. Literally, a "victorious one" who has conquered the afflictive and cognitive obscurations; this is another term for a buddha.

40. The first two quotations are from Nāgārjuna's *Mūlamadhyamakakārikā*, while the third is from Jñānagarbha's *Satyadvayavibhaṅgavṛtti* and the last is from Śāntarakṣita's *Madhyamakālaṃkāra*.

1. "Whatever occurs in a dependently related manner is unceasing and unoriginated."
2. "Nothing arises from itself or from something else, or from both, or without a cause. Nothing whatsoever comes into being at any time."
3. "Many things do not produce a single entity, nor do many things produce many. One thing does not produce many things, nor does one thing produce one thing."
4. "Since these entities postulated by our own and others' [philosophical schools] are devoid of any nature of being either authentically singular or authentically plural, they have no inherent nature—like reflections."

These represent just a fraction of the arguments, but they are in accord with the more elaborate discussions presented elsewhere.

The **deconstruction**[41] and **negation** [of whatever appears obscuratively] is done by way of dividing them into their directional components and analyzing them in terms of sixteen parts, or ten parts, and so on. Their **dimensions** after **splitting** them **down to something one-hundredth the size of the tip of a hair** are extremely minute. The word **comprehend** indicates that "with the knowledge gained from hearing and thinking, one should train in seeing all phenomena in terms of the two realities." Moreover, what precedes [239] such training is the understanding derived from hearing and thinking; once one has listened and thought about it, one meditates. As it is taught: "For those of great learning the inner purity of the forest is a joyful place to grow old," and, "Begin by seeking genuine knowledge."

Now I shall present the stages of meditation on the pith instructions.[42]

While sitting cross-legged on a comfortable cushion, consider

41. Reading the Tibetan *gshegs* as *gzhigs*, as in the edition of the root text currently available.

42. This may be a line from Atiśa's root text that is no longer extant, as indicated by the words "pith instructions" and "meditation" glossed in the commentary that follows.

> **for a while that there are two kinds of entities: physical and nonphysical. Physical things are aggregations of elementary particles, but if those are broken down and deconstructed by way of their directional components, not even the subtlest remains, nor does it appear at all. Something nonphysical is the mind. But even with this, the past mind has ceased and is no more, the future mind has not yet arisen nor has it emerged, and the present mind is extremely difficult to investigate. It has no color and is devoid of form. Being like space, it is indeterminate. Moreover, since it is neither singular nor plural, or else since it is unoriginated, or else since it is by nature clear light, and so forth, when you analyze and deconstruct it with the weapons of reasoning, you will realize that it is indeterminate.**

The meaning of "pith instructions" is as explained above. "Meditation" has the three aspects of the preparation, the actual practice, and the conclusion. **Sitting cross-legged on a comfortable cushion** indicates the preparation for samādhi, which includes the resolve never to forsake any sentient being and the intention—set with great, immeasurable enthusiasm—to achieve great enlightenment. **Consider for a while that there are two kinds of entities** refers to the investigation. **Physical and nonphysical** are mutually exclusive, for the defining characteristics by which they exist are incompatible, and since they include all phenomena, there can be no third alternative. **Physical things** indicates that they are indeterminate as physical form, while we accept them in terms of causes and effects. In this regard, causes consist of the most minute particles of the four elements, but because one can focus on them as having many parts, a single, partless particle cannot be determined to exist. If one single thing is not determined to exist, "the many" cannot be determined either, for the many are of the essential nature of the one and so forth. Thus, apart from being singular or plural, there is no other alternative, as it is said [in Śāntarakṣita's *Madhyamakālaṃkāra*], "Apart from being singular or plural, no entity can be anything else, because these two are mutually exclusive."

Therefore, if elementary particles are indeterminate, the resultant physical phenomena are also indeterminate, just as there is no sprout if there is no seed. This is demonstrated by the statement [in Śrīgupta's *Tattvāvatāravṛtti*], "Thus, because there is nothing that initiates them, substantial entities and so on are negated." This is the meaning of **nor does it appear at all**, as well as of the words, "Appearances are signs, and insofar as they are causes of bondage, signs will no longer emerge."

Now the characteristics of the mind are themselves shown to be invisible, so it is said to be **nonphysical.** [240] In this regard, that which can perform a function is momentary, so the parts of a moment are what are to be divided. **But even** here: **the past** is something that **is no more**, so it does not exist. If it were to exist, it would turn into the present. The **future** is something that has **not yet arisen**, so it does not exist. If it were to exist, then, like the present, it would not be something that has not yet come [that is, not "the future"]. Therefore, the text says, **the present mind is extremely difficult to investigate**. It is difficult to investigate because when it is sought out, it is unobservable. **It has no color and is devoid of form** means that it [has no color], such as blue or yellow, or [any shape], such as long or short. Since it is **neither singular nor plural**, it does not bear analysis as being one or many, as explained elsewhere. **It is unoriginated**, since it does not arise either as something existent or nonexistent. **It is by nature clear light** because it is nonconceptual with respect to itself and is untainted. The phrase **and so forth** refers to the absence of any of the four modes of arising, including the absence of arising from self, from other, from both, from no cause, and so on. In actuality, it transcends the extremes of existence and nonexistence, so it is like an illusion. The phrase, **with the weapons of reasoning**, likens reasoning to weapons because they cut and destroy. The *Jñānālokālaṃkāra* [*Sūtra*] states,

> Homage and praise to the buddhas,
> who have never, at any time, among all phenomena,
> found the mind, and who, knowing all phenomena,
> never objectify anything at all.

The phrase **realize that it is indeterminate** means to realize this through understanding the arguments.

> **Thus, if neither can be determined to have any essential nature at all and both are simply nonexistent, then discerning wisdom itself is also indeterminate. As an analogy, by rubbing two sticks together, fire emerges, which serves as the condition for the two sticks to burn up and become nonexistent. Afterward, just as the very fire that incinerated them dies out by itself, exactly when all phenomena are determined to be nonexistent by means of their individual and general characteristics, wisdom itself disappears and the clear light is not determined to have any essential nature at all. Consequently, anything that could turn into a fault, such as laxity and excitation, is dispelled. During that period, consciousness does not conceive of anything and does not apprehend anything. All kinds of mindfulness and mental engagement are relinquished, and until enemies or thieves—signs or concepts—rise up, consciousness should remain in that way. When you wish to arise, gently uncross your legs and get up, and with a mind that is like an illusion, engage in as much virtue as you can with your body, speech, and mind.**

Thus, if neither can be determined to have any essential nature at all means that this is revealed with samādhi. **Both** refers to physical and nonphysical phenomena. **Neither can be determined** means that they cannot be determined ultimately, and this refutes and stops conceptualizations regarding other things. **Discerning wisdom itself is also indeterminate** refutes and puts a stop to conceptualizations regarding itself. Wisdom is a specific instance of functioning phenomena, so if functioning phenomena are indeterminate, wisdom itself will also be indeterminate, just as if trees are not determined, then the aśoka tree and so forth are refuted thus. [241] Moreover, it is said, "Just as the fire that burns fuel does not remain after the fuel is consumed . . . ," and as summarized above, if the mind is indeterminate, so the mental processes that emerge from it are unable to be determined, like the sun and its rays. As it is said [in Śrīgupta's *Tattvāvatāravṛtti*], "Since the mind is refuted in that way, so are mental processes negated." The statement **As an analogy, by rubbing two sticks together, fire emerges, which serves as the condition for the two sticks to burn up and become nonexistent** expresses this point based on textual authority.[43] Discerning wisdom is said to be like fire, and all conceptualization is like fuel. As it is written, "We assert that all the phenomena of living beings are fuel for the fire of consciousness. When they are incinerated with the fire of thorough analysis, they subside," and "All nonvirtuous thoughts are incinerated in the fire of discernment."

Regarding **individual and general characteristics**, general characteristics include emptiness, identitylessness, and so forth. Individual characteristics include pleasure, distress, and so on. **Wisdom itself** is the consciousness of meditative equipoise. **Disappears** means it is free from conceptualizations of itself or other [phenomena]. The point being made here is also revealed in the following verse [from Jñānagarbha's *Satyadvayavibhaṅgakārikā*]:

> When one does not subsequently perceive
> an identity in the knower or the known,
> because at that time signs do not emerge,
> and because one's attentional stability is firm,
> one does not rise [from meditation].

The clear light refers to that which by nature is pristinely pure. "Free of extremes" refers to freedom from the extremes of permanence, annihilation, and so on.[44] **Is not determined . . . at all** means that it is not determined

43. This precise analogy appears in the forty-third chapter of the *Ratnakūṭa Sūtra* (the chapter on Kāśyapa) as well as in Kamalaśīla's second volume of the *Bhāvanākrama*, though those quotations are not exactly the same as the quotations cited here.

44. This reference to freedom from extremes is not found in the extant version of Atiśa's root

to be singular, plural, or anything else. All **laxity**, **excitation**, and so on are **faults** of samādhi. Laxity is inner dullness, excitation is mental distraction, and **such as** indicates other characteristics. **During that period** refers to the period of meditative equipoise. **Consciousness . . . does not apprehend anything** means that it is free from concepts of an apprehender and what is apprehended. **All kinds of mindfulness and mental engagement are relinquished** means that all thoughts focused on the past and the future are abandoned, [242] as are [thoughts of] beautiful forms and so on. **Conceptual enemies or thieves** are like enemies or thieves because they steal the treasures of samādhi, so they are to be warded off by the sentry of introspection, as it is written [in Bhāviveka's *Madhyamakahṛdaya*]:

> With the rope of mindfulness,
> firmly tether the wayward elephant of the mind
> to the post of the meditative object,
> and gradually bring it under control
> with the hook of wisdom.

Conventionally, this is like the situation in which, when one looks intently at a bonfire, the specific instance of one's hair standing on end in bristling anger will stop.[45] For this reason, it would make no sense for one's accumulation of the two collections [of merit and knowledge] to generate dualistic appearances!

If someone were to say, "Since the Bhagavān is like an illusionist who knows illusions to be illusions and for whom clinging to them as being real does not occur, then he is not mistaken toward those very objects."

[Atiśa would respond,] "If that were the case, then just as proponents of a self know the self as a permanent identity, śrāvakas know things as real enti-

text.

45. That is, just as one's individual anger will be calmed by gazing into the great blaze of a bonfire, the specific instances of the faults of samādhi will all be calmed by the "fire" of the wisdom realizing emptiness.

ties, and Cittamātrins know reflexive awareness as ultimately real, so they would not be mistaken toward those very things. If you say this, try to quote something that will support you!"

If the interlocutor then says, "Since a self and so on are not among objects that can be known as real entities, are refuted by valid cognition, and are not determined by valid cognition, they are mere projections, so the apprehension of them would be mistaken. But they are determined to be mere illusions by valid cognition, and that is not refuted by valid cognition. So, such accurate knowledge would not be mistaken."

[Atiśa would respond,] "That is incorrect. Objects known by unmistaken primordial consciousness are not in any way determined to abide as illusions, just as hallucinations and so on do not abide as objects of unmistaken [conditioned] consciousness."

If the interlocutor then says, "If [buddhas] had no knowledge of obscurative phenomena as they appear, it would follow that there would be no omniscient primordial consciousness."

[Atiśa would respond,] "But if that were the case, then since illusory horses, hallucinations, and so on do not appear to the direct perception of someone with undefective sense faculties, then it would turn out that it is not direct perception [for those who do see them].[46] Therefore, it is incorrect to say that primordial consciousness, which has abandoned all error, is false. If something false were to appear, the primordial

46. The inclusion of "illusory horses" seems to be anomalous here, since the example primarily refers to the situations where those with impaired sense faculties—specifically in the case of cataracts or another eye disease—perceive with direct sensory perception hallucinatory objects such as "falling hairs," which are not seen by those with undefective sense faculties. But there are also cases in which a large group of people with sound sense faculties could collectively perceive a magician's conjured "illusory horses" on the basis of a stick or other innocuous object, and with the conditions of mantra and samādhi. The point here is that simply because hallucinatory objects do not appear to those with healthy sense faculties does not mean that those with defective sense faculties did not have direct sensory perception of those appearances—for they did. Likewise, simply because that which is false does not appear to the omniscient primordial consciousness of a buddha does not negate the fact the false appearances appear to those deluded by ignorance.

consciousness of it would also be mistaken, like apprehending a mirage as water. If that were not so, that object would have to be a real entity, and consciousness [243] would not be mistaken toward it in any way. Therefore, how could the signs of dualistic appearances ever emerge for the final primordial consciousness [of a buddha]? 'Dualistic appearances' and 'delusive signs' are merely different names, but they do not have different referents. As it is stated in a sūtra, 'Subhūti, forms are signs, and sounds are signs.' In addition, as it is stated [in the *Vairocanābhisambodhi Tantra*], 'The samādhi of the buddhas, *mahārṣis*, and *jinaputras* has completely abandoned signs, along with the features of all the worlds.' And there are other statements like these."

If, due to fear and terror that obscurative phenomena do not exist, someone then says, "If what is obscurative does not appear to primordial consciousness, appearances would end up being eliminated[47]—"

[Atiśa would respond,] "That is incorrect. It does not necessarily follow that what does not appear is eliminated, so it is the epitome of what cannot be ascertained. This is like cases of a double moon, hallucinations, and so on not appearing to the consciousness of undefective sense faculties; that consciousness does not eliminate them. When examined by wisdom and primordial consciousness, there is nothing that is true or false, existent or nonexistent, and phenomena do not abide anywhere, so this is called the nonabiding Middle Way. As it is written [in Nāgārjuna's *Yuktiṣaṣṭikā*]:

> Those whose cognition transcends existence and nonexistence
> and does not abide [in any extreme]
> meditate thoroughly on the meaning of 'conditionality,'
> which is profound and devoid of objectification."

This also explains the stages of hearing and thinking. Apart from that, all

47. Reading *bsal bar* for *gsal bar* here and in the next paragraph.

obscurative phenomena are present as objects of conventional valid cognition, so their existence is not denied.

> **If those of good fortune practice with reverence uninterruptedly for a long time, they will see reality[48] in this very lifetime, and without striving or exertion, they will naturally and spontaneously make manifest all phenomena, like the vault of space. By achieving the post-meditative state, they will know all phenomena to be like illusions and so on. From the time that they make manifest the vajra-like samādhi, they will no longer have any post-meditative states, for they will rest in meditative equipoise at all times. I shall not speak here of reasonings and scriptures regarding such questions as "If that were not the case, how would they be any different from bodhisattvas?" By the power of accumulating the collections for the sake of others for countless eons, and by the power of offering prayers, they become what is needed in accordance with the inclinations of disciples. There are a great number of scriptures and reasonings [on this topic], but I shall not elaborate on them here.**

Samādhi is the one-pointedness of the mind upon its object, and it has unobstructed potency as the immediately preceding cause for accomplishing the inconceivable three kāyas. **From the time that they make manifest [the vajra-like samādhi]** means that from the time one achieves the state of an authentically and perfectly enlightened buddha, because one is enlightened in the actual nature of equality, while there are specific instances of primordial consciousness, within the nature of the absolute space of phenomena they are one. Likewise, although the Ganges, Sindhu,

48. The Degé Tengyur edition has "will see bliss" (*bde ba mthong bar 'gyur*), but the Peking and Narthang editions of the Tengyur have "will see reality" (*bden pa mthong bar 'gyur*), which seems a preferable reading given the context.

Pakṣu, and so on are different rivers, in the nature of the great ocean they are one; as it is said [in the *Abhisamayālaṃkāra*], "Because there are no divisions within the absolute space of phenomena, there cannot be different lineages," [244] and "Divisions are made in terms of the phenomena that serve as bases."

They will no longer have any post-meditative states because signs do not emerge. **Times** refers to earlier, later, and so forth. **Meditative equipoise** does not waver from the absolute space of phenomena; as it is written [in Vasubandhu's *Abhidharmakośabhāṣya*], "An elephant is in equipoise whether it is resting or gets up." **If that were not the case** means, "If the signs of dualistic appearances were to emerge," then, **how would they be any different [from bodhisattvas]?** This means [buddhas] would then be no different from those who are on the path of training, for they would not have abandoned the delusive conceptualizations of dualistic grasping. Since they would not have become enlightened in the actual nature of equality, the signs of dualistic appearances would emerge, but this is not correct. As it is said [in the *Vairocanābhisambodhi Tantra*], "Enlightenment has the defining characteristic of space, because all signs have been abandoned." Since, as it is also said, "Subhūti, primordial consciousness has no object. If primordial consciousness were to have an object, it would not be known as primordial consciousness," then how could signs ever emerge?

The phrase **for the sake of others**, and so on, addresses the following qualm: "If dualistic appearances were not to emerge, the stream of appearances to primordial consciousness would cease, so offering prayers and accumulating the collections would be pointless." It is stated here that from a nonconceptual domain the two *rūpakāyas* emerge and inconceivably serve the needs of sentient beings. There is no contradiction in [the buddhas] being without conceptualization while benefit for sentient beings emerges, just as waves emerge from the ocean, light emerges from the sun, and all that one needs and wants emerges from a wish-fulfilling jewel. In addition, this is indicated by examples such as that of a stūpa, from which benefit for sentient beings emerges, even though it is without conceptualization.

Reasonings refer to valid cognitions that can refute [contrary assertions]. **Scriptures** are the words of the Buddha. **I shall not speak here** refers to his concern with being too verbose. **For the sake of others** refers to their mundane and supramundane well-being. **Countless eons** are innumerable. **Collections** means the collections of merit and knowledge, which are the causes [of enlightenment]. **Offering prayers** [245] is for others' welfare. **Disciples** indicates the eyes and so forth of those with pure mindstreams. **In accordance with the inclinations** means that [the buddhas] appear in specific ways to train each disciple, for they **become what is needed** in accordance with what different types of beings admire, as it is said [in the *Saṃvarodaya Tantra*, the *Source of Vows*]:

> Various types of behavior are displayed
> for sentient beings with many different inclinations.
> In response to teachings on the profound, actual nature of
> reality,
> even if they are not appealing to you, do not disparage them,
> for the actual nature of reality is inconceivable.

In reality, the Bhagavān does not possess the *buddhakāyas* and so on, nor any of the signs of dualistic appearances. In this regard, it is said, "Not wavering from the absolute space of phenomena, one remains in a state of nonconceptuality," and as it is also said [in the *Vajracchedikā Sūtra*], "Some see me as form." Therefore, although the *dharmakāya* is like space, which has no distinctions such as a periphery or center, various colors, and so on, sentient beings conceive of it as having a periphery and center, as being blue and yellow, and as having many distinctions.

If someone were to say, "If the rūpakāyas and so on are without conceptualization, it would be implausible for them to be able to serve the needs of sentient beings."

[Atiśa would respond,] "This issue has already been explained above. Although the sun is without conceptualization, rays of light emerge and illuminate things. The sphere of the sun itself is not its light rays. If the sphere of the sun itself were its light rays, it would be inside houses and so on, it would be located in this [or that] particular region, and that sphere itself would become diverse [that is, be located wherever its light rays reached]. The light rays themselves are also not the sphere of the sun, for if they were, they would remain right there in the sky and would not illuminate all things. Therefore, although the sun is not its light rays, light rays emerge from it and illuminate all things. To make this same point, a sūtra states, 'The Buddha is like space, and sentient beings are like mountains.' This is inconceivable."

The enlightened view of Dīpaṃkara is difficult [246] to fathom,
and the great meaning of the Middle Way is not an object of cognition.
Nevertheless, Prajñāmokṣa has clearly presented these pith instructions
to reveal the meaning to those who do not know it and desire instruction.

By whatever merit has been acquired from this virtue,
may the precious teaching remain in this world
for as long as earth, water, fire, air, and space remain,
and may all beings achieve the state of enlightenment.

This completes the text called *Pith Instructions on the Middle Way* composed by the paṇḍita Dīpaṃkara Śrījñāna. That same Indian preceptor[49] and I, the translator and bhikṣu, Lotsāwa Tsultrim Gyalwa, translated, edited, and set the final version at the Trulnang temple in Lhasa. It was at a request to the paṇḍita named Dīpaṃkara Śrījñāna by Lekpé Sherab of the Tibetan noble Ngok clan that I have translated this text in the Rasa [Lhasa] Trulnang Tsuklag Khangchen. I, Naktso Tsultrim Gyalwa, affirm that the Elder Dīpaṃkara Śrījñāna,

49. This phrase appears only in the Peking and Narthang editions of the Tengyur.

who holds the scriptural tradition of individuals of the three capacities, does not go astray on errant paths.

This completes the commentary to *Pith Instructions on the Middle Way* composed by the paṇḍita Prajñāmokṣa. It was translated [into Tibetan], edited, and finalized by the Indian preceptor Prajñāmokṣa himself and the Bhikṣu Tsultrim Gyalwa [that is, Naktso Lotsāwa].

Translated by B. Alan Wallace and Eva Natanya

5. The Eight-Verse Mind Training

Geshé Langri Thangpa Dorjé Sengé

With the resolve to accomplish
the highest welfare for all sentient beings
who surpass even a wish-fulfilling jewel,
may I always hold them dear.

Whenever I associate with anyone,
may I regard myself as the lowest among all
and cherish them as supreme
from the very depths of my heart.

In all activities may I examine my mindstream
and as soon as a mental affliction arises,
since it is malignant for myself and others,
may I forcefully turn away from it.

When I encounter sentient beings of a miserable nature,
seeing that they are oppressed by strong vices and misery,
may I cherish these beings so difficult to find,
as if I had found a precious treasure.

When others out of envy treat me unreasonably
with abuse, slander, and the like,
may I accept defeat
and offer the victory to them.

Even when one to whom I had brought benefit
and in whom I had great hopes, without any reason harms me,
may I regard that person
as my sublime spiritual friend.

In short, may I directly and indirectly
offer benefit and happiness to all my mothers,
and may I secretly take upon myself
all their harm and suffering.

May all this be undefiled by the conceptual stains
of the eight mundane concerns,
and by recognizing all phenomena as illusions,
without clinging, may we be freed from bondage.

Translated by B. Alan Wallace

The Words of Mañjuśrī

Sakya Pith Instructions to Transform One's Life

The Sakya order is an illustrious lineage, whose eleventh-century founder, Khön Könchok Gyalpo (1034–1102), was a member of the ancient Khön clan, which is understood to have descended from celestial deities during the time of the Tibetan empire. Khön Könchok Gyalpo's recorded ancestors include a minister of the eighth-century Tibetan king Trisong Detsen, and a brother who was one of the first seven monks ordained under Śāntarakṣita. The Khön family thus held and had maintained many of the secret Vajrayāna rites passed down from the time that Padmasambhava had granted empowerments in the Tibetan imperial court. But by the eleventh century, after the collapse of the Tibetan empire and the ensuing period of fragmentation, some of the Nyingma traditions had been weakened or become corrupt. Dismayed by witnessing the public display of rituals meant to be kept strictly private, Khön Könchok Gyalpo set out to study first the Hevajra tantric cycle and later the Cakrasaṃvara and Guhyasamāja cycles with esteemed translators who were newly importing lineages of Indian Vajrayāna into Tibet. In 1073, Khön Könchok Gyalpo founded Sakya Monastery in a valley known for its extraordinary geographical features (including "pale grey earth," the meaning of the Tibetan word, *sa kya*), which Jowo Atiśa had visited a few decades earlier. There Atiśa had made prostrations and offerings before a vision of sacred syllables and explained, "This is a sign that in the future one emanation of Avalokiteśvara, seven emanations of Mañjuśrī, and one emanation of Vajrapāṇi will come to this place, and that from that time forward, emanations of these three enlightened beings will come in an unbroken stream and work for the sake of living creatures."[50]

It was Khön Könchok Gyalpo's son, Sachen Kunga Nyingpo (1092–1158), who is regarded by the Sakyapas to have been an emanation of Ārya Avalokiteśvara. As a boy, Sachen Kunga Nyingpo received early training from his father, who passed away when he was just ten years old. He continued his training in both sūtra and tantra under the great translator Bari Lotsāwa, and at the age of twelve, entered an intensive retreat to meditate on the deity Mañjuśrī, the embodiment of the wisdom of all buddhas. While sitting in a cave at Sakya, reciting Mañjuśrī's *Arapatsana* mantra, the boy experienced some disturbing visions, which appeared "sometimes in the form of a man made of conch shell and at other times in the form of a great lion." When the boy shared this with his teacher, Bari Lotsāwa, he was told that there was a harmful spirit trying to obstruct his practice "and that he could dispel these interferences by meditating on Akṣobhya. He then received the appropriate teachings, permission to practice, and the method for blessing water with the power to protect. By putting these into practice, the obstacles disappeared. Lord Mañjuśrī then appeared to him, his body the color of pure gold, one hand displaying the mudrā of turning the Wheel of Dharma, while sitting in the lotus posture on a precious throne. To Mañjuśrī's sides appeared his companions, the golden colored bodhisattvas Akṣayamati and Pratibhānakūta."[51]

It was at this moment that the divine being appearing before him spoke the verses to Sachen Kunga Nyingpo that are translated below as *Parting from the Four Types of Clinging*. Sachen Kunga Nyingpo went on to become an incomparable master of many lineages of sūtra and tantra that would

50. Sherab Gyaltsen Amipa, *Waterdrop from the Glorious Sea: A History of the Sakya Tradition of Tibetan Buddhism*, trans. B. Alan Wallace (Rikon, Switzerland: Tibet Institute, 1976), 9.

51. Sherab Gyaltsen Amipa, 22.

form the bedrock of the Sakya tradition, especially the oral lamdré tradition of the path and its fruition, which stems from the Indian mahāsiddha Virūpa.[52] Nevertheless, the four lines spoken to the young Sachen by Mañjuśrī (also known as Mañjughoṣa) continue to form the core pith instructions for Sakya teachings on the steps of the non-tantric Mahāyāna, for which innumerable commentaries have been written and taught over the centuries.

Following the root verses spoken to Sachen Kunga Nyingpo, we include a brief and authoritative commentary by the most renowned of the early Sakya masters, Sakya Paṇḍita Kunga Gyaltsen (1182–1251). Sakya Paṇḍita was Sachen Kunga Nyingpo's grandson and was trained closely by his uncle, Jetsun Drakpa Gyaltsen (1147–1216). Sakya Paṇḍita was a child prodigy, displaying the ability to speak Sanskrit while still a toddler and memorizing key texts of the Hevajra cycle by the age of ten. In addition to his vast knowledge of Dharma, he became a master of medicine, the arts, and various languages, as well as being a superlative logician. Thus, he earned the title of *mahāpaṇḍita* when he was able to recite a text in Sanskrit that he had just heard from the Kashmiri mahāpaṇḍita Śākyaśrībhadra (1140–1225), while having the same text only in Tibetan in front of him.[53] Sakya Paṇḍita became renowned for his writings in the fields of valid cognition, the Middle Way, the three sets of vows (that is, the *prātimokṣa*, bodhisattva, and Vajrayāna vows), linguistics, and tantra. Over time, he was recognized as an actual embodiment of Mañjuśrī, thus revealing himself as one of the seven emanations of Mañjuśrī prophesied by Atiśa to appear in the land of Sakya. As written by Sherab Gyaltsen Amipa:[54]

> When the great being Kunga Gyaltsen [Sakya Paṇḍita] translated his treatise *The Treasure of Knowledge Concerning Ideal Cognition* into Sanskrit, its fame spread throughout eastern,

52. For a more extensive biography, see https://treasuryoflives.org/biographies/view/Sachen-Kunga-Nyingpo/2916.

53. Sherab Gyaltsen Amipa, *Waterdrop from the Glorious Sea*, 36.

54. Sherab Gyaltsen Amipa, 38–39.

> western, and central India. At that time, several non-Buddhist *paṇḍits* including Harinanda came to debate with him in the town of Kyirong in the western Tibetan region of Mangyül. For thirteen days they debated, with the result that the non-Buddhists lost. Then Harinanda saw Lord Mañjuśrī appear by the right shoulder of Sakya Paṇḍita, and he said to the *paṇḍit*, "It was not you that I could not defeat, but rather the orange being with the sword by your right shoulder. It's because of him that you won and I was defeated. You have won in terms of debate, but now let us compete in supernormal powers!" And he flew into the sky. Sakya Paṇḍita clapped his hands and Harinanda fell to the earth. Then Harinanda cut off his long hair, took the vows of a Buddhist monk and served the Buddhadharma. The well-known statue of the deity (as he appeared at that time) called "Mañjuśrī, the Victor in Debate," is found today in the Lhachen Temple.

At the age of sixty-three, Sakya Paṇḍita was invited to the royal camp of the Mongolian prince Godan Khan, who was overlord of the regions of the Mongolian empire bordering on Tibet at that time. Godan Khan sought a spiritual guide in Sakya Paṇḍita, who remained in the region of the Mongolian court from 1246 until he passed away amid miraculous signs in 1251. Sakya Paṇḍita's influence there would contribute significantly to the lasting establishment of Buddhism in Mongolia.[55]

The Sakya tradition is famed for its conscientious observance of monasticism existing side-by-side with the esteemed family lineage at its helm and for its tradition of thorough education in classical Sūtrayāna topics as they had been taught in the Indian Buddhist monasteries (following Sakya Paṇḍita's rigorous example). These were conjoined with the practice of the

55. For further biographical details, see https://treasuryoflives.org/biographies/view/Sakya-Pandita-Kunga-Gyeltsen/2137.

profound tantric lineages of Hevajra, Cakrasaṃvara and Guhyasamāja—culminating in the pith instructions of lamdré, which were kept strictly secret until each disciple was prepared to receive them. Through the legacy of Sakya Paṇḍita and then his nephew Chögyal Phakpa (1235–1280) in their relationship with Mongolian Khans, Sakya Monastery would also become the seat of substantial political influence in Tibet for about a century (until the mid-fourteenth century), paving the way for the type of "priest–patron" relationship that would protect Tibetan freedom for centuries in the face of its more politically powerful neighbors.

We include here as well excerpts from a commentary on *Parting from the Four Types of Clinging* by the twentieth-century Sakya master Khenchen Appey Rinpoché, Ngakwang Yönten Zangpo (1927–2010). Khenchen Appey Rinpoché studied extensively in his youth, especially under the nonsectarian Sakya master Jamyang Khyentsé Chökyi Lodrö, and became a highly respected abbot and teacher in Tibet before going into exile in Sikkim in 1959. Over the following decades, Khenchen Appey Rinpoché helped to found and was a principal teacher first at Sakya College and later at the International Buddhist Academy (IBD), in India and Nepal respectively, spending about five years in meditation retreat in Pharping in between.[56] The passages included here, in English translation, consist of two brief excerpts from transcripts of teachings he offered orally in Tibetan to a gathering of hundreds of monks at the International Buddhist Academy in Kathmandu in June 2007. Khenchen Appey Rinpoché shares a classical lineage on several different types of meditation, including very important points on how to put the key topics of the Mahāyāna path into practice through analytical meditation, even long before one has achieved the full fruits of stabilizing meditation in śamatha.

Thus, the teachings based upon *Parting from the Four Types of Clinging* serve as preparation for every other practice of the Mahāyāna and

56. For a more extensive biography, see https://www.khenpoappey.org/en/khenpo-appey-rinpoche.

Vajrayāna. If one knows how to look, one can find all the stages of the path to enlightenment right there in these four lines. If we can put them into practice through stabilizing meditation and analytical meditation, the realizations that ensue from fully comprehending these lines will make every subsequent Buddhist practice authentic.

6. Practical Instructions on *Parting from the Four Types of Clinging*

Sachen Kunga Nyingpo

Oṃ svasti siddhi.

When the Great Sakyapa Lama (Sachen Kunga Nyingpo) was twelve years old, for six months he engaged in the practice of the noble Mañjughoṣa, such that on one occasion he directly perceived the noble Mañjughoṣa in the midst of an array of light, sitting upon a jeweled throne, orange in color, displaying the excellent mudrā of teaching the Dharma, with two bodhisattvas on his right and left. And the Lord spoke:

> If you cling to this life, you are not a Dharma practitioner.
> If you cling to the three realms, that is not the spirit of emergence.
> If you cling to your own concerns, you are not a bodhisattva.
> Where there is grasping, that is not the view.

By examining the meaning of this utterance, he recognized that all the practices of the path of the transcendences are synthesized in the mind training of parting from the four types of clinging, and he attained an extraordinary certainty with respect to all dharmas. *Samāptaṃ ithi.*

Translated by B. Alan Wallace

7. Unmistaken Practical Instructions on *Parting from the Four Types of Clinging*

Sakya Paṇḍita Kunga Gyaltsen

I bow at the feet of the sublime Guru!

Upon having acquired a body with leisure and opportunity in general, having encountered the precious teachings of the Buddha, and having aroused an uncontrived [virtuous] attitude, one should engage in an unmistaken sublime Dharma. So in that regard, one should practice parting from the four types of clinging. What are they? Not clinging to this life, not clinging to the three realms of saṃsāra,[57] not clinging to one's own concerns, and not clinging to phenomena and signs. To explain them:

This life is like a water bubble, so the time of death is uncertain. Therefore, clinging to this life is not worth its price.

The three realms of saṃsāra are like poisonous fruit, which is momentarily tasty but eventually inflicts harm. Anyone who clings to them is fooled.

If you cling to your own concerns, this is like letting an enemy take care of your child. Although it may seem to be fun for a while, eventually this will definitely hurt you. Thus, if you cling to your own concerns, while

57. This refers to the three realms of conditioned existence known as the desire, form, and formless realms. See the discussion below in the section on the view in "A Lamp for Dispelling the Five Obscurations."

temporarily there is pleasure, eventually you will go to a miserable state of existence.

If you cling tenaciously to things and signs, this is like mistaking a mirage for water. Although it temporarily looks like water, when you come upon it, there is nothing to drink. Although this saṃsāra appears to a deluded mind, if it is examined with intelligence, there is nothing that can be determined as having any essential nature. Thus, by understanding that the mind does not enter into the past, nor does it enter into the future, and consciousness does not enter the present, you should come to know that all phenomena are free of elaborations.

By so doing, you will not cling to this very life and consequently will not be born in a miserable state of existence.

By not clinging to the three realms of saṃsāra, you will not be born in saṃsāra.

By not clinging to your own concerns, you will not take birth as a śrāvaka or *pratyekabuddha*.

By not clinging to things or signs, you will swiftly achieve manifest, perfect enlightenment.

This unmistaken practical instruction on *Parting from the Four Types of Clinging* is the view of the mind of the glorious Great Sakaypa (Sachen Kunga Nyingpo), and this completes the composition by Sakya Paṇḍita.

Translated by B. Alan Wallace

Excerpts from

8. Meditation Guidance on the Mahāyāna *Parting from the Four Types of Clinging*

Khenchen Appey Ngakwang Yönten Zangpo

Generating the Mind of Bodhicitta at the Outset

Please listen to this Dharma teaching by generating the mind of bodhicitta, thinking, "I shall achieve buddhahood for the sake of all sentient beings. In order to do so, I shall listen to the Dharma." Those of you gathered here have come from afar out of great interest in and concern for the Dharma, and I am delighted you have come.

At this time, the Dharma I shall explain is principally *Parting from the Four Types of Clinging*. In general, there are three aspects of the Buddhadharma: (1) the collections of the teachings of the sūtras spoken by the Bhagavān Buddha, (2) commentarial treatises on the enlightened view of the Buddha that were composed by paṇḍitas of India and so on, and (3) pith instructions that arrange the order of the discourses within those teachings and treatises on the many paths to achieving fortunate rebirths and liberation, and explain how to practice, principally for the sake of beginners. There are, moreover, many pith instructions; even in Tibet there are many pith instructions on the Śrāvakayāna and the non-Mantrayāna Mahāyāna. Among them, in Tibet the two most renowned are *Parting from the Four Types of Clinging*, granted by the noble Mañjughoṣa to Sachen Kunga

Nyingpo, and the mind training granted by Serlingpa [Dharmakīrti of Suvarṇadvīpa] to the glorious Lord Atiśa.[58] *Parting from the Four Types of Clinging* was taught by the noble Mañjughoṣa. On the occasions where the greatness of Mañjughoṣa is extolled in the sūtras, there are also teachings such as the following: It is said that if one utters the name of one buddha, there is great merit. Even more so, if one utters the names of many buddhas, one hardly needs to explain that there is yet greater merit. But it is said that if one utters the name of Mañjughoṣa one time, there is greater merit than saying for an eon as many names of buddhas as the grains of sand on the banks of the Ganges River. Such assertions are made because Mañjughoṣa performs the same number of enlightened activities as those of all the buddhas.

He is the one who inspired many buddhas, including our Teacher, to first generate the aspiration for supreme enlightenment and then aroused them to follow the path. Because of this, Mañjughoṣa is said to be the father of all the buddhas. Another reason is this: the "definitive Mañjughoṣa" is said to be the mind, or wisdom, of all the buddhas. For that reason as well, Mañjughoṣa is called the "father of all the buddhas." The noble Protector Maitreya stated, "Even if many bodhisattvas on the tenth *bhūmi* like me were to observe very carefully, we would not be able to fathom even the warrior's stance displayed by Mañjughoṣa." Many such accounts of the magnificence of Mañjughoṣa are presented in the sūtras.

Śamatha and Vipaśyanā in the Context of Meditation

Regarding meditation, there are the two: śamatha and vipaśyanā. With the cultivation of dhyāna, one achieves stillness in the mind; specifically, if one achieves śamatha, taking that as one's basis, whatever one cultivates, such as loving-kindness, compassion, and so on, the mind will swiftly become accomplished in the training, and the attainments that are the fruition of

58. That is, what was later written down by Geshé Chekawa as *The Seven-Point Mind Training*. See B. Alan Wallace, *The Art of Transforming the Mind*.

each practice will emerge. Śamatha is indispensable as a basis for the higher paths of the three yānas [Śrāvakayāna, Pratyekabuddhayāna, and Bodhisattvayāna]. However, those who lack śamatha may single-pointedly meditate on death and impermanence, cultivate loving-kindness, compassion, and so on. If they meditate again and again, they can gain clear realization of death and impermanence, and loving-kindness, compassion, and so on can arise.

As for methods of meditation, there are two: analytical meditation and stabilizing meditation. For instance, if one cultivates śamatha, one needs to meditate repeatedly by focusing the mind on a single object without letting it disperse elsewhere. In that practice there is no need for analysis. On the other hand, if one cultivates vipaśyanā or meditates on identitylessness, that way of meditating includes both analytical meditation and stabilizing meditation. For instance, in the case of identitylessness, upon reflecting upon one or many reasons for identitylessness, the single-pointed engagement with the reality that cuts through false superimpositions is called "analytical meditation." For someone who has previously gained ascertainment regarding those reasons and has also gained familiarization, then, without thinking about the reasons for the mode of existence of identitylessness, simply focusing one's attention on that identitylessness is called "stabilizing meditation."

For instance, if one meditatively cultivates compassion, by first reflecting upon the reasons why compassion for all sentient beings is necessary, upon all sentient beings as our mothers, upon how much suffering there is, and so forth, this cultivation of compassion is analytical meditation. Without reflecting upon any such reasons, continuously focusing one's mind on the thought "O what compassion for all sentient beings! What compassion I have for each one!" is called "stabilizing meditation." Recite phrases such as "May all sentient beings be free of suffering and the causes of suffering!" Count on your rosary, recite them a hundred times, and if you also bear them in mind a hundred times, those phrases will be of benefit. Those are simply general examples.

Translated by B. Alan Wallace and edited by Eva Natanya

The Words of Mañjuśrī and Vajrapāṇi

View, Meditation, and Conduct as Taught to Tsongkhapa

Jé Tsongkhapa was born in the tenth month of the Tibetan Fire Bird year, 1357, in the region of Tsongkha in the far-eastern corner of the Amdo region of eastern Tibet. He took the novice vows of a monk by the age of six, receiving the name Losang Drakpa, after having begun his formal studies with a respected local teacher, Chöjé Dhöndrup Rinchen. According to some accounts, he had already received several Vajrayāna empowerments and was engaging in mantra retreats even before becoming ordained.[59] By the age of about sixteen he had left home for central Tibet, never to return. For at least the next twenty years, Tsongkhapa traveled from monastery to monastery throughout central Tibet, studying with many of the most respected Buddhist teachers of his time, mainly in the Sakya, Kadam, and Kagyü traditions. His fierce and captivating performance in debate became legendary, and he is said to have had a phenomenal capacity for memorization as well as for samādhi. From the time he was about twenty, his root teacher was a renowned teacher from the Sakya lineage, Jetsun Rendawa Shönu Lodrö (1349–1412). Tsongkhapa maintained a close relationship with this teacher throughout his life; in addition to studying with him all the major topics of sūtra philosophy, Tsongkhapa received a thorough explanation of the Guhyasamāja root tantra from Rendawa in 1390.

59. See Thupten Jinpa, *Tsongkhapa: A Buddha in the Land of Snows* (Boulder, CO: Shambhala Publications, 2019), 25, 27.

Earlier that year, Tsongkhapa had his first meeting with Lama Umapa Pawo Dorjé, a former yak herder from eastern Tibet who had experienced visions of Mañjuśrī since his youth. Lama Umapa sought from Tsongkhapa the blessing of Sarasvatī (and then also received from him teachings on the autocommentary of Candrakīrti's *Madhyamakāvatāra*),[60] while Tsongkhapa, once ascertaining that Umapa's visions were authentic, expressed the aspiration to receive teachings from Mañjuśrī through Umapa as a medium. While Tsongkhapa did not yet have the capacity to see and speak with Mañjuśrī directly, he already had the scriptural knowledge and spiritual authority to tell Umapa, "You should fervently pray to Mañjuśrī, but you must remember that the form that one sees with the eyes is not actually Mañjuśrī himself. The genuine form of a meditation deity appears only at the level of mental cognition, not sensory perception."[61]

The second time Tsongkhapa met with Umapa was in 1392, when they entered an intensive retreat together at Gadong, a Kadampa monastery near Lhasa. They each made fervent prayers and supplications to Mañjuśrī, and then the deity would sometimes appear spontaneously to Umapa, so that he could pose Tsongkhapa's questions to the deity and relay the answers. Tsongkhapa's deepest qualms at the time concerned (1) the correct view of emptiness according to the system of Nāgārjuna and (2) the details of how to understand and manifest the illusory body within the five stages of the completion stage of Guhyasamāja. Regarding the view of emptiness, Tsongkhapa learned from Mañjuśrī that his current view (which reflected an interpretation of Candrakīrti that was prevalent among scholars in Tibet at the time) was *neither* authentically Prāsaṅgika *nor* authentically Svātantrika Madhyamaka. Mañjuśrī then granted Tsongkhapa "a series of teachings on the distinction between the views of Prāsaṅgika Madhyamaka and the Svātantrika; the differences between [connate] versus intellectually acquired forms of grasping at self-existence; the levels of subtlety involved

60. Jinpa, *Tsongkhapa*, 77, 107.

61. Jinpa, 78.

in understanding what is being negated in the context of emptiness; the criteria of finding the correct view of emptiness; and how [obscurative reality] needs to be understood according to Prāsaṅgika Madhyamaka."[62] Tsongkhapa admitted that he could not yet fully understand the teachings he received, but Mañjuśrī exhorted him to continue to supplicate his gurus and engage in sādhana practices, to strive in accumulating merit and in purifying negative karma, and to reflect deeply upon the meaning of the great Indian treatises. It was Mañjuśrī who then directed Tsongkhapa to withdraw from his teaching activities and become a solitary hermit, devoting all his time to these spiritual practices and to meditation.[63] This is what Tsongkhapa would go on to do later that year, taking eight of his disciples with him into long-term retreat in the region of Wölkha.

Meanwhile, at a certain point during that earlier retreat with Umapa at Gadong, Tsongkhapa was inspired to temporarily shift from his primary practice of śamatha to make repeated supplications to Mañjuśrī through visualization and mantra recitation. Only a few days later, Tsongkhapa experienced his own direct vision of the deity's resplendent form,[64] the first of many such visions that would come throughout his life.

The first set of root verses translated below dates to this retreat with Lama Umapa at Gadong, and indeed Umapa Pawo Dorjé is cited as the scribe.[65] Tsongkhapa later composed an extensive commentary to these verses, titled *Guidance in the View of the Middle Way*, which elaborates a sequential practice of śamatha and vipaśyanā that provides detailed instruction for a year or more of intensive, single-pointed retreat practice. It is this *Guidance in the View of the Middle Way* that also forms the structural basis for the poetic verses titled *A Shower of Siddhis: Guidance in the View of the Middle Way as a Song of the Four Recollections*, written by the Seventh Dalai Lama, Losang

62. Jinpa, 109–10.

63. Jinpa, 110.

64. Jinpa, 112.

65. See Jinpa, 112–14, including an alternative translation of these verses.

Kalsang Gyatso, over three hundred years later. Hence, we have included *A Shower of Siddhis* immediately following the root verses for Tsongkhapa's *Guidance in the View of the Middle Way*, though of course it was written centuries later.

The second set of verses from Tsongkhapa that are translated below, *The Synthesis of Practice*, is said to have been spoken by Mañjuśrī directly to Tsongkhapa himself during a vision that took place at Gya Sokphu Hermitage in 1393, after Tsongkhapa and his eight close disciples had spent their first year in retreat together in the region of the Wölkha Valley, southeast of Lhasa. In this vision, Mañjuśrī was surrounded by a host of buddhas, bodhisattvas, and the great masters of India, and a sword of light extended from the deity's heart into Tsongkhapa's own heart, carrying a stream of silver nectar that flowed into his heart, pervading his body and mind with great bliss. The initial verse that begins, "In the city of Katara," is likely a coded poetic allusion to this transcendent experience of divine joy.[66]

It was during this three-year period of retreat in the Wölkha region (from late 1392 to late 1395) that Tsongkhapa was able to devote himself to developing the single-pointed samādhi that would serve as the basis for his later realizations, which would in turn become the source of his piercing clarity and confidence in writing and teaching throughout the last two decades of his life, until his passing in 1419.[67]

It was during a later year-long retreat in the Wölkha Valley, which took place from 1397 to 1398, that Tsongkhapa gained irreversible clarity in his understanding and realization of emptiness.[68] It was only after this transformative experience that Tsongkhapa began writing his major and definitive works on the Middle Way view, including his masterpiece, *The Great*

66. See Jinpa, 129–33, especially note 230, and Thupten Jinpa's alternative translation of these verses on 131–32.

67. As there is no space here to recount the full arc of Tsongkhapa's lifework, much less his "four great deeds," we encourage the reader to turn to Thupten Jinpa's masterful biography *Tsongkhapa*.

68. See Jinpa, *Tsongkhapa*, 166–71.

Treatise on the Stages of the Path to Enlightenment (*Lamrim Chenmo*), completed in 1402. But it was not until 1415 that Tsongkhapa composed an abbreviated version of this work: *The Concise Presentation of the Stages on the Path to Enlightenment*, which was intended more as a handbook for practice in retreat than a comprehensive treatise and omits many of the formal debates and quotations from scripture that support Tsongkhapa's points in the *Great Treatise*.

Nevertheless, in this *Concise Presentation* Tsongkhapa treats a few points in more detail than he had earlier. One such point concerns the precise nature of the nonconceptuality and relinquishment of mental engagement that occur upon actually achieving śamatha, which are *not* the same as the nonconceptuality that emerges from actual vipaśyanā with respect to emptiness.[69] Another crucial point that Tsongkhapa highlights in the *Concise Presentation* is the place of both conceptuality and nonconceptuality in leading to the union of śamatha and vipaśyanā, which is the culminating phase of both transcendent meditation and transcendent wisdom (among the six transcendences that form the entire structure of the bodhisattva's way of life). It is the crucial sections on how to cultivate vipaśyanā in dependence upon śamatha and then on how to achieve the union of śamatha and vipaśyanā that we include here.[70]

Tsongkhapa lived at a special juncture in Tibetan history: at a time when

69. See B. Alan Wallace, *Balancing the Mind: A Tibetan Buddhist Approach to Refining Attention* (Ithaca, NY: Snow Lion Publications, 2005), 207–213, and Jinpa, *Tsongkhapa*, 286–88, for detailed explanations of this point.

70. For the corresponding section in Tsongkhapa's *Lam rim chen mo*, see "Uniting Serenity and Insight" in his *Great Treatise on the Stages of the Path to Enlightenment*, vol. 3 (Ithaca, NY: Snow Lion, 2004), 351–61. Within the *Great Treatise* Tsongkhapa treats many of the points on the importance of analysis earlier, in the section on "Insight Requires Analysis" (327–50), but the way that he integrates these points within the actual section on how to cultivate vipaśyanā within the *Concise Presentation* is especially helpful for practice. For a translation of the entire śamatha section of the *Concise Presentation*, see Wallace, *Balancing the Mind*, chapter 2, and for a translation of the entire vipaśyanā section, including the concluding phase on "How calm abiding and special insight are unified," see Jeffrey Hopkins and Kevin Vose, *Tsong-kha-pa's Final Exposition of Wisdom* (Ithaca, NY: Snow Lion Publications, 2008), 27–179.

there was relative political peace, when there were many thriving monasteries of diverse lineages among which he could move freely—apparently without encountering intersectarian conflict, even as he did meet with a significant diversity of views and interpretations. His comprehensive education took place within the first fifty years after the Tibetan canons of Indian Buddhist works in translation—the Kangyur and Tengyur—had been fully compiled by Butön Rinchen Drup (1290–1364), and these collections then served as the basis for Tsongkhapa's continuous study and memorization of canonical works. There is no doubt that Tsongkhapa brought to his education a truly extraordinary mind and capacity for memorization, critical inquiry, and profound practice. But he also had the fortune to meet with an array of texts and a variety of qualified teachers steeped in an already-confident Buddhist tradition such as he would not have found in Tibet even a century earlier.

On the other hand, it is clear that Tsongkhapa's insatiable hunger for learning was in part due to his dissatisfaction with many of the explanations he received. His written works show him grappling with diverse points of view, and he repeatedly takes it upon himself to resolve apparent contradictions among various ways of interpreting key passages of Indian Buddhist literature. It is also evident that Tsongkhapa did not write most of his major works until the last two decades of his life. He waited until he was sure of his position—based not only on intellectual inquiry but on profound meditative insight and realization—before writing most of the major treatises on both sūtra and tantra that are associated with his name today.

In the excerpts we have chosen for this volume, we glimpse the vivid presence and influence of Mañjuśrī that pervaded Tsongkhapa's mindstream. The view of emptiness expressed in Mañjuśrī's pith instructions to Tsongkhapa resonates deeply with articulations of the view that later Tibetan history more explicitly associates with the Mahāmudrā and Dzokchen traditions. It is crucial for us to recognize that the detailed explanations of the Middle Way view that appear in Tsongkhapa's mature treatises emphasize the compatibility and indivisibility of ultimate and obscurative reality—

indeed the inextricable complementarity of emptiness and dependently related events. Tsongkhapa emphasizes these points as representing the authentic understanding of Candrakīrti's interpretation of Nāgārjuna, and through familiarity with Tsongkhapa's biographies (especially as compiled and integrated by Thupten Jinpa in *Tsongkhapa: A Buddha in the Land of Snows*), we can recognize that he himself had finally come to understand these crucial points only in dependence upon the personal guidance of Mañjuśrī at critical junctures in his life. But we should also recognize that Tsongkhapa emphasizes these points in ways he saw were needed as a corrective to subtle varieties of extreme views that had crept into Tibetan understanding since the introduction of Candrakīrti's work into the Tibetan language in the eleventh century. Tsongkhapa revered Atiśa, and Tsongkhapa's mature view of the Middle Way would not have differed from Atiśa's, but given differences in time and circumstances, Tsongkhapa saw the need to articulate the Middle Way view with far more elaboration, all in order to guide disciples to the same realization: utterly beyond elaboration.

Thus we come to the mystery of the text transmitted to Tsongkhapa by Lhodrak Drupchen Namkha Gyaltsen (1326–1401).[71] Tsongkhapa and his group of eight close disciples visited Lhodrak Drupchen at his invitation in 1395, soon after emerging from their initial three-year period of strict retreat in Wölkha. Tsongkhapa had already heard from one of Drupchen's teachers that he was said to be an emanation of Nāgārjuna's famed student Āryadeva and that he had visions of Vajrapāṇi. When Tsongkhapa first met Lhodrak Drupchen, biographies report that Tsongkhapa actually saw Drupchen in the form of Vajrapāṇi, while Drupchen saw Tsongkhapa in the form of Mañjuśrī. Tsongkhapa received several empowerments from Drupchen, as well as extensive transmissions of the three Kadam lineages of teachings on the stages of the path to enlightenment (*lamrim*), which traced back to Atiśa. Drupchen also received teachings from Tsongkhapa, and there

71. For biographical details, see https://treasuryoflives.org/biographies/view/Drubchen-Namkha-Gyeltsen/2592.

was a deep mutuality in their reverence for and trust in one another. Even after his three-year retreat and numerous direct interactions with Mañjuśrī, Tsongkhapa still had unresolved questions, and Drupchen posed these to Vajrapāṇi on his behalf. The revelation that came as a response is translated here as *Garland of Supreme Medicinal Nectar: Questions and Answers*, which Drupchen sent to Tsongkhapa in writing sometime after the seven months they spent together.[72]

Tsongkhapa's response to the divine teaching is recorded in a letter that he sent to Drupchen, in which he praises these secret vajra words of Ārya Vajrapāṇi, which are "pith instructions that encapsulate the crucial points of the enlightened view of the buddhas and bodhisattvas," as being "without excess, omission, or error." The verse of blissful praise with which he thanks Drupchen includes the phrase "The nectar of the Lord of Mysteries' speech / completely fulfilled my inner hopes"; but here "completely fulfilled" is *dzok par jé*, which in Tsongkhapa's adept use of poetic allusion is very likely not an accidental reference to "completely perfected," as in the "Great Perfection," which is the subject of the teaching.[73]

It is important to note that a large part of the instructional portion of the text matches verbatim a treasure revelation from the *Khandro Nyingtik* (*Heart Essence of the Ḍākinīs*), found in the collected works of Longchenpa (1308–64). There, the conversation is between Guru Padmasambhava and Yeshé Tsogyal, and the text is called *Golden Garland of Nectar: Questions and Answers*.[74] Though Longchenpa preceded Tsongkhapa historically, we have no evidence that Tsongkhapa—or even Lhodrak Drupchen—was

72. See Jinpa, *Tsongkhapa*, 139–44.

73. Tib. *gsang bdag gsung gi bdud rtis yis, yid kyi re ba rdzogs par byas. Lho brag mkhan chen phyag rdor ba la phul ba*, in *Rje'i gsung 'bum, bkras lhun par rnying*, vol. *kha* (*Bka' 'bum thor bu*, 83a) (Dharamsala, India: Sherig Parkhang, c. 1997), 379. See Jinpa, *Tsongkhapa*, 144, for an alternative English translation of the entire verse.

74. See Longchen Rabjam Drimé Öser (1308–63), *Zhus len bdud rtsi gser phreng* (*Golden Garland of Nectar: Questions and Answers*), in *Snying thig ya bzhi, Mkha' 'gro snying tig*, vol. *waṃ*, reproduced from prints from the A 'dzom chos sgar par khang woodblocks (Delhi, India: Sherab Gyaltsen Lama, 1975), 1–34.

aware of Longchenpa's writings or treasures. Lhodrak Drupchen's father was a Nyingmapa, and he had received a Nyingma empowerment when he was five years old, but he spent the majority of his life in Kadam monasteries as a lineage holder of the works of Atiśa.[75]

For what remains in the intricacies of the text, we invite the reader to entertain the possibility that insofar as Lhodrak Drupchen may indeed have received a direct transmission from Vajrapāṇi in a pure vision, there would be nothing in principle to prohibit the omniscient Guru Padmasambhava from transmitting a mind treasure to Tsongkhapa through Lhodrak Drupchen in the form of a pure vision of Vajrapāṇi, whether or not Drupchen already knew of the existing treasure in the *Khandro Nyingtik*. It is important to recognize that in the text here, "Karmavajra" refers to Lhodrak Drupchen as the questioner, and "Matibhadra" (which is Sanskrit for Losang, "Excellent Mind") is the intended recipient of the answers—namely, Tsongkhapa Losang Drakpa. We have relied primarily on the edition of the text that appears in Tsongkhapa's collected works (Tashi Lhünpo woodblocks) while consulting the same text as it appears in two manuscript editions of Lhodrak Drupchen's collected works and incorporating a few alternative readings from those manuscripts in the translation here.

The Seventh Dalai Lama, Losang Kalsang Gyatso

Losang Kalsang Gyatso was born in 1708 in the Litang region of Kham in Tibet. As an infant, he manifested many wondrous signs that displayed the spiritual momentum with which he entered that life. Shortly after his birth, a resident monk who channeled a protective deity, Öden Karpo, named the young boy as the incarnation of the Sixth Dalai Lama.[76]

Amid political conflicts with Lhazang Khang (the *de facto* ruler of Tibet

75. See Jinpa, *Tsongkhapa*, 147. For further significant details about the relationship between Tsongkhapa and Lhodrak Drupchen, see the whole of chapter 7.

76. See https://treasuryoflives.org/biographies/view/Seventh-Dalai-Lama-Kelzang-Gyatso/3107.

at the time) as to who was actually the Seventh Dalai Lama, Kalsang Gyatso was thoroughly examined by the central Tibetan Geluk monasteries in 1714 and officially, but secretly, recognized as the new Dalai Lama. Only in 1720 was it safe for the young boy to arrive at the Potala Palace, where he was soon ordained by the renowned Geluk master the Fifth Paṇchen Lama Losang Yeshé, and given the monastic name Losang Kalsang Gyatso.

In the face of continued political adversity, he was discreetly sent into exile from Lhasa and placed in Gartar Monastery in eastern Kham in order to further his religious studies. He then wholeheartedly devoted himself to study, meditation, teaching, and writing. It was at this time that he wrote his most extensive and highly regarded work, a great commentary on the maṇḍala and initiation rites of the *Guhyasamāja Tantra*.

In addition to being a prolific writer, poet, and scholar, Kalsang Gyatso emerged as a successful political leader for Tibet, while providing new opportunities for laypeople involved in government service to be educated in the fine arts. In 1757, he passed away at the age of fifty, having become the teacher and guide for many notable Geluk lamas of his day.

Root Verses from

9. Guidance in the View of the Middle Way

Spoken by the Noble Mañjughoṣa
to Lama Umapa Pawo Dorjé and Jé Tsongkhapa

Namo Guru Ārya Mañjuśriye.

In reliance upon various dependent relationships,
reveal the nature of existence, just as it is.

Having gone for refuge, gathered the collections, and purified obscurations,
meditate upon dependent relationships, in their forward and reverse order:

I, the fortunate one who practices to accomplish enlightenment,
once settled in the samādhi of meditative equipoise
upon the manifest nature of the sacred body, speech, and mind,
and upon the profound practical instructions—
that all phenomena, whether appearances or emptiness, whether of saṃsāra or nirvāṇa,
are dependently related and lack any nature at all—

shall come to know the meaning of identitylessness:
since the collection of aggregates—body, speech, and mind—
is not determined as a self in any way at all,
and because there is no self apart from these.

The five aggregates, the doors of senses,
the elements, and what emerges from the elements, virtue and nonvirtue:
all phenomena, whether appearances or emptiness, whether of saṃsāra or nirvāṇa,
are dependently related and lack any nature at all.

Free of arising, ceasing, or remaining,
beyond saying *it exists* or *it does not exist*, *it is* or *it is not*,
free of elaboration, indivisible, profound peace:
whoever understands this passes beyond all sorrow.

These are the vajra words of the *Guidance in the View of the Equality of Mundane Existence and Peace*. May there be virtue. . . .

This was written down by [Lama Umapa] Pawo Dorjé exactly according to what was spoken by the noble Mañjughoṣa.[77]

Translated by Eva Natanya

77. This translation follows the version of the verses found in the Tashi Lhünpo and the Zhol editions of Jé Tsongkhapa's collected works, though there are differing versions of the verses recorded in early texts by Tsongkhapa's disciples.

10. A Shower of Siddhis: Guidance in the View of the Middle Way as a Song of the Four Recollections

Losang Kalsang Gyatso, the Seventh Dalai Lama

Upon the immutable seat of skillful means and wisdom united as one
sits the kind guru who is of the essential nature of all sources of refuge,
a buddha, replete in the abandonment [of all obscurations] and realization [of all things], right there.
Abandoning all critical thoughts, supplicate him or her with pure perception.
Without letting your mind wander, rest in a state of admiration and reverence.
Recalling this without forgetting it, sustain this state of admiration and reverence.

Within the prison of limitless saṃsāra's agony
wander sentient beings of the six classes, bereft of happiness:
your very own parents who have nurtured you with such care, right there.
Abandoning attachment and aversion, cherish and arouse compassion for them.
Without letting your mind wander, rest in a state of compassion.
Recalling this without forgetting it, sustain this state of compassion.

Within the divine palace of great bliss, delightful to experience,
dwells your own body—with its pure aggregates and elements—as a divine body,
a personal deity in whom the three kāyas are indivisible, right there.
Without grasping to the ordinary, train in divine pride and luminous appearances.
Without letting your mind wander, rest in a state of the profound and the luminous.
Recalling this without forgetting it, sustain this state of the profound and the luminous.

The maṇḍala of knowable appearances and possible worlds
is pervaded by the space of the actual nature of reality, the ultimate clear light,
the ineffable, actual nature of existence, right there.
Abandoning mental fabrications, attend to the essential nature of sheer emptiness.
Without letting your mind wander, rest in a state of the actual nature of reality.
Recalling this without forgetting it, sustain this state of the actual nature of reality.

At the crossroads of the various appearances to the six collections of consciousness,
observe the haze of dualistic phenomena, devoid of any basis or root,
a deceptive, illusory spectacle, right there.
Without thinking of it as real, attend to the essential nature of emptiness.
Without letting your mind wander, rest in a state of appearances and emptiness.
Recalling this without forgetting it, sustain this state of appearances and emptiness.

Thus, so that I and others may establish habitual propensities for becoming familiar with the authentic view, I, Losang Kalsang Gyatso, a bhikṣu follower of Śākyamuni, composed this song, guidance on the four recollections, consisting of special, practical instructions that the noble Mañjuśrī directly bestowed upon the great Dharma king Tsongkhapa.

Translated by B. Alan Wallace

11. The Synthesis of Practice

Jé Tsongkhapa

Homage to the Noble One who is the Treasury of Knowledge.

You, whose supreme body arose by the power of gathering the two
collections,
whose eyes, delighting in divine compassion, gaze in the ten directions
upon all that is,
who rips out from its root all the delusion that is the foundation of mundane existence,
please grant to sentient beings great wisdom, the life force of liberation.

In the city of Katara,
when the grove of blossoms was in full bloom,
and many bees were dancing in them,
they appeared to drink their fill
of the deathless nectar, supreme.

This is in praise of the occasion when the Omniscient Noble One [Tsongkhapa] saw the face of the noble Mañjughoṣa in a most extraordinary way at Gya Sokphu Hermitage, the time at which he uttered the synthesis of practice.

This, exactly, is the synthesis of practice that the Noble One [Mañjughoṣa] himself spoke at that time:

> Meditate upon the actual nature of the mind,
> which, like space, is not located anywhere.
> Strive in all that assists you in this.
> Like the rhinoceros, remain alone.
>
> Abandon all busy and distracting activity
> and settle inwardly, in meditative equipoise.
> Take your joy in great enlightenment.
> Have no doubt about the ripening of karma.
>
> Meditate upon the spirit of emergence and bodhicitta.
> Continuously ignite the great fire of mindfulness.
> The kindling of the six objects will certainly be consumed.
> Because all phenomena of saṃsāra and nirvāṇa
>
> were never seen by anyone in the past, nor are they seen now,
> they are free of extremes, like space.
> The appearance of objects is like a lotus growing in the sky.
> Who among the tathāgatas has ever found the apprehending mind?
>
> Awareness and its space being identical was established by the barren woman's son.
> Whatever is in accord with this constitutes the path of the jinas.

For the path that leads to enlightenment, there are the two: method and wisdom.

For method, from among the common and the uncommon, for the uncommon there is (1) the main topic, (2) how to meditate upon it, and (3) its benefits. For wisdom, from among the abbreviated and extensive explanation, for the extensive explanation there is (1) the refutation of what is apprehended, (2) the refutation of what apprehends, (3) the refutation of a reflexive awareness in which awareness and the space of awareness are identical, and (4) the teaching on the greatness of the path.

In this way, the synthesis of practice spoken by the noble Mañjughoṣa is encapsulated in four verses and two lines.

This was composed by the Omniscient Noble One, Tsongkhapa himself.

Translated by Eva Natanya

12. On the Union of Śamatha and Vipaśyanā

FROM *THE CONCISE PRESENTATION OF THE STAGES ON THE PATH TO ENLIGHTENMENT*

Jé Tsongkhapa

[421] Here is the third part [of the section on how to cultivate vipaśyanā: the main presentation of how to cultivate vipaśyanā in dependence upon śamatha.]

If you do not find the view of identitylessness, then no matter what kind of meditation you undertake, that meditation will not rest in the meaning of suchness. Therefore, you must find this view. But even if you come to understand this view, when it comes time to meditate upon suchness, if you do not first bear that view in mind and then meditate by settling upon it, it will not turn into a meditation upon suchness. Therefore, if, after each session in which you begin by analyzing the view, you just place yourself in a state of not thinking of anything, this is not what it means to sustain [the view of] suchness.

While bearing the view in mind, if you merely familiarize yourself with settling in your recollection of the view, this is nothing but the practice of sustaining śamatha as explained earlier. It is not, however, the point of the scriptures that explain how to sustain vipaśyanā as distinct from śamatha. Therefore, [422] you should maintain this vipaśyanā through analyzing the meaning of identitylessness with wisdom, as explained before.

If you practice only analytical meditation, the śamatha you developed previously will decline. Thus, you should analyze and then sustain it while mounted on the horse of śamatha and continue to alternate with periods of stabilizing meditation.

Furthermore, if, by doing too much analytical meditation, your stillness decreases, then you should restore this stillness by practicing stabilizing meditation again and again. But if you do too much stabilizing meditation, you will become averse to analysis, and even when you do analyze, it will be of no use. If it happens that you get entirely wrapped up in stillness, then you should do a lot of analytical meditation. If you meditate in this way, all the while balancing the aspects of śamatha and vipaśyanā, then your practice will gain great force.

As it says in the final volume of the *Stages of Meditation* [Kamalaśīla's *Bhāvanākrama*],

> Moreover, when one has cultivated vipaśyanā, and wisdom has become predominant, then at the same time, the śamatha decreases. Therefore, like a butter lamp placed in the wind, the mind keeps moving, so it cannot see suchness very clearly. Therefore, at that point one must cultivate śamatha. But if the śamatha becomes predominant, then, like a person falling asleep, one will not be able to see suchness very clearly. Similarly, then, when this takes place, one should cultivate wisdom.

When you sustain analysis in this way, it makes no sense to maintain that "whatever conceptualizations pertain to this are necessarily conceptualizations by which one holds things to be real by grasping to signs, so they should be stopped." This is because, as I have demonstrated many times before, the conceptualizations that hold things to be real are only one kind of conceptualization.

If you believe that *anything* held by conceptualization must be crushed with reasoning, [423] this means you have fallen into the fault of repudiating what actually exists, by denying with your reasoning something that is too broad. I have demonstrated that this is not the meaning of the scriptures.

Now you may think, "It is not like that with regard to other entities, but with regard to their actual nature, whatever way in which it is held by cognition must involve a grasping to signs in the form of clinging to things as real." Indeed, the mode of grasping is a problematic fault, but not everything held by cognition is a problem. This is proven by the statement "Those with a confined outlook who strive for liberation must investigate suchness through many doors of scripture and reasoning."

In this case, you may think, "If meditation on suchness is practiced in order to give rise to nonconceptuality, it will not arise from discerning conceptual analysis, since cause and effect must be similar in nature." On this point, the Bhagavān himself has given a clear answer. As it says in the Kāśyapa chapter [the forty-third chapter of the *Ratnakūṭa Sūtra*],

> O Kāśyapa, it is like this: If, for example, two sticks were rubbed against each other by the wind, fire would spring up from them. Once fire has emerged, the two sticks burn away. In the same way, O Kāśyapa, if there is authentically discerning conceptual analysis, the faculty of an ārya's wisdom will arise. When it has arisen, it burns away that authentically discerning conceptual analysis itself.

Thus he states that the wisdom of an ārya arises from discerning conceptual analysis.

As it says in the middle volume of the *Stages of Meditation*:

> For this reason, when a yogin investigates thoroughly with wisdom, he finds that, ultimately, he cannot definitely apprehend any essential nature in any functioning thing. At that moment the yogin enters a totally nonconceptual samādhi. He then realizes the very nonexistence of essential natures in all phenomena.

> [424] If someone does not meditate after analyzing, discerningly and with wisdom, the essential nature of functioning things, but rather completely abandons bringing anything to mind and just meditates, this will never overcome conceptualization. Nor will such a person ever realize the very nonexistence of essential natures, because there is no light of wisdom. Thus, from authentically discerning conceptual analysis itself comes the fire of knowing what is, authentically, as it is. If that emerges, it burns the stick of concepts as does the fire that comes from rubbing sticks together. This was declared by the Bhagavān.

If this were not so, then the stainless could never emerge from the stained, that which is beyond the world could never emerge from the world, buddhas could never emerge from sentient beings, and āryas could never emerge from ordinary people. Because in each of those pairs, cause and effect are dissimilar.

In the *Commentary on Bodhicitta* [*Bodhicittavivaraṇa*] it is said,

> Wherever conceptualization appears,
> how could there be emptiness?
> Neither the aspect of a mind that analyzes
> nor that which is analyzed
> is seen by any of the tathāgatas.
> Where there is analysis
> or something analyzed,
> there is no enlightenment.

Here [Nāgārjuna] teaches that while reifying that which is analyzed and that which analyzes, there is no achievement of enlightenment. However, if one were to reject the wisdom of discerning analysis and simply reject that which is analyzed and that which analyzes, this would contradict the scriptural statement that one establishes suchness through the many doors of discerning conceptual analysis. Furthermore, [425] if neither of those two [that is, neither the mind that analyzes nor that which is analyzed] were seen by the buddhas, then it would follow that they do not exist at all.

As it states in the same work:

> Whoever meditates on emptiness—known as
> *non-arising*, *emptiness*, or *identitylessness*—
> as one of an inferior nature
> is not meditating on any of them.

This statement does not reject meditation that focuses upon identitylessness—the emptiness that is the absence of something arising by an inherent nature. But it does reject a lesser meditation on emptiness—one which is of an inferior nature because it holds onto those [absences] as being real.

It is just as it says in the *Praise of the One Who Has Gone Beyond the World* [Nāgārjuna's *Lokātītastava*]:

> You revealed the nectar of emptiness
> in order to clear away every kind
> of conceptual fabrication.
> But if anyone were to cling to that,
> you would reproach him severely.

Similarly, it says in [Nāgārjuna's] *Jewel Garland* [*Ratnāvalī*]:

> Thus there is nothing to focus upon
> in *identity* or *identitylessness*,
> absolutely, just as it is.
> For this reason, the Great Sage refuted
> views of both identity and identitylessness.

According to Ārya Nāgārjuna, since one cannot establish either "identity" or "identitylessness" as existing absolutely, the view that either option could exist absolutely must be refuted. But this does not reject the view that things are without identity.

As quoted previously from *Ending All Debates* [Nāgārjuna's *Vigrahavyāvartanīkārikā*], this is true because of the following: If it were not the case that there is no inherent nature by which phenomena can be inherently determined, then phenomena would be determined as inherently existent!

On this point, it says in the *Summary* [*of the Exalted Transcendent Wisdom Sūtra*]:

> Even if a bodhisattva thinks,
> "These aggregates are empty,"
> he engages with signs.
> This is not faith in
> the place of non-arising.

The *Great Mother* [*Sūtra*] says [426]:

> If you engage with "empty forms"
> or "identitylessness," then you are engaging with signs.
> But this is not engaging with transcendent wisdom.

Suppose you say that the meaning of all these quotations is that one *should* hold emptiness and the like to exist as real, because if one did not do so, then one would have no faith in the place of non-arising. But this is untenable, because then, to have faith in that place would automatically mean you are acting with signs. As it says in that same sūtra:

> When you have thoroughly understood that
> no phenomenon has any nature of its own,

then this is the activity of supreme
transcendent wisdom.

Also:

When with wisdom you have destroyed both things
composed
and uncomposed, as well as things either positive or negative,
until not even one atom remains upon which to focus,
if this purifies the world, then it can be classified
as transcendent wisdom.

As it says in the *King of Samādhi* [*Samādhirāja Sūtra*]:

If you investigate with discernment the identitylessness of
phenomena,
and, having analyzed, you meditate on what you discovered:
this is a cause for attaining the fruition of nirvāṇa.
No other cause can bring you to this peace.

Then, in the *Heart of Transcendent Wisdom*, when Śāriputra asks how he should train, as someone who wants to act in the profound transcendent wisdom of a bodhisattva, Avalokiteśvara answers,

> You must regard these five aggregates as being absolutely and completely empty of any inherent nature.

[If you hold that previous position] then you would contradict these and many other scriptural passages.

Furthermore, it states in the *Praise of the Absolute Space of Phenomena* [Nāgārjuna's *Dharmadhātustava*],

> The highest state of mind,
> the dharma that purifies,
> is the absence of any nature.

Also:

> As long as you hold to a "me" and a "mine,"
> [427] so long will you impute an outer world.
> But if you see the two ways in which no identity exists,
> then the seeds for cyclic existence will come to an end.

As it says in *A Guide to the Middle Way* [Candrakīrti's *Madhyamakāvatāra*]:

> Therefore, viewing "me" and "mine" as empty,
> the yogin becomes totally free.

You should come to an understanding according to these statements, and then continuously sustain your ascertainment of identitylessness and the nonexistence of inherent nature.

On this point, it says in the first volume of the *Stages of Meditation*,

> In the *Dhāraṇī for Entering into Nonconceptuality* [*Avikalpapraveśa Dhāraṇī*] it is said, "By not directing your attention, you will abandon the signs of form and so forth." Here, the intent of the phrase "not directing attention," is that whatever you investigate with wisdom will disappear. But this does not mean that you are simply not directing attention at all. Nor does it mean that just by abandoning mental engagement,[78] as in the meditative absorption [*samāpatti*] "devoid of discernment," you could

78. Note that "directing the attention" and "mental engagement" translate the same Tibetan term: *yid la byed pa* (Skt. *manasikāra*). We have chosen both translations to draw out different nuances from this important term.

> abandon the insistent clinging to form and so on that you have had since time without beginning.

So, with regard to all the statements in scripture where it says that "by meditating without mental engagement, one abandons holding to signs," the true intent is this: Once you have investigated correctly with analytical wisdom, and not one atom of that upon which you had been focusing—when grasping to things as real—any longer appears, then you enter into meditative equipoise on the meaning of this realization. Furthermore, the middle volume of the *Stages of Meditation* states,

> Whatever the mind may be, when you seek it out, you realize it as empty. Whatever state of mind with which you realize, when you thoroughly seek out its essential nature, you will realize it as empty. [428] Realizing in this way, you enter into the yoga without signs.

This teaches that one should enter into signlessness itself precisely after doing a thorough analysis beforehand. It shows with extreme clarity that, with nothing more than the complete absence of mental engagement, or without analyzing the essential nature of functioning things with wisdom, it is impossible to enter into total nonconceptuality itself. *The Jewel Cloud* [*Ratnamegha Sūtra*] states this, and accordingly says that if you do not discover the view of suchness by correctly analyzing beforehand, then it will be impossible to enter into a nonconceptual state with regard to the meaning of suchness.

It says in the last volume of the *Stages of Meditation*:

> Those scriptural statements about it being "inconceivable" and "beyond cognition" are meant to prevent the false presumption that one could realize the meaning of the profound just by hearing or thinking about it. Because these profound realities are to be known by each ārya, by each one's own awareness, it is taught

> that they are inconceivable, and so forth, *by someone else*. Those phrases were stated in order to prevent the inappropriate attitude that comes from holding the meaning of the profound to exist as real.
>
> However, they are not said to stop one from carrying out appropriate investigation using the wisdom of discerning analysis. If they were to reject that, then these sayings would be in contradiction to reasoning and to very many authoritative scriptures. Although such investigation is indeed of the essential nature of conceptuality, it is also of the essential nature of the appropriate method of mental engagement. Therefore, because a thoroughly nonconceptual primordial wisdom will emerge, if you long for such primordial wisdom, [429] then you should rely upon that method.

All these scriptural statements refute the sayings of those learned monks from China, who claimed that "You will never find the view that establishes suchness by relying on scriptures and reasoning; it is by settling into meditative equipoise, without directing your attention to anything at all, that you will realize suchness." It is extremely important for you to understand the ways that this idea is refuted.

Moreover, these methods of meditation appear in all the early practical instructions for the steps on the path [to enlightenment]. They appear in [the Kadampa] Geshé Potowa's *Spiritual Nursery* as follows:

> Some claim that when listening and reflecting, one should by reasoning
> establish the nonexistence of inherent nature,
> but that when meditating, there should just be no concepts.
>
> But according to them, it would be a disconnected emptiness.
> Since they meditate off to the side,

it will never act as an antidote.

Therefore, precisely when you meditate,
analyze with discernment "the One and the Many,"
"Dependence and Relationship,"
or whichever reasoning you are familiar with.
Then stay there for just a little while, without any conceptualization.

If you meditate in that way, it will be an antidote to the mental afflictions.
Whether you wish to follow a divine being
or you wish to practice according to the Pāramitāyāna,
this is the way to cultivate wisdom.

Then, because you have become familiar with the identitylessness of a person,
you will be able to apply the practice in this way.

Furthermore, the Lord [Atiśa] says [in *A Guide to the Two Realities*],

Who has realized emptiness? Nāgārjuna, prophesied by the Tathāgata, and his disciple, Candrakīrti, who both saw the actual nature of reality.
By means of the lineage of pith instructions received from them, you can realize the actual nature of reality.

On this method of teaching, [430] what the Lord [Atiśa] said in his *Pith Instructions on the Middle Way*[79] appears to be similar to, and to accord with, the view of Ācārya Kamalaśīla.

79. Tib. *Dbu ma'i gdams ngag* vs. the textual title *D'bu ma'i man ngag*, so Tsongkhapa may

Thus you should understand all the methods for sustaining insight as explained previously: You should know how to rely upon the six preparatory practices, how to carry out the actual session and the conclusion to each session, how to proceed between sessions, and especially how to guard your practice so that it is free of both excitation and laxity.

Here is the fourth part [from the main fourfold division of the presentation of vipaśyanā]: The criterion of whether you have achieved vipaśyanā through meditation.

If you meditate by investigating with the wisdom of discerning analysis, then, until such time as pliancy has arisen in you, as described before,[80] it is an approximation of vipaśyanā. But once this pliancy has arisen, it is the definitive form of vipaśyanā. The essential nature of pliancy, and the way in which it arises, are just as they were described before.

Now, if you have achieved śamatha and it has not declined in quality, then insofar as the pliancy that follows from śamatha is still present, here, this is not merely a matter of having pliancy. You may wonder, "What is it, then?" When you have been practicing analytical meditation, if by its own force this automatically brings on an experience of pliancy, then it will turn into vipaśyanā. It is the same whether your vipaśyanā focuses upon the qualities of a wide range of phenomena, or upon the nature of phenomena as they actually exist.

As it says in the *Sūtra Commenting on the True Intent* [*Saṃdhinirmocana Sūtra*],

> O Bhagavān, what do you call it when a bodhisattva internally brings to mind again and again, as an object of samādhi, an image of phenomena about which he has undertaken thorough

either be referring to the specific text, *Madhyamopadeśa*, or to the genre of Atiśa's pith instructions/practical instructions on the Middle Way.

80. In the section on stillness, not translated here. See B. Alan Wallace, *Balancing the Mind*, 198–203.

> consideration—so long as he has not yet gained pliancy of body and mind?
>
> [431] O Maitreya, this is not vipaśyanā. You must call it an orientation that approximates vipaśyanā and is concomitant with it.

The *Pith Instructions on Transcendent Wisdom* [*Prajñāpāramitopadeśa*, by Ratnākaraśānti] says,

> Thus, once you have achieved pliancy of body and mind [in śamatha], and you remain in it, you should engage in discerning analysis, with intense conviction, on the meaning of those phenomena you have been considering thoroughly, as images that are the objects of internally directed samādhi. As long as pliancy of body and mind have not arisen, this is a mental engagement that approximates vipaśyanā. Once these have arisen, then it is vipaśyanā.

If it can automatically lead to pliancy, and furthermore, insofar as it is able to lead to a single-pointed state of mind, the discerning analysis leads to śamatha by force of its own analytical meditation. This is a sublime quality of having attained śamatha previously. Therefore, when someone who has properly achieved śamatha practices analytical meditation, it amplifies the śamatha in an extraordinary manner. So you should never hold the position that "If I practice the analytical meditation of the discerning analysis, then the stillness of my meditation will deteriorate."

Here is [the major division on] how to unite the pair of śamatha and vipaśyanā.

If you have not attained each of the two—śamatha and vipaśyanā—according to the criteria of achievement as explained for each of those two, respectively, then you will not have the cause to forge them together as a pair. Thus, it is definitely necessary for you to achieve each of the two in order to have a *pair* to unite.

Now, since you can achieve the union of the pair from the time that you first achieve vipaśyanā, the way to do so is as follows: [432] By the power of having practiced analytical meditation on the basis of the śamatha you gained previously, then, as explained previously in the section on śamatha,[81] you achieve a type of attention that engages of its own accord, without the manifest action of mental formations.[82] If you can achieve this, then it will go on to be the union of the pair.

As it says in [Asaṅga's] *Śrāvakabhūmi*:

> Now suppose someone asks, "Just how are śamatha and vipaśyanā united, or engaged equally as a pair? Why is it called a path of entry into the union of a pair?"
>
> It is said that through the nine stages of mental stillness, you will achieve the ninth stage—"attentional balance"—and there you thoroughly achieve samādhi. On that basis, you will make tremendous efforts at higher wisdom by thoroughly distinguishing phenomena.
>
> At that point, the mind will begin to engage of its own accord, and without any effort, in the path of thoroughly distinguishing phenomena. Because a proper path of śamatha such as this lacks the manifest action of mental formations, the vipaśyanā will be totally pure, will be thoroughly trained, will follow after śamatha, and will be imbued with a meditative experience of bliss. It is in this way that the two of śamatha and vipaśyanā are united and engaged equally, and this is called the path of entry into the union of the pair of śamatha and vipaśyanā.

81. See Wallace, *Balancing the Mind*, 203–11.

82. Tib. *mngon par 'du byed pa med par*.

The last volume of the *Stages of Meditation* states,

> At a certain point, because you are freed from both excitation and laxity, your mind will rest evenly in meditative equipoise, and engage of its own accord. [433] Thus, your mind will become extremely clear with regard to suchness, and at that time, you can relax your effort, settling into a state of equanimity. You should know that at this point you have attained the path of the union of the pair of śamatha and vipaśyanā.

According to these statements, this comes about once you have crossed the threshold of achieving the definitive form of vipaśyanā.

Moreover, [Ratnākaraśānti's] *Pith Instructions on Transcendent Wisdom* says,

> After [you have generated vipaśyanā], you will focus on a conceptual image, and regarding that very state of mind, when, with the stream of its mental engagement—which continues in an unbroken continuum, without interruption—it experiences both, it is called the path of the union of the pair of śamatha and vipaśyanā. Śamatha and vipaśyanā are the "pair"; the "union" means being imbued with, or engaging, [in their object] while being mutually bound to one another.

Here, "without interruption" means that you do not have to settle your mind into nonconceptuality after halting a period of analytical meditation, but rather that the analytical meditation itself ushers you into nonconceptuality. "Experiences both" means that your mind experiences both (1) the śamatha that focuses upon a nonconceptual image, and (2) the vipaśyanā that focuses upon a conceptual image. "With the stream" refers to the fact that the analytical vipaśyanā and the śamatha that rests at the end of analysis do not occur at exactly the same time, but rather, during the period of the śamatha that is ushered in directly by the power of analysis: you are engaging concomitantly in both (1) the vipaśyanā that thoroughly investigates the phenomena upon which it focuses just as they actually exist, [434] and (2) the śamatha that rests stably in single-pointed concentration upon those phenomena, just as they actually exist.

When you reach a point like this, śamatha and vipaśyanā are merged, or engaged equally. This is required for one to be able to attain the realizations born from meditation. Therefore, when you analyze with discernment the meaning of identitylessness from within a state that does not destroy the quality of a nonconceptuality that has a stable aspect of stillness, like a small fish darting here and there through motionless water, this "gathers" the two in a way that is permissible. However, apart from positing this as an approximation of śamatha and vipaśyanā, it is not the meaning of the union of the pair of actual śamatha and actual vipaśyanā.

As for how to unite the pair of śamatha and vipaśyanā in this way, you should learn it as it comes down from the authentic and reliable treatises, but you should not put your trust in explanations drawn from false superimpositions that are alternatives to these scriptures. You should learn the extensive logical examination of the steps of the path to enlightenment, the scriptural passages that elicit knowledge, and the expanded explanation of how to meditate, all in my longer book on the steps of the path.

Translated by Eva Natanya

13. Garland of Supreme Medicinal Nectar: Questions and Answers

Lhodrak Drupchen Namkha Gyaltsen,
Reporting on a Revelation by Vajrapāṇi
on Behalf of Jé Tsongkhapa

[302] "I pay homage to Vajrapāṇi, the Lord of Mysteries. You whose essential nature is the mind of all buddhas of the past, present, and future, O Lord of Mysteries, Great Vajradhara, blessed by buddhas as numerous as the sands of the Ganges River, since you are the one with the ears of the great elephant, I supplicate you, please reveal the pinnacle of the yānas.

"Since you are the one finely adorned, please reveal the unique view, an authentic view that is rid of all confusion.

"Since you are the one who subdues all, please reveal a Dharma that slices through the web of doubts regarding view, meditation, and conduct.

"Since you are the precious wellspring of sublime qualities,[83] please reveal a Dharma that will enable the inconceivable samādhi uniting śamatha and vipaśyanā to arise in one's mindstream.

[303] "Since you are the cloud of truth, please reveal an instruction that will let fall a great rain of the Dharma that extinguishes the fire of afflicted conceptualization.

83. Including an additional word from the edition of this text in Lhodrak Drupchen Namkha Gyaltsen's collected works, *Zhu lan sman mchog bdud rtsi phreng ba*, in *Lho brag nam mkha' rgyal mtshan gyi gsung 'bum*, reproduced from a rare manuscript preserved at Orgyan Chöling Monastery in Bumthang (Thimphu, Bhutan: Kunsang Tobgey, Druk Sherig Press, 1985), vol. 1, 582, line 3: *yon tan*.

"Since you are the one with a tongue of blazing fire, please reveal a profound instruction that will burn the fuel of grasping to entities and grasping to signs.

"Since you are the one of exquisite form, please reveal an instruction that will make one's eyes fill with tears upon seeing the practical guidance that will give rise to immaculate bliss.

"Since you are the precious wish-fulfilling jewel, for the sake of Matibhadraśrī, who has made the request, and as I, Karmavajra, make supplication to you, please reveal an extraordinary instruction, consisting of Dharma in clear language, with few words and vast meaning, that will enable those of sharp faculties to sever their doubts and comprehend the meaning, and will enable even dull-witted cowboys to grasp the words and comprehend the meaning, a Dharma that enables them all to realize swiftly the dharmakāya of the buddhas."

Thus I made supplication, and an extraordinary taste slipped between my teeth [304] and swirled upon my tongue. Then I swallowed. It seemed this was from your compassion, my lama. Then, without showing any bodily form, came the steady sound of a voice, which spoke these words:

"Karmavajra, convey my secret words to the ears of Matibhadraśrī. This is the enlightened view of the father, Samantabhadra, and the heart advice of the mother, Samantabhadrī. I, Vajradhara, say that these, my secret words, are the pinnacle of the yānas. In order to accomplish the great, supreme medicine, search out the actual nature of the mind, the clear light."

I, Karmavajra, asked, "What is the essential nature of the clear light?"

"Karmavajra, it is encapsulated in terms of the essential nature, manifest nature, and compassion of the clear light."

Karmavajra asked, "When meditating on the clear light, are there ways to go astray or not?"

"Your question is excellent. If someone does not understand, there are pitfalls. In this regard, there are four: (1) the way of going wrong, (2) the signs of the mistake, (3) the detriments, and (4) the consequences of the mistake.

"The way one goes wrong with respect to the essential nature is this. In general, what is known as the *essential nature* is as follows: within the luminous emptiness that is the nature of existence of one's own pristine awareness, which is not determined as anything at all, the consciousness of the present moment—primordially and forever free of modification or contamination—is present in the manner of *ka*.[84] When someone meditates on emptiness without resting upon that *ka*, then, since one is not free of the mind that grasps to emptiness, this is said to be *mistaking emptiness for being nihilism*.

"As a sign of this mistake, one claims, 'There are no buddhas above; there are no hells below; everything is indeterminate emptiness.'

"The detriments of this mistake are as follows: With the attitude of thinking, 'Everything is empty,' at best, one casts aside all Dharma practices, such as the cultivation of admiration and reverence, pure vision, refuge, [305] bodhicitta, loving-kindness and compassion, and engages in the activities of this present life. At worst, one wantonly engages in nonvirtue. Here, since one is acting in contradiction to reality, there is nowhere to go but vajra hell.

"Accordingly, the consequences of such misconduct are as follows: At best, if one is engaging with reality in the wrong way, but in the direction of virtue, this will give rise to the extremist view of nihilism. At worst, if one has engaged with reality in the wrong way with respect to cause and effect, one will wander in the ocean of suffering.

"Karmavajra, there are many who say, 'I have realized emptiness,' but there are few who have realized the ultimate nature of existence.

"Karmavajra, with respect to the *manifest nature*, there are four ways to go astray. For the first, the pitfall regarding the manifest nature is this: With respect to the natural glow of empty pristine awareness, which becomes

84. That is, the first of the consonants in both the Sanskrit and Tibetan languages.

manifest as kāyas and facets of primordial consciousness, the kāyas are not determined with faces and arms; primordial consciousness is not determined with colors; and these are not determined as families with characteristics. Rather, the natural glow of emptiness abides indivisibly as luminosity and emptiness within just the aspect of luminosity. In the case whereby someone does not recognize indivisible luminosity and emptiness as a union, this is said to be *mistaking pristine awareness for appearances.*

"As a sign of this mistake, one will be estranged from all Dharma language, and if one is taught the language of *union*, it will not be comprehended.

"The detriments of this mistake are as follows: With the attitude of thinking, 'Everything exists as appearances that are real entities,' such individuals cannot engage with the Dharma teachings on the mind. Becoming caught up in dogmatism around philosophical tenets, they are separated from the path to omniscience. Since they reify appearances, there is no way for them to be liberated.

"The consequences of this mistake are as follows: [306] Since they become attached to the outer appearances of the clear light, they are born in the realms of form. Inwardly, since they do not recognize pristine awareness as luminosity and emptiness, their minds revolve exclusively in one direction, so they will never be liberated.

"Karmavajra, there are many who say, 'I have recognized the clear light,' but there are few who have become thoroughly trained in luminosity and emptiness as a union.

"Karmavajra, with respect to *compassion*, also, there are four pitfalls. The way one goes wrong is this: These thoughts that either do not arise or arise in all manner of ways are the natural glow of pristine awareness—emptiness and luminosity. When someone does not understand how it is that however many such thoughts appear, they cannot fall beyond the scope of pristine awareness and emptiness, this is said to be *mistaking pristine awareness for emptiness.*

"As a sign of this mistake, with one's body, speech, and mind one engages exclusively in activities concerned with this present life.

"The detriments of this mistake are as follows: With the attitude that a person's thoughts can never arise as the dharmakāya, one is bound by the web of whatever thoughts arise and becomes cynical with respect to virtuous practices. Since one is primarily familiar with negative habitual propensities, one acts only for this life. Since one is bound by the chains of dualistic grasping, doubts, hopes, and fears, one has bound oneself.

"The consequences of this mistake are as follows: Since one does not recognize the place in which thoughts are released,[85] they are reinforced as habitual propensities. Not understanding the grave consequences of cause and effect, one wastes this life in distraction. After death, one strays off to the three realms.

"Karmavajra, there are many who say, 'I am without thoughts,' but there are few who realize the deepest meaning of 'release upon arising.'"

Karmavajra asked, "Since if one does not eliminate those three pitfalls, practice becomes meaningless, how does one eliminate those three pitfalls?

The Lord of Mysteries spoke thus: "Karmavajra, this empty essential nature of pristine awareness has not been modified by anyone. [307] It is without causes or conditions. It abides primordially and forever. In this regard, without modifying or correcting it in any way, settle upon it right where it is, and you will be enlightened in the vast expanse of original purity, where there are no pitfalls. In the same way, this luminous manifest nature[86] is primordially, spontaneously actualized, indivisible from emptiness. Its creative power is unimpeded compassion. Since whatever arises is not determined by any inherent nature, know all three as a great union and you will be enlightened in them indivisibly."

85. Following the reading in *Lho brag nam mkha' rgyal mtshan*, *Zhu lan sman mchog bdud rtsi phreng ba* (Thimphu) vol. 1, 584, line 7: *rnam rtog gi grol sa* (instead of *rnam rtog gi gol sa* in Tsongkhapa's collected works).

86. Following *Lho brag nam mkha' rgyal mtshan*, vol. 1, 585, line 2: *rang bzhin gsal ba* (instead of *rang bzhin 'od gsal ba*).

Then I, Karmavajra, asked, "What are the pitfalls with respect to (A) the view, (B) meditation, and (C) conduct?"

A. Pitfalls with Respect to the View

The Lord of Mysteries spoke thus: "Listen, O Karmavajra. First, there are five types of pitfalls with respect to the view: (1) the pitfall regarding the view itself, (2) the pitfall in terms of one's abode, (3) the pitfall regarding companions, (4) the pitfall of mental afflictions, and (5) the pitfall of sectarianism.

"First, here is the pitfall regarding the view itself. The view of Dharma in general is asserted to be that of emptiness, free of extremes, whereas for a yogin of this tradition of Secret Mantra, it is asserted to be direct and naked. If one realizes these two ultimately, there is no difference between them. If one does not realize them, then with regard to the view in general, if one does not establish the analytical view that is expressed with words in actuality, within one's own experience, then this is a mistaken view.

"If one does not have confidence in the direct view, and instead, one settles firmly on the analytical view expressed in words, claiming that 'nothing has any point of reference' and 'everything is free of activity and free of extremes,' and thereby engages wantonly in virtue and evil, and furthermore, if while claiming that 'there are no good or bad deeds,' 'doing virtue is of no benefit,' 'doing evil won't bring any harm,' and 'everything is unimpeded equality,' [308] one makes one's home in what is utterly ordinary, these are called *demonic*[87] *views replete with dark, empty words*. This is the root of mistakes with respect to all views.

87. Though *bdud* (lit. "māras") is missing in the extant editions of the *Garland of Supreme Medicinal Nectar*, this is the classical form of the phrase in Dzokchen literature (*nag po kha 'byams bdud kyi lta ba*) and is what appears in the parallel form of this teaching in the *Khandro Nyingtik* revealed by Longchenpa. Cf. Longchen Rabjam, *Zhu len bdud rtsi gser phreng* (*Golden Garland of Nectar: Questions and Answers*), 10.

"Matibhadraśrī, you must engage in the union of the direct, nondual, naturally luminous view and profound cause and effect.

"Here is the pitfall in terms of abode. In general, for someone who has realized the view in a fleeting way, in order for this to turn into the expanse, the final view, one should go to a place that is isolated, clean, and clear, such as a remote mountain hermitage. Even though one has a fleeting view, in order to sustain it, if [one feels] one must wander among mountain ranges, this is a mistaken view due to having a poor location.

"Matibhadraśrī, you must sustain a fleeting view in a mountain hermitage.

"Here is the pitfall regarding companions. Someone who has a fleeting view must associate with friends who share a compatible Dharma practice and who do not provoke an increase in mental afflictions. If one associates with bad friends, it is impossible not to become contaminated with negative conduct. They lead you through this life, and do not give you any chance to sustain the view. The increase of mental afflictions is the root of mistakes.

"Karmavajra and Matibhadraśrī, if you wish not to go astray, then, [like] cutting the string of a rosary, separate yourself from irrelevant friends and remain alone.

"Fourth is the pitfall of mental afflictions. Suppose someone with a fleeting view vanquishes mental afflictions as soon as they arise but does not take them onto the path. Then, any kind of outer circumstances will arouse mental afflictions. In that case, as karma is accumulated moment by moment, eventually one engages in negative behavior and accumulates negative karma by way of the five poisons regarding appearances to the six configurations of consciousness.

"Therefore—since the consequences of those actions will emerge both in the near term and long term—whatever mental afflictions arise, instantly bear them in mind with mindfulness [309] and then loosely relax your consciousness. Cultivate loving-kindness and compassion for all sentient beings, who are brought about from such mental afflictions. Make supplications to receive the blessings to take such mental afflictions onto the path.

In particular, pray to your guru from the depths of your heart. Once you have purified the seeds of those mental afflictions with mantras, meditate upon your yidam and count recitations of your personal deity's heart mantra. After that, relax into the experience of the view, and then make extensive prayers of dedication.

"By taking [mental afflictions] onto the path in this way, you will achieve temporal and ultimate sublime qualities as their results. If you do not take them onto the path in this way, you will sink into the swamp of mental afflictions, and your view will not turn into the expanse. So this is the great root of mistakes.

"Karmavajra and Matibhadraśrī, if you wish not to go astray, devote yourself to the antidotes for whatever mental afflictions arise, and take them onto the path!

"Fifth is the pitfall of sectarianism. All those who have a fleeting view, moreover, having mistaken the view of their philosophical system and texts as the 'only one,' takes refuge in their own transmissions while distinguishing between us and them, higher and lower, this side and that side, and between good and bad. Thus, regarding the great view of the buddhas, free of extremes, individuals cognitively assess that view as if evaluating it by the fistful. This is the root of the mistake.

"Karmavajra and Matibhadraśrī, if you wish not to go astray in that way, recognize the view free of extremes as the great, vast emptiness."

B. Pitfalls with Respect to Meditation

"For the second part, there are four types of pitfalls with respect to meditation: (1) pitfalls regarding the essential nature of meditation, (2) pitfalls in terms of one's abode and companions, (3) pitfall of faults, and (4) pitfalls of the mental afflictions.

"First, here are the pitfalls regarding the essential nature of meditation. [310] The guru nakedly introduces the essential nature, manifest nature, and compassion, but the disciple does not understand. The disciple does not get the point of the essential nature, manifest nature, and compassion. The disciple goes astray by not recognizing the indivisibility of luminosity and emptiness. Moreover, the disciple may practice according to the guru's tradition of practical instructions, but by clinging to a smattering of bliss in the body or mind, goes astray as a human being of the desire realm. If one becomes attached to a state of mind in which there are simply no thoughts at all, one will go astray as a god of the pure abodes. If one becomes attached simply to luminosity that is nonconceptual, one will go astray as a god of the form realm. If one becomes attached to a bliss that is nonconceptual, one will go astray as a god of the desire realm. If one becomes attached to a vacuity that is nonconceptual, one will go astray as a god of the formless realm. These cases constitute going astray in the three realms.

"If the objects of the sense faculties are continuously impeded, one will go astray in the domain of boundless space. If they are impeded so that one does not feel anything, as in deep sleep, one will go astray in the domain of nothingness. If luminous appearances to consciousness are impeded, one will go astray in the domain of boundless consciousness. If there continuously arises a mere glow of bliss with respect to luminosity, and nothingness in terms of appearances, one goes astray in the domain of neither existence nor nonexistence. These cases constitute what is known as *falling exclusively into śamatha*. From here, when one has died and consciousness is transferred, one revolves in the three realms and the six classes of sentient beings.

"Karmavajra and Matibhadraśrī, if you do not know how to avoid the pitfalls of meditation, since you will revolve in the three realms due to foolish meditation,[88] it is useless. Moreover, if you affirm the existence of the body and mind as ordinary people[89] see them, you will go astray in thinking the ordinary is autonomous. If you grasp exclusively to existence or nonexistence, you will go astray in the eternalism or nihilism of the extremists. [311]

88. Following *Lho brag nam mkha' rgyal mtshan*, vol. 1, 587, line 5–6: *glen sgom gyis khams gsum du 'khor bas* (instead of *glen sgom gyi khams ldog 'khor bas*).

89. That is, those who are not āryas.

If you affirm the existence of objects as being separate from the mind, you will go astray as a śrāvaka or a pratyekabuddha. If you assert appearances to be the mind, you will go astray as a Cittamātrin. If you assert the physical worlds and their sentient inhabitants to be deities [and their maṇḍalas], you will go astray in the Mantrayāna. What is the point of meditation that does not eliminate mistaken extremes?"

Then I requested a method for avoiding these pitfalls.

The Lord of Mysteries spoke thus: "If you wish not to go astray in those ways, then, like Matibhadraśrī, first expand your mind by way of hearing. Then, strike the crucial points by means of the pointing-out instructions. Finally, at the time of practice, as it is true that all the pitfalls described above involve clinging and attachment to samādhi, so—as in the case of a rabbit sleeping in a hawk's nest or as in the samādhi of an arrow-maker—there is no chance for liberation.[90] Therefore, whatever appearances of meditative experiences may arise, right there in whatever arises, relax and settle, without correcting or modifying, without hope or fear, and without rejecting or affirming them. If there is no grasping to anything that arises, you will not plummet into the pitfall.

"Second, here are the pitfalls in terms of one's abode and companions. For one who is meditating, it is important to meditate in a place with the appropriate characteristics, such as being away from other people. If one stays in a hermitage where there is a lot of busy activity, or in a place where the field of mental afflictions expands, one will go astray due to defilements and material donations, as well as attachment and hatred.

"If you associate with bad friends, progress in meditation will halt, for you have purchased your own misery. Karmavajra and Matibhadraśrī, if you

90. Following *Zhu len bdud rtsi gser phreng* (*Golden Garland of Nectar: Questions and Answers*), in *Snying thig ya bzhi, Mkha' 'gro snying tig*, vol. *waṃ*, 14–15: *grol rgyu med* (instead of *gol du med*). We have chosen this alternative reading from the *Khandro Nyingtik* form of this revelation, since the meaning that appears in the Lhodrak Drupchen form of the revelation is highly problematic, finishing the analogy to the rabbit and the hunter instead with the phrase, "so you will not go astray." Rather, the rabbit's sleep will inevitably end in its being eaten by the hawk, and the arrow-maker's samādhi will end in his being shot by an arrow, as in the paradigmatic Tibetan saying, "the arrow-maker will be killed by his own arrow" (*mda' mkhan rang gi mda' yis bsad*).

practice an authentic Dharma, you forcefully cut your ties to poor abodes and bad friends and leave them behind. This is profound.

"Third, here are the pitfalls in terms of faults in meditation. When sustaining meditation, [312] there are the three faults of laxity, excitation, and dispersion. In terms of laxity, there are (a) laxity due to one's abode, (b) laxity due to companions, (c) laxity due to season, (d) laxity due to food, (e) laxity due to posture, and (f) laxity due to meditation.

"First, as for laxity due to one's abode, if you stay in a forest within a deep ravine or in a dilapidated and defiled village monastery, your consciousness will become confused, the *bindus* will be unclear, awareness will be cloaked, your sleep will be too deep, and your body will feel heavy. In that case, perform a cleansing ritual and confess misdeeds. Go to a higher place that is clean and clear. Meditate upon your seat as being luminous. Cut holes in the windows to allow for a fresh breeze. Then, meditating with a snowy mountain peak as your object while sitting with your body naked will dispel laxity.

"Second, laxity due to companions will arise if you stay together with people who have [karmic] defilements. Perform a confession and cleansing ritual. Since this protects you from those who have degenerated in their *samayas* or who have [karmic] defilements, it will dispel laxity.

"Third, as for laxity due to season, if you become dull and lax in spring and summer, going to a high elevation—such as the snow-covered mountains—and meditating there will dispel laxity.

"Fourth, as for laxity due to food and clothing, since human food or clothing that has a defilement will cause laxity, then, when you are practicing, if you take care to avoid human food or clothing that has a defilement, this will dispel laxity.

"Fifth, as for laxity due to posture, if beginners walk around, sit, lie down, and so on, this will lead to laxity. Therefore, when meditating, while assuming one of the three postures [taught for tögal practice] or the *vajrāsana*, arouse your consciousness, clear your sense faculties, and meditate with vivid presence and lucidity. This will dispel laxity.

"Sixth, as for laxity due to meditation, if you meditate with your consciousness downcast, it will eventually lose clarity and become hazy. [313] Since this is laxity, by elevating your [visual] faculty into space, focused on the light of a lamp, this will intensify your awareness, arousing the luminosity of the actual nature of your mind. That will dispel laxity.

"Karmavajra, if the person removing hindrances to meditation lacks enthusiastic perseverance, the hindrances will not be dispelled.

"[Fourth,] here are the pitfalls of the mental afflictions. For someone sustaining meditation, there are many robbers and enemies—namely, the mental afflictions. At root, they are generated by the five poisons and arise as the eighty-four thousand mental afflictions. Thus, they won't give you any chance to meditate but will lead you back into saṃsāra.

"With an attitude like that of a mother who has lost her only son, remain undistracted, and abandon [mental afflictions] as if they were a poisonous snake that had shown up in your lap. Apprehending them with introspective mindfulness, practice taking them onto the path, exactly as [taught] in the section on the view. If you do not do this, you will collect negative karma moment by moment.

"If you wish not to go astray in this way, then, without being separated from the fire of introspection throughout your entire life, strive in abandoning [what is to be abandoned] and adopting [what is to be adopted]. In general, until the view and meditation are stable, go off by yourself and remain alone, like a wounded deer. It is a very important crucial point that you see mental afflictions as being like a poisonous snake and flee.

"Regarding the fault of excitation,[91] there are two kinds: (a) excitation due to one's abode and (b) excitation due to circumstances.

"As for excitation due to one's abode, if you meditate in a place at a high elevation, where it is very clear, your awareness will be very clear, so that consciousness will not settle. Thus, conceptualization will become excited

91. Note that this continues the explanation of the three faults of meditation (the first of which was laxity), now grouped under the heading of the pitfall of the mental afflictions.

and scattered. If you allow your mind to scatter wherever it will, it will come under the power of mental afflictions, so settle your awareness within a clear boundary. If that does not subdue it, tame it with the gaze of the śrāvakas.[92] Occasionally direct your consciousness to your seat and subdue it in that way. At night, [314] within the round area formed by the channels at the soles of your feet, as it were, rest your mind within a black bindu, and thus fall asleep.

"When thoughts come quickly and briefly, once you have identified them, utter *phaṭ*, and then hold the energies. Afterward, loosely relax and rest there. Alternatively, once you have chased solely after a thought, rest in the state of not finding it. This will dispel excitation.

"Secondly, as for excitation due to circumstances: If, aroused by thinking about some external circumstance, the mind becomes agitated and scattered in a mentally afflicted way, set the intention "There is nothing I need to do," and reverse clinging with loving-kindness and compassion. Then practice with method and wisdom, and with admiration and reverence. Earnestly practice taking [mental afflictions] onto the path, as in the section on the view.

"For the third [type of fault in meditation], there are two varieties of the fault of dispersion: (a) dispersion due to not understanding and (b) dispersion due to circumstances.

"First, as for dispersion from not understanding, if you do not know how to divide your meditation into sessions, no matter how much you meditate, it will not improve. There will arise wrong views regarding the practical instructions and toward your guru. If you do not draw a fine distinction between understanding, meditative experience, and realization, you will fall into dull-witted meditation.

"Therefore, make supplication to your guru; develop a confident understanding of the practical instructions; divide your meditation into sessions,

92. This almost certainly refers to placing the gaze in the space in front of one, resting at a distance of about a plow's length ahead.

and have many of them. Without mixing it up with activities, meditate with vivid presence and lucidity. When there is clarity, stop the session before there is scattering. Meditate thus. Once you halt dispersion in this way, your practice will progress to higher and higher levels.

"Secondly, as for dispersion due to circumstances: Due to the condition of external circumstances, the five poisons proliferate regarding appearances to the six configurations of consciousness. You then become distracted and cannot hold them with mindfulness. By immediately arriving [at mindfulness] by means of an antidote, disperse piecemeal your grasping at appearances, and know them to be like illusions.

"Karmavajra, if you wish to avoid these pitfalls, [315] hit the pig on the snout with a pestle."[93]

Then Karmavajra asked the Lord of Mysteries, "Shouldn't a practitioner of Mantrayāna take mental afflictions as the path?"

The Lord of Mysteries spoke thus: "Of course you must take mental afflictions as the path! But apart from a peacock, there is no one who can take poison as food. Someone who can take mental afflictions as the path without abandoning them is rarer than the *uḍumbara* flower. For a person of superior faculties, mental afflictions arise as aids to practice, but for those of lowest faculties, mental afflictions become poisonous, so they must be abandoned. This is profound.

"First, as many [mental afflictions] as you abandon, they will turn into the expanse. Then, both mental afflictions and the sublime qualities that you seek will all appear as illusions, so that clinging and attachment will not arise at all. Even if they emerge, there is no need to block them. No harm is done. And if they do not emerge, a mind to embrace this does not arise. There is nothing to hope for. This is the measure of having taken [mental

93. This refers to a common situation in rural Tibet, where a pig might try to enter the family kitchen on the second floor of a house where animals were often kept inside on the first floor of the same house. The lady of the kitchen would have to smack the pig on the snout before it had even entered the door of the kitchen; otherwise, she would have a major problem on her hands!

afflictions] as the path. But until you have reversed manifest clinging, taking mental afflictions as the path will be like a bee that becomes stuck to flower nectar by circling around it.

"Karmavajra and Matibhadraśrī, let this be your way of evaluating progress along the grounds and paths."

C. Pitfalls with Respect to Conduct

"For the third part, there are two pitfalls with respect to conduct: (1) the pitfall of conduct performed at the wrong time, and (2) the general pitfall of conduct.

"First, as for the pitfall of conduct performed at the wrong time:[94]

a. Since conduct like that of a bee is a preliminary for hearing, reflection, and meditation, it is the conduct of a beginner. If it is performed during the period of austerities, that is the wrong time.
b. Conduct like that of a deer is for the time of experiential practice, but if it is performed during the period of austerities, since you will come under the influence of another samādhi, that is the wrong time.
c. Conduct like that of a mute [316] is for striking the crucial points of experiential practice, but if it is performed during the time of acting like a bee, since you will not be able to distinguish the

94. The following seven forms of conduct are explained as follows in the *Khandro Yangtik* compiled by Longchenpa, citing *The Union of the Sun and Moon*: "With the conduct like that of a bee, taste the flavor of all phenomena. With the conduct like that of a deer, abandon all conditions for delusive objects. With the conduct like that of a mute, abandon all delusive speech, without exception. With the conduct like that of a swallow, eliminate all doubts regarding the secret method. With the conduct like that of a madman, abandon all stationary objects. With the conduct like that of a lion, wander in charnel grounds, abandoning fear. With the conduct like that of a dog and pig, abandon all thoughts of clean and unclean." *Zab don rgya mtsho'i sprin*, in *Snying thig ya bzhi, Mkha' 'gro yang tig*, vol. *āḥ*, reproduced from prints from the A 'dzom chos sgar par khang woodblocks (Delhi, India: Sherab Gyaltsen Lama, 1975), 395.

meanings of words, that is the wrong time.

d. Conduct like that of a swallow entering its nest is conduct for the time when one's own experiences have arisen, but since it will become an obstacle for samādhi, if one does not yet have the heat [of experience], it is the wrong time.
e. Conduct like that of a madman is for the time when you have devoted yourself to experience, but if it is performed when just a tiny bit of experience has arisen, you will not discover the final meaning, so that is the wrong time.
f. Conduct like that of a lion is for the time when the view has turned into the expanse, but if it is performed at the time of gaining experience through practice, it is the wrong time. Since it will not be based upon suchness and since you will be led astray by other appearances, it is wrong.
g. The conduct like that of a dog and pig is conduct for the occasion of empowerment, but if it is performed at an inappropriate time, since the *ḍākinīs* will be absent, it is wrong.

"If you perform the conduct correctly, since your own appearances will arise as the actual nature of reality, you will be able to transform the appearances of others who have no faith.[95] You will be able to resuscitate the dead.[96] You will be able to accomplish every kind of miraculous deed, which will enable you to transform the elements and appearances. You should understand that if you go wrong with respect to the types of conduct described above, this is the pitfall of conduct, and the fruition will not emerge.

"Karmavajra and Matibhadraśrī, practice in accord with the treatises on Dharma conduct in general.

"Secondly, here is the pitfall of Dharma conduct in general. You may be

95. That is, you will be able to perform extraordinary deeds that appear to others, even if they are without faith.

96. Following *Lho brag nam mkha' rgyal mtshan*, vol. 1, 591, line 4: *gsad pa gso nus* (instead of *gsang ba gol nus*, which is clearly a miscarving).

mindful of your present conduct, but if it is not in accord with Dharma, then it does not follow along the path of the buddhas, so it is called *hypocrisy*. This is the pitfall of conduct.

"Karmavajra, in general, if you wish not to go astray at the time of conduct, then whatever conduct you may engage in, let it follow along the path of the buddhas."

D. Pitfalls with Respect to the Fruition

"For the fourth part,"[97] pitfalls with respect to the fruition, there are two: (1) temporary and (2) ultimate. [317]

"First, for the temporary pitfall, if, by holding as supreme the common fruition of practicing the profound instructions, pride and presumption then arise, this is the pitfall by which the ultimate fruition is blocked. Though you may [think that you] have achieved the fruition, if hope and fear have not been destroyed, this is mistaking the result for its cause.

"Karmavajra and Matibhadraśrī, know that any cause for hope or fear is groundless."

Then Karmavajra asked, "If one directly realizes this crucial point of pristine awareness, is bodhicitta necessary or not?"

The Lord of Mysteries spoke thus: "It is true that the Secret Mantra of the Mahāyāna is distinguished by bodhicitta. Nevertheless, if, throughout the four times of day, you do not bear in mind death, impermanence, karmic causes and their consequences, and the disadvantages of saṃsāra, this life will slip away by itself. If you do not at all times cultivate loving-kindness and compassion for all sentient beings, you may take up the name of the Mahāyāna, but you have mistaken it for the Śrāvakayāna and the Pratyekabuddhayāna. If you do not know what to reject and what to practice each moment with respect to the subtlest aspects of cause and effect, though you may have high realizations, various nonvirtues will emerge.

97. This fourth part was not listed in the earlier outline of the text but is introduced here.

"Karmavajra, if you practice an authentic Dharma, both realization and all that precedes it are necessary."

Then Karmavajra asked, "What are the greatest obstacles to practice along the path?"

The Lord of Mysteries said, "At first, when you are entering the path, whatever conditions emerge that lead your mind in the opposite direction are obstacles. In particular, for a man, a woman may become a formidable māra. For a woman, a man may become a formidable māra. For both, food and clothing may become formidable māras." [318]

Then I said, "Most practitioners of Secret Mantra claim that it brings a great enhancement to practice if one devotes oneself to a female partner. How is that so?"

The Lord of Mysteries said, "A female partner who enhances one's progress on the path is rarer than gold. Admiration and reverence for an evil woman turns you into an adulterer. You turn your pure vision into a girlfriend. You offer the merit you have accumulated to an adulteress. You turn your revulsion against the divine Dharma. If you listen to teachings, you behave like a dog. You talk about faith with your mouth. But if you turn away, you turn away from your heart. There is stinginess and ferocious jealousy. Without collecting the karma that will take you upward, it turns into an iron hook that will drag you downward. While the enhancement to augment your Dharma never arrives, you open the door to welcome attachment, hatred, and suffering. With the hope to be liberated by means of passion, you devote yourself to it, and that becomes a cause for augmenting your mental afflictions. While you hope it will serve as the basis for improving the health of your constitution, it will carry you away in a cloak of defilements from violated samayas. A woman who does not guard samayas is a prostitute or a māra."

I asked, "To what kind of woman is it appropriate to devote oneself?"

The Lord of Mysteries said, "To one who is the reverse of all the faults described above. In particular, she has admiration for the Dharma, her mind has great aptitude, she is patient and good-natured, and she has tremendous faith and compassion. The six transcendences are complete within her mindstream. She does not go against the guru's word. She has reverence for practitioners. She guards the samayas of the Mantrayāna as one protects one's own eyes. Except during an empowerment, she does not engage in intercourse.[98] She dwells in the practices of ritual purity. If such a woman appears, then she will be an aid to your path. But such a woman is extremely rare, and to call something like this [a path] 'with passion' is provisional.[99] It is the Dharma fortune of those with highest faculties.[100]

"For all ordinary people, [319] since they naturally fall into mental afflictions, they must turn away from them. Once you have entered the door of

98. This refers to a way of granting empowerment that took place in Indian Vajrayāna Buddhism during the first millennium of the common era and which was enacted at the time when Guru Padmasambhava transmitted Vajrayāna empowerments in the royal court of Tibet, relying upon such a superbly qualified partner as Yeshé Tsogyal. Out of reverence for the extremely rare circumstances under which a guru and partner are qualified to grant the highest empowerments of Mahāyoga and Anuyoga in definitive form, Vajrayāna empowerments have been transmitted primarily in ritually symbolic form for centuries in Tibet and in recent times around the globe.

99. In the stage of completion (Tib. *rdzogs rim*), there is a classical distinction between practice "with passion" (Tib. *chags can*), which involves advanced and subtle practices performed with a human partner, and practice "without passion" (Tib. *chags bral*), which focuses entirely on visualized practices of the channels, energies, and bindus of the subtle body. The point here is that even the path "with passion" is actually in name only, for in order to practice it authentically, one must have transcended the mentally afflicted aspect of passion.

100. Venerable Gyatrul Rinpoché makes a parallel point in contemporary terms: "It is not exactly clear how Westerners got the idea that married couples, or, for that matter, any couple having a lot of desire for each other, could practice the Vajrayana techniques taken from tantric Buddhism or some other spiritual tradition. They try to visualize themselves as deities but then engage in an ordinary sexual act based on attachment/desire. They want an experience of something more blissful than ever before. This is one of the biggest mistakes a person can make. This activity does not even approximate the practices we are discussing. One who attempts tantric practices in this way, lacking the proper prerequisites and permission from the vajra guru, just accumulates causes for lower rebirth—even, perhaps, cause for the lowest possible rebirth, since this is to misuse and disrespect pure Dharma practice. Pure Dharma has nothing to do with ordinary sexual desire. . . . To perform these secret practices, a practitioner must be on a very high level and must practice solely for the sake of sentient beings. When a practitioner arrives at this level of practice, it is very wonderful, but one must wait until the right time arrives." Gyatrul Rinpoche, *The Generation Stage in Buddhist Tantra*, trans. Sangye Khandro (Ithaca, NY: Snow Lion Publications, 2005), 77–78.

the Mantrayāna, if you do not guard your samayas, do not even hope for buddhahood."

Then Karmavajra asked, "For a Dharma practitioner, since food, clothing, and grasping to the identity of one's body can lead to harm, please grant an instruction on how to cast these three away with one's mind."

The Lord of Mysteries said, "Karmavajra, all of these bodies are destroyed. Each lifespan, moreover, was determined beforehand. There is no certainty as to [when it will end,] whether you are old or young. Nothing is beyond dying, so even for one who has a fine form, I've never seen a case in which, through being attached to one's fine form, one could remain without dying. In order to cast away all inordinate attachment to one's body, wander among mountain ranges.

"For clothing, it is sufficient if you wear tattered garments. For food, it can even come from rocks and water, but human beings cannot practice this Dharma.

"Now, if you practice virtue motivated by loving-kindness, compassion, and bodhicitta, it will have great strength. This, too, is very rare.

"This, my Dharma of secret words, is the heart advice of the ḍākinīs. I, Vajradhara, have revealed these my secret words for Matibhadraśrī, who is blessed outwardly by the female deity Sarasvatī and inwardly by the divine Queen of Secret Primordial Consciousness.[101] Keep this instruction sealed for three years, without speaking of it to anyone else. The name of this instruction is *Garland of Supreme Medicinal Nectar: Questions and Answers*.

"Regarding this medicine, there is the analogy that at first, it will not be appetizing to its intended disciples. Once they have the appetite for it, there is the analogy that they will vomit it out. This medicinal compound [320] can dispel the chronic disease of saṃsāra, and it is said that there is nothing better than this. Once you have first partaken of this medicine, please do not vomit it out in the meantime. If you can proceed in this way, then the tightly constricting, chronic disease of saṃsāra will be released."

101. Tib. *ye shes gsang ba'i dbang phyug ma*.

Once again, Karmavajra posed a question to the Lord of Mysteries: "Who is Matibhadraśrī and what is the scope of his mindstream? When will he become enlightened? By which personal deity is he specially cared for? Where was he born in his previous lives?"

The Lord of Mysteries replied, "This Losang Drakpa is someone who has amassed the two collections [of merit and knowledge] on a vast scale. For seven previous lifetimes he displayed the role of a paṇḍita and thus accomplished the benefit of sentient beings. In the life just before this present one, he took birth in the land of Kashmir and was known as Paṇḍita Matibhadraśrī. He gathered a consummate entourage of five hundred disciples and was known to ordinary people to be on the path of preparation.

"Even I, Vajrapāṇi, cannot fathom his sublime qualities. As for his special personal deity, he is cared for by the outer and inner female deities, and he is also cared for by the protectors of the three lineages.[102] These are his special personal deities. I cannot reveal when he will be enlightened. Mañjuśrī and Avalokiteśvara will make this prophecy. Since he is someone with respect to whom just seeing, hearing, recalling, or touching him brings transformative benefit, another being cannot assess the scope of his mindstream."[103]

Then Karmavajra asked the Lord of Mysteries, "How long will the teachings that he revealed here in the Land of Snows last?"

"From now on we are in the period of scriptural transmission. Within that, this is the period of the collection of the sūtras. For those who have the *vinaya* (monastic discipline), [Losang Drakpa's teachings] will remain for one thousand three hundred years." [321]

Then Karmavajra asked the Lord of Mysteries, "Here in snowy Tibet, what joys and sorrows will come?"

"The forces of evil will grow and the forces of goodness will be defeated, so that all the peoples of the borderlands will come to the center. For this

102. Tib. *rigs gsum mgon po*. This is a well-known Tibetan term that refers specifically to Avalokiteśvara, Mañjuśrī, and Vajrapāṇi.

103. That is, because one is already transformed for the better through any contact with Tsongkhapa's mindstream, no one can assess it "objectively."

reason, all the gods and demons of the borderlands will come to the center. All the people from the center of the land will go to foreign lands. All the gods and demons from the center of the land will go to foreign lands. For this reason, the gods and demons will not be in harmony with one another. Many people will experience famine and epidemic diseases. There will be no happiness for sentient beings. How worthy of compassion are you teachers who grasp to crumbling sects!

"The time when armies from the borderlands will arrive and conquer is now. Nevertheless, by keeping just a tiny part of the general ritual services going, the regions of central Tibet and the ordained monks and nuns will stave it off. Even now, if the preventative practices are performed, it is possible to stave it off. Due to sentient beings' karma, it cannot be postponed for more than ten years. If there is quarreling among factions within the sangha, this is the sign that it will come quickly.

"By sustaining the samādhi of nonconceptuality and so forth that belongs to the supreme vehicle,[104] the experience of vipaśyanā arises, and because the profound method is distinguished by compassion, it will arise quickly. Through the profound method of mantra recitation, by striking the crucial points in the body, you will realize [vipaśyanā] right there on the mind. As for the point that it arises involuntarily, since the [Mantrayāna] has the inconceivable, supreme guidance on the profound method for great compassion, it will arise. If one lacks learning through hearing, since there are many pitfalls in Secret Mantra alone, it is extremely important to listen carefully when one is a beginner. [322] Even with this method for arousing bodhicitta—as it is practiced by most meditators nowadays[105]—what else would you expect apart from a trifling experience of vipaśyanā? By reciting the *dhāraṇīs* and mantras of profound Secret Mantra, a smattering of common siddhis may emerge. But the supreme siddhi arises in a continu-

104. This seems to indicate a samādhi that has identified pristine awareness.

105. Following *Lho brag nam mkha' rgyal mtshan*, vol. 1, 595, line 1: *bsam gtan pa byin po'i sems bskyed lugs* (instead of *bsam gtan pa byin gyis sems bskyed lugs*).

ous stream from the depths. Therefore, you must develop pure vision with respect to everything. In order for the experience of authentic vipaśyanā to arise, you must depend upon a guru in whom authentic vipaśyanā has arisen. If authentic vipaśyanā does not arise, rely upon my secret words. You must put an end to all of the pitfalls. So it is.

"For someone without śamatha, that which is to be understood in the view is concealed. Therefore, regarding those who assert that they are imbued with vipaśyanā, none of the *jinas* have ever said this! It does not emerge that way.

"The extraordinary method for causing an experience of vipaśyanā to come forth is in the unique teaching of Secret Mantra: the six yogas [of Kālacakra][106] and the Great Perfection. In general, there are inconceivably many divisions of the individual causes for liberation and omniscience. But if one summarizes them, they can be encapsulated into three.[107] There are many instances of this within my secret words.

"The distinction between whether a Dharma practitioner is or is not on the path is a matter of the magnitude of one's unique bodhicitta. (1) The essential nature of bodhicitta is great compassion. (2) Its function is to accomplish the needs of sentient beings, and (3) this is unique. The measure of whether one has understood those three and gained authentic experience of them is that, having severed the bonds of one's own needs, one thinks only of the needs of others and practices only for the benefit of others."

I asked, "Is this Great Perfection an authentic view?" [323]

"The Great Perfection is indeed an exalted view, but with respect to the view, that which the Ācāryas Nāgārjuna and Candrakīrti have elucidated is

106. Tib. *sbyor ba drug*, which is an abbreviation for *sbyor ba yan lag drug*, the name for the six-phased yoga (*ṣaḍaṅgayoga*) of the completion stage of Kālacakra: withdrawal (*pratyāhāra*), meditative stabilization (*dhyāna*), control of the life-sustaining energy (*prāṇāyāma*), retention (*dhāraṇā*), recollection (*anusmṛti*), and meditative concentration (*samādhi*). These terms have very specific meanings in these advanced practices, which are quite distinct from the general meanings of these words in other Buddhist and non-Buddhist contexts.

107. From context, it seems the "three" referred to here are śamatha, vipaśyanā, and bodhicitta.

without error. It is impossible for definitive[108] vipaśyanā to arise that does not depend upon their explanations.

"Nowadays in Ü and Tsang[109] there are inconceivably many people who, having eliminated false superimpositions regarding the unerring path of the buddhas by means of scripture and reasoning, have the opportunity to guide others on the authentic path. But those who have the opportunity to guide may still lack confident understanding of the guidance. Since they are unable to guide, if they do so anyway, all such teachers and students will go to the miserable realms of existence. How worthy of compassion!"

Then Karmavajra asked the Lord of Mysteries, "How long will Losang Drakpa live? Who will be exceptional among his entourage? Where will he increase the good of living beings? Where will he act for the good of living beings in his next lifetime? Please reveal this to us."

The Lord of Mysteries said, "If he does not remain in one region, the welfare of living beings will increase. But then he will not be able to live longer than forty-five years. If he devotes himself solely to practice, he can live to seventy-one years. If he acts for the welfare of living beings, then, since the practices of White Tārā and Amitābha do not include Mañjuśrī,[110] if he practices Mañjuśrī-Red Yamāri, this will lengthen his life. If he does not practice this, there is a danger of obstacles from evil forces. Those practices are to be greatly cherished.

"Among his entourage, three will be superlative, and there will be many among his entourage who enter the path of accumulation. As for his path, since it will surpass what was prophesied in previous lifetimes, it cannot be measured. He will swiftly see the holy faces of the personal deities mentioned earlier. [324] There are three ways of seeing. The highest is to see the holy face directly. Middling is to see the holy face within a meditative expe-

108. Following *Lho brag nam mkha' rgyal mtshan*, vol. 1, 595, line 7, which adds *mtshan nyid pa*.

109. The two main provinces in central Tibet.

110. Following *Lho brag nam mkha' rgyal mtshan*, vol. 1, 596, line 2: *'jam dpal dang 'bral ba yod pas* (instead of *'jam dpal dang 'brel ba yod pas*).

rience. Lowest is to see the holy face in a dream. Before one sees the holy face of the personal deity, extremely ferocious apparitions can arise. It can even happen that a type of formidable māra emanates in the form of one's personal deity. In that regard, from a stable state of samādhi, one should invite the beings of primordial consciousness (*jñānasattvas*) and dissolve them into [the form appearing in one's vision]. Then, if it is indeed the personal deity, that being will blaze in ever greater glory. If it is a māra, it will disappear." (There are many inconceivable points in this regard, but this one is easy for me to understand.)[111] "If, however much you see the holy face of the personal deity, you experience no joy or inspiration, you have been carried away by a māra."

Once again I asked, "Where will this Losang Drakpa be born in his subsequent lifetimes?"

"He will be born in Tuṣita, in the direct presence of Maitreya, and will be known as Mañjuśrīgarbha.[112] Then, from Tuṣita, he will bear in mind the needs of sentient beings in the Jambudvīpa continent of another world system, and will take birth there as a Dharma king. Immeasurable benefit will arise for the sentient beings there. In the third lifetime [after this present one], here in this Jambudvīpa he will be born in the east of India and be known as Paṇḍita Jñānaśrī, abbot of a monastery called 'At the foot of a mountain.'[113] He will gather an entourage of two thousand disciples. Everyone in his entourage will either be on the great stage of the path of accumulation or be on the path of preparation."

Since it is possible that the words spoken by the Lord of Mysteries himself will be incomprehensible to others, he asked me to keep them hidden. Although he spoke of the greatness of your holy body and about some of your sublime qualities, since I did not have time to put his words to writing,

111. Given Lhodrak Drupchen's comments at the end about what he was able to include in writing based on much more that Vajrapāṇi spoke, this is likely an interpolation of Lhodrak Drupchen's voice, rather than part of Vajrapāṇi's statements.

112. Tib. *'Jam dpal snying po*.

113. Following *Lho brag nam mkha' rgyal mtshan*, vol. 1, 596, line 7: *ri ṛtsa* (instead of *ri tsa*).

[325] only a fraction of them are written here. As for the questions, these are all the questions that I asked, but he said that you yourself are very familiar with it, so, since it is but a fraction, this is what I have written. So be it.

Maṅgalaṃ bhavantu

Translated by Eva Natanya and edited by B. Alan Wallace

The Words of Avalokiteśvara

Śamatha and Vipaśyanā in the Mahāmudrā Tradition of Mingyur Dorjé and Karma Chakmé

Karma Chakmé was given the name Wangdrag Sung ("Fiercely Powerful Speech") at his birth in 1613 and was immersed in the Dharma from early childhood, as his father—who was a Nyingma practitioner descended from the great Dharma kings of Tibet—guided his early education and granted him oral transmissions, minor empowerments, and training in ritual activities. The young Karma Chakmé experienced numerous visions of Padmasambhava, Vajravārāhī, and other deities.

At the age of eleven, he met his root guru, Pravaśara, from whom he received major empowerments and transmissions. Through very diligent practice, including meditating seated on a stool throughout the night, he became adept in Vajrayāna, experiencing pure visions and receiving siddhis from every deity that he practiced. At the age of nineteen, he took refuge and the upāsaka vows, and later the same year received a great number of Vajrayāna transmissions and empowerments in the Kagyü tradition from the second Gyalwang Karmapa Karma Rakshi. During that time he took the novice monastic vows during the day and that same evening took the *gelong*, or full monastic ordination, receiving the name Karma Chakmé. He joined the Thupten Nyinling Monastery of the Zurmang Kagyü tradition, where he practiced as an impeccable monk, becoming a master of the five great scriptures of Indian Mahāyāna Buddhism, and was greatly skilled in logic.

At the age of thirty-seven, he entered strict retreat focused on the deity Avalokiteśvara and the practice of Mahāmudrā. He remained in this intensive, solitary retreat for thirteen years, occasionally granting empowerments and commentaries to disciples through an opening in the wall of his retreat hut. During this time, many deities appeared to him in pure visions, granting countless blessings.

He recognized and enthroned the great *tertön* Namchö Mingyur Dorjé (1645–1667)[114] when Mingyur Dorjé was about ten years old, and they would go on to share a mutual teacher–student relationship, each revering the other. Karma Chakmé served as the scribe for Mingyur Dorjé's revelation of the thirteen volumes of the Namchö, or Sky Dharma, cycle of teachings, which became widely practiced in both the Karma Kagyü and Nyingma traditions (especially those of Kathok and Palyul Monasteries) down to the present day; two chapters of Karma Chakmé's own extensive commentary on this enormous body of teachings is translated below. Mingyur Dorjé revealed the Namchö—which he received as mind treasures in pure visions—while still a boy of eleven or twelve years old, often accompanied by states of trance. Karma Chakmé cared for the boy and also made possible the preservation of the myriad empowerments and transmissions that Mingyur Dorjé received from Samantabhadra, Amitābha, Avalokiteśvara, and Padmasambhava by writing them down.

It is clear from Karma Chakmé's commentary to the Namchö that this explanation was originally shared in the context of a multi-day teaching, with numerous disciples present, some more senior than others—that is, the "stewards" who had received the teaching previously. This commentary is specifically with respect to the *Cycle on the Avalokiteśvara Body Maṇḍala* within the Namchö revelations, and it is an "aural lineage," namely, the

114. For biographical details see https://treasuryoflives.org/biographies/view/Namcho-Mingyur-Dorje/9190 and https://www.namdroling.net/Portal/Page/Terton-Mingyur-Dorje.

teachings ideally needed to be heard directly from a lineage holder. Yet tradition preserves this as a text, which allows suitable excerpts to be translated and thus understood and practiced by many more people than might ever have the fortune to receive the aural lineage in person.

Karma Chakmé had an especially close connection to Avalokiteśvara and also granted public guidance for those yearning to be reborn in the buddhafield of Amitābha, called Sukhāvatī. When Karma Chakmé was sixty-five years old, in 1678, the Buddha Amitābha appeared to him in a pure vision, expressing discontent that he had not yet come. It was then that he realized it was time for him to go to Amitābha's pure land of Sukhāvatī. The mahāsiddha manifested illness that same day, and soon afterward passed away, displaying many auspicious signs.[115]

In the two chapters that follow, where Mingyur Dorjé's revealed root text is represented in bold type, we see a foundational presentation on the path of śamatha and vipaśyanā as they are held in common across the traditions of the sūtra Mahāyāna, Mahāmudrā, and Dzokchen. We witness Karma Chakmé's inspiring erudition as he cites myriad sūtras and tantras to illustrate and support each point, as well as his direct instructions from experience—which can guide us straight to the heart of meditative stability and realization of emptiness, if we can take each page presented here as personal instruction for practice.

115. For further biographical details see https://www.namdroling.net/Portal/Page/Mahasiddha-Karma-Chagmed.

14. The Cultivation of Śamatha

FROM *THE GREAT COMMENTARY TO MINGYUR DORJÉ'S BUDDHAHOOD IN THE PALM OF YOUR HAND*, CHAPTER 15

Karma Chakmé

Then, for the presentation of the instructions on the main topic, there are (1) the instructions on cutting through, which are held in common by śamatha-vipaśyanā, Mahāmudrā, and Dzokchen; and (2) there are the uncommon instructions on the direct crossing over. Moreover, within the first of these there are the three topics of śamatha, vipaśyanā, and the union of these two.

First there is a presentation of śamatha, for without śamatha the mental afflictions are not suppressed, the fine qualities of extrasensory perception do not arise, and the wisdom of emptiness is not realized. First, śamatha must be cultivated, as stated in [Śāntideva's] *Bodhicaryāvatāra*:

> Someone whose mind is distracted dwells between the fangs
> of the mental afflictions.

[Atiśa's] *Bodhipathapradīpa* says,

> If śamatha is not achieved, extrasensory perception does not
> occur.
> Accordingly, without the power of extrasensory perception,
> the needs of sentient beings cannot be accomplished.

And [Nāgārjuna's] *Suhṛllekha* states,

> Without dhyāna there is no wisdom.

As for the immeasurable benefits of śamatha, craving for [416] mundane activities is averted; many avenues of samādhi arise in one's mindstream; mental afflictions are calmed; compassion arises; one realizes the meaning of emptiness, which is wisdom; and so on. The *Prajñāpāramitāsaṃcayagāthā* states,

> Due to dhyāna, one disparagingly rejects the attractions of the desire realm,
> and one manifestly accomplishes sound reasoning, extrasensory perception, and samādhi.

The *Bodhicaryāvatāra* states,

> Once you know that vipaśyanā perfectly imbued with śamatha completely destroys the mental afflictions . . .

And the *Dharmasaṃgīti Sūtra* states,

> The mind settled in meditative equipoise sees reality as it is. Due to seeing reality as it is, the mind of a bodhisattva dwells in great compassion for sentient beings.

The *Mahāyānasūtrālaṃkāra* states,

> By this very dhyāna, all beings are brought to the three kinds of enlightenment.

Moreover, it is said that if one cultivates śamatha alone and achieves the fourth dhyāna and so on, one can display an uncanny variety of tainted paranormal abilities. The *Śatasāhasrikāprajñāpāramitā Sūtra* states,

> One fully accomplishes the first dhyāna [417] and then abides therein; one fully accomplishes the second dhyāna and then abides therein; one fully accomplishes the third dhyāna and then abides therein; one fully accomplishes the fourth dhyāna and then abides therein. Then one settles in meditative equipoise in that fourth dhyāna and experiences numerous types of paranormal abilities. One causes even this great earth to quake; one transforms from one to many; one transforms from many to one; one experiences becoming visible and invisible. Passing through walls, passing through fences, and passing through mountains, one moves about with a body that is unimpeded, as one would through space. One moves through space with one's legs crossed, like a feathered bird. One moves up through the earth and down into the earth, as one would through water. One walks upon water without sinking, as one would on land. One billows forth smoke and blazes with light, like a bonfire.
>
> Moreover, those endowed with such great paranormal abilities, with such great might, and with such great power, stroke the sun and moon with their hands, [418] and their bodies wield dominion as far as the world of Brahmā. Those endowed with such physical zeal use these types of paranormal abilities to go wherever the bhagavān buddhas in incalculable, innumerable, immeasurable realms in the ten directions of the world may reside, may nurture [disciples], or may teach the Dharma, and they venerate those bhagavān buddhas [by offering] bountiful garments, alms, bedding, medicine for the ill, and essential items. Moreover, those many garments, alms, bedding, medicines for

> the ill, and essential items are not exhausted until one becomes a manifestly perfected buddha in supreme, perfect enlightenment.

The meaning of this and further passages is that if one has cultivated faultless śamatha alone, such signs that one has achieved the fourth dhyāna will occur. They are tainted paranormal abilities, which also occur for non-Buddhists, Bönpos, and so forth. If the achievement of such śamatha is imbued with vipaśyanā, then there are untainted paranormal abilities, but the basis of all the paranormal abilities and sublime qualities [419] of the mahāsiddhas of India and Tibet is śamatha.

Furthermore, if one does not cultivate dhyāna, even though one may strive for other roots of virtue, one will not be fit to be included within the class of the Muni's teachings. The *Kuśalamūlasaṃparigraha Sūtra* states,

> Even though one may guard ethical discipline for an eon and
> cultivate patience for a long time,
> if one does not become acquainted with the actual nature of
> reality, one is an extremist in relation to my teachings.

The *Nandagarbhāvakrāntinirdeśa Sūtra* states,

> Whoever lacks the mind of meditative equipoise
> lacks pure, primordial wisdom,
> so the contaminations will not be eliminated.
> By all means, then, accomplish it!

The *Pitāputrasamāgama Sūtra* states,

> With respect to any of the dharmas of the Buddha,
> they will not be seen by any other path:
> If śamatha and great primordial wisdom are achieved,
> self-emergent realization will certainly occur.

In the *Mahāprātihāryanirdeśa Sūtra* it is said,

> No movement of the body, no movement of the speech, no movement of the mind, and the complete purity of these three spheres: it is truly a miracle!

For the cultivation [420] of such śamatha one must abandon entertainment and distractions, as the *Adhyāśayasaṃcodana Sūtra* states,

> Maitreya, these are the twenty faults of idle entertainment: the body is unrestrained, the speech is unrestrained, the mind is unrestrained, mental afflictions are strong, one is polluted by mundane talk, māras find their opportunity to enter, one resorts to unconscientious behavior, and śamatha and vipaśyanā are not achieved . . .

The *Candrapradīpa* [*Samādhirāja*] *Sūtra* states,

> The Supreme Jina is not venerated with food or with drink,
> with garments, flowers, incense, or garlands.
> Superior to such merit is that of one who earnestly yearns for
> enlightenment, is disillusioned with vile composites,
> and for the sake of sentient beings dwells in the wilderness,
> taking the seven steps [to liberation].
> . . .
> Such a person continually turns away from composites,
> has no desire for anything in the mundane world,
> and his contaminations do not increase.
> . . .
> Forsake delight in towns and cities, [421] remain in solitude,
> and dwell in the forest.

Like a rhinoceros, always be alone.
Before long, you will achieve supreme samādhi.

Therefore, now for these few days you should avoid all distractions, including invitations, business, prejudiced conversation, asking questions, and so on. Not only that, dispense with all physical, verbal, and mental distractions, including the religious practices of prostrations, circumambulations, and chanting. The *Bodhicaryāvatāra* also says,

The One Who Realizes Suchness stated that all recitations and austerities,
even though performed for a long time, are meaningless if the mind is distracted elsewhere.
. . .
You who wish to guard your practice, guard your mind with great care!
If you do not guard this mind, you will also not be able to guard your practice.
. . .
By restraining this mind alone, all those will be restrained.
By subduing this mind alone, all those will be subdued.
Apart from the discipline of guarding the mind, what's the use of many austere disciplines? [422]
. . .
If the elephant of the mind is let loose, it inflicts the harm of Avīci Hell.
If this elephant of the mind is restrained with the rope of thorough mindfulness, all fears will vanish,
and all joys will come into your hands.
. . .
My possessions and honor, my body and livelihood may

> decline, but never will I let the mind, which is above all, decline.
> To you who wish to guard your minds, guard mindfulness and introspection, even at the cost of your life!
> This I ask with folded hands.
> Repeatedly examining the condition of the body and mind—just that, in short, is the definition of guarding introspection.

Well then, how is śamatha to be cultivated? There is (I) śamatha with a sign and (II) śamatha without a sign. For both of these, the posture is very important. The *Ārya Avalokiteśvara Padmajāla Tantra* states,

> When you are sitting upright in the vajrāsana on a very soft cushion,
> cast your gaze down over the tip of the nose.
> With mindful, free-flowing respiration,
> touch the tip of the tongue against the palate,
> slightly draw [423] the navel inward,
> and rest your mind conscientiously.

In the *Vajramālā Tantra* it is said,

> The practitioner should sit upon a comfortable cushion, and direct both eyes over the tip of the nose. The nose should just be in view.
> Let the shoulders be even, and touch the tongue to the palate.
> Let the teeth and lips be comfortable, and the exhalation and inhalation be relaxed.
> By incrementally releasing effort, the exhalation and inhalation will flow naturally as you sit properly in the *bodhisattvāsana*.

Here is the meaning: A vital point is that with the physical posture as a contributing factor, realizations arise in the mind. Thus, due to the legs being either in the vajrāsana or the bodhisattvāsana, the downward-clearing vital energy is directed into the central channel, envy is calmed, and one is not troubled by interferences. Due to the hands being in the mudrā of meditative equipoise four finger-widths below the navel, the water vital energy is directed into the central channel, and hatred is calmed. Due to the spine being straight like an arrow and the shoulders being spread like the wings of a vulture, the earth vital energy is directed into the central channel, and delusion is calmed. By tucking the chin slightly down toward the chest, the fire vital energy is directed into the central channel, and attachment is calmed.

With the eyes partially open, direct the gaze to a point four finger-widths below the tip of the nose, [424] and by touching the tongue to the upper palate, the vital energy of air is directed into the central channel, pride is calmed, and consciousness becomes clear. In that way if you correctly adopt the seven points of the posture, the vital energies are directed into the central channel, resulting in the natural arising of realizations.

If the body leans to the right, there first occurs a sense of clarity, but thereafter anger arises, and you are afflicted by masculine demonic forces such as *pārthivas*.[116] If you lean to the left, there first occurs a sense of joy, but thereafter attachment arises, and you are afflicted by female demonic forces. If you lean forward, there first occurs a sense of nonconceptuality, but thereafter delusion arises, you are afflicted by *kṣamāpati*s,[117] the mind becomes unhappy, and the vital energy of the heart becomes disturbed. If the body leans backward, there first occurs a sense of vacuity, but thereafter obstacles occur, including the arising of pride, strong conceptualization, scattering,

116. Tib. *rgyal po*. Demonic forces or beings that emerge from the aggregates to which one grasps as being "me," and which consist of the conceptual mental processes that reify appearances. They arise as apparitions of ignorance.

117. Tib. *sa bdag*. An earth spirit whose actual nature is that of delusions produced by the causes and conditions of ignorance.

and excitation, the body becomes bluish and thin, the vital fluids seep out, and so forth. Therefore, be sure not to err with respect to the posture.

I. The Cultivation of Śamatha with a Sign

Whether you place an enlightened form, a stick, or a pebble in front of you,
encircle it with the consciousness [208] that has generated a deity.
Do your best to rest your mind in that sphere.
Resting in the center, momentary movements, and awareness of them both—
are the dharmakāya, sambhogakāya, and nirmāṇakāya.

Place the form of Śākyamuni or any golden image of a deity, or a lotus, or else a stick, a pebble, or the like in front of you. In any case, generate it as the divine Śākyamuni, Vajrasattva, Samantabhadra, or Vajradhara—whichever is suitable—and then let your consciousness encircle it. Then do your best to rest your mind within its sphere. Remaining in the center is stillness. Momentary dispersions are movements. Mental awareness of them both is awareness. Stillness is the dharmakāya. Awareness is the sambhogakāya. Movement is the nirmāṇakāya.[118]

Then, to cultivate śamatha with a sign, the *Samādhirāja Sūtra* states that if you meditate on Bhagavān Śākyamuni in front of you, there are

118. The bold indented text is from Mingyur Dorjé's *Guidance in the Great Perfection called Buddhahood in the Palm of Your Hand, from The Cycle on the Body Maṇḍala in the Profound Aural Lineage of the Sky Dharma (Namchö) Mind Treasure*, in *Gnam chos*, vol. 1 (Paro Kyichu, Bhutan: Dilgo Khyentsey Rinpoché, 1983), 207–209.

immeasurable benefits, and it says to hold in mind each of the thirty-two signs and eighty symbols of [the Buddha's body]. The same sūtra states,

> When a bodhisattva sustains his or her attention on the object
> [425] of the magnificent Protector of the World,
> whose enlightened body is like the color of gold, that is called
> meditative equipoise.

The meaning of this is stated in the verse of vajra words [from the root text]:

> **Whether you place an enlightened form, a stick, or a pebble**
> **in front of you,**
> **encircle it with the consciousness that has generated a deity.**
> **Do your best to rest your mind in that sphere.**

And its commentary, taught by the Great Compassionate One [Avalokiteśvara] himself, states,

> **Place the form of Śākyamuni or any golden image of a deity, or a lotus, or else a stick, a pebble, or the like [in front of you]. In any case, generate it as the divine Śākyamuni, Vajrasattva, Samantabhadra, or Vajradhara—whichever is suitable—and then let your consciousness encircle it. Then do your best to rest your mind within its sphere.**

Here is the meaning: Place in front of you—or before a group of people—an enlightened representation so it can be seen. If you do not have one, use a pebble, a stick, or a flower. For just a few people, place a pebble in front of each one. There are four techniques for sustaining the attention: (A) sustaining the attention on the nirmāṇakāya, (B) sustaining the attention on the sambhogakāya, and (C) sustaining the attention on the dharmakāya, [426] as well as (II) sustaining the attention without any referent.

A. Sustaining the Attention on the Nirmāṇakāya

Now envision this enlightened representation, or the pebble, lotus, or stick, as a small, enlightened body of the Bhagavān, the nirmāṇakāya Śākyamuni, just four finger-widths in height. Single-pointedly focus your mind on that, and just for a moment stay there without distraction. Now just for a moment hold your attention on the coil of hair on Śākyamuni's forehead. Now just for a moment direct your mind to the eternity knot on Śākyamuni's chest. Now focus your mind on the vajra in front of Śākyamuni. Now hold your attention on Śākyamuni's entire body. The meaning of this is stated, moreover, in [Kamalaśīla's] *Bhāvanāyogāvatāra*:

> Cultivate an attraction for the enlightened form of the Buddha, yellow like refined gold, adorned with its signs and symbols, emitting rays of light. Get rid of desires and the afflictions of the mind, and keep the body straight and erect. Place in front of you a cast metal statue or painting of such an enlightened form. If you attend to it continually, you will perceptually see that very form completely, or else see it completely by way of its limbs and so on. When that becomes an object on which you can focus, [427] rely on it without distraction, uninterruptedly throughout the day and night. If the mind becomes lax or excited and so forth, or tight, take delight in yearning for the sublime qualities of the Buddha. Practice diligently in that way. By so doing you will succeed.

Moreover, if the mind, lacking clarity, becomes lax and dull, sustain your attention on the Buddha's crown-protrusion. If your mind cannot be made to settle down due to strong scattering and excitation, direct your attention to the Buddha's navel, the soles of his feet, or the edge of his seat. If there is no laxity or excitation, sustain your attention on the eternity knot on the Buddha's chest. Then that constitutes sustaining the mind on the nirmāṇakāya.

B. Sustaining the Attention on the Sambhogakāya

Then you may place in front of you a pebble or a stick, or it is also suitable if you do not. In either case, imagine the Bhagavān Vajrasattva, his body white in color, holding a vajra and bell, four finger-widths in height, adorned with silks and jewels, and seated in the bodhisattvāsana. Sustaining your attention on him, encircle him with your mind as much as you can.

Now to give a clear explanation of the teachings on the nine stages of mental stillness as taught in the sūtras by the Bhagavān:

1. Placement: The mind is focused single-pointedly on an enlightened form or a stick, and so on. [428]
2. Thorough placement: Attention is maintained continuously for a protracted period.
3. Definite placement: If the mind is scattered by conceptualization, it is immediately restrained with mindfulness and settled in meditative equipoise.
4. Close placement: The mind of meditative equipoise is fused with the previous locus of attention and placed in equipoise.
5. Subduing: Delight is brought forth from being clearly mindful of the fine qualities of sustained attention and resting in that state.
6. Pacifying: The individual conditions that lead to scattering off to specific objects are ascertained, and by rejecting craving for them, attention is sustained.
7. Fully pacifying: Each of the causes of distraction, such as avarice, and all the results of distractions, such as unpleasant feelings, are recognized in their essential nature, and they are released by themselves.

8. Unification of the mindstream: By the power of such meditation, the mind automatically engages with the meditative object, and it remains there without reliance upon strong effort.
9. Meditative equipoise: Finally, there is no distraction [429] either during meditative equipoise or when not meditating.

Those are the nine stages of mental stillness. The practices devoted to the nirmāṇakāya and sambhogakāya entail the mind apprehending something external.

C. Sustaining the Attention on the Dharmakāya

Then, for the mind to apprehend inwardly: At the center of your heart imagine the dharmakāya Vajradhara, his body deep blue and the size of the outer thumb-joint, holding a vajra and bell crossed at his heart, seated in the vajrāsana on a lotus and moon seat, and adorned with silks and jewels. Do your best to sustain your attention on this without distraction.

Now "serene,"[119] refers to calming the mind from being drawn away to various thoughts. The vivid stillness[120] of the mind wherever it is focused is śamatha.

II. Śamatha without a Sign

Then, for śamatha without a sign, focus your mind on Samantabhadra. Samantabhadra is emptiness devoid of form, color, and substantiality. Do not imagine or think about anything in the mind. Do not pursue traces from the past, nor anticipate the future. Relax, simply without distraction, in the consciousness of the present, without rejecting or affirming anything. Relax and rest. The *Bhadrakarātrī Sūtra* states,

119. This is the meaning of the first syllable, *zhi*, of the Tibetan term for śamatha.

120. This is the meaning of the second syllable, *gnas*, of the Tibetan term for śamatha.

> Do not follow after the past, [430] and have no hopes for the future.

The *Avaivartacakra Sūtra* states,

> The mind of the past is not found, and likewise for the future.
> Achieve equanimity regarding events in the present.

And in the *Saṃdhinirmocana Sūtra*:

> "Bhagavān, what sort of śamatha objects are there?" He replied, "There is one: It has the form of nonconceptualization." . . . "How is one to cultivate this singular śamatha?" "When, with continuous mental engagement, uninterruptedly attending to the actual nature of the mind, there is samādhi uninterrupted by laxity or excitation . . . that is flawless mental engagement with the actual nature of the mind."

The *Prajñāpāramitāsaṃcayagāthā* states,

> Bodhisattvas who do not focus upon the limits of the past, the limits of the future, or the events of the present purify the three times.
> They experience the unconditioned, without elaboration, and they experience supreme transcendent wisdom.

The *Kālacakra Mūla Tantra* states,

> The mahāmudrā of withdrawal (*pratyāhāra*)
> has the defining characteristic of empty space.

Paṇḍita Dharmakīrti states,

> Mindfulness of thoughts eradicates them, [431]
> so they appear as luminosity itself.

The *Mahāyānasūtrālaṃkāra* states,

> The limpidity of turbid water does not arise from the outset
> but appears only when it is freed of impurities.
> So it is with natural purity, and the way to it is this.

The *Samādhirāja Sūtra* also states,

> Without thoughts, without conceptualization,
> without an apprehended object, and with nothing to show,
> the mind, too, is without a referent.
> Therefore, this is called "samādhi."
> If jinaputras cultivate this king of the samādhis of bodhisattvas,
> they go beyond conceptualization, which is difficult to transcend,
> and gradually nonconceptual primordial wisdom arises.

The *Kāyatrayastotra* states,

> Nonconceptual primordial wisdom alone
> is asserted by the wise to be samādhi.
> Any other samādhi does not dwell
> in authentic reality, but is a distraction.

The *Śatasāhasrikāprajñāpāramitā Sūtra* states,

> What is the samādhi of mental stillness? Abiding in that samādhi, the mind is unwavering, nonconceptual, and does

not become despondent or unhappy. There does not arise the thought "This is what is called 'the mind.'" [432] This is the samādhi called "mental stillness."

The Mother *Prajñāpāramitā Sūtra* states,

> When bodhisattvas experience transcendent wisdom, they have the samādhi called "isolation." Bodhisattvas who experience that samādhi swiftly become manifestly, perfectly enlightened. In similar fashion, they have the samādhi that is "without mind," that is "without mental activity," that is "unwavering," and which "does not see any essential nature with respect to any phenomena." Bodhisattvas, mahāsattvas, who experience that samādhi swiftly become manifestly, perfectly enlightened. This is the consummation of the causes that are dhyāna and śamatha. . . .
>
> It is profound due to its isolation, and profound because its depths are difficult to fathom. Subhūti, this which is without form is the profundity of form. Subhūti, this which is without feeling, discernment, mental formations, or consciousness is the profundity of consciousness. . . .
>
> Subhūti, this transcendent wisdom is totally nonconceptual. The total absence of conceptualization [433] is called "buddha." The total absence of conceptualization is called "enlightenment."

In the *Aṣṭasāhasrikāprajñāpāramitā Sūtra* it is said,

> By cultivating transcendent wisdom, one does not dwell in form, nor in feeling, nor in discernment, nor in mental formations, nor in consciousness.

The *Pradarśanānumatoddeśaparīkṣā* states,

> By their own nature, meditation and recitation with mudrās,
> maṇḍalas, and mantras,
> even over many tens of millions of eons, will never bring any
> attainment of siddhis.
> One who dwells in suchness upon abandoning all
> conceptualization
> achieves [siddhis] in this very life and reaches supreme
> enlightenment.

The *Sampuṭa Tantra* states,

> Upon examining the status of conceptualization,
> if, in accord with the teachings of the Mind Vajra,
> an intelligent person then does not engage in
> conceptualization,
> for that person there will without doubt be siddhis.
> Conceptualization takes one to the hell realms,
> and one circles around in the ocean of the six classes of
> existence.
> If freed from conceptualization,
> one goes to the absolute space of unstained peace.
> So cut the web of conceptualization!

[434] The *Vairocanābhisambodhi Tantra* states,

> Conceptualization acts as the cause of suffering.
> For as long as it is not eliminated,
> one is not a buddha in this world,
> and one cannot be called "omniscient."

In the *Vajramālā Tantra* it is said,

> With the exhaustion of all conceptualization,
> great bliss arises authentically.

The *Vajrapāṇyabhiṣeka Tantra* states,

> In primordial consciousness free of conceptualization,
> the jinas of the past have become manifest buddhas.
> In that freedom from conceptualization,
> it is taught that one gains success in secret Mantrayāna.
> Its pure fruition naturally turns into clear light.
> For one who practices from conceptualization, siddhis will not emerge.
> So meditate upon the forms of the Mantrayāna
> by eliminating conceptualization.

The *Abhidhānottara Tantra* states,

> In order to actualize the kāya of primordial consciousness,
> the Tathāgata taught meditation that eliminates all conceptual fabrications.

In the *Vairocanābhisambodhi Tantra* it is said,

> Those who long for the state of omniscience
> should continuously strive for the total elimination
> of the various forms of conceptualization.

[435] The *Vajraśekhara Tantra* states,

> Malevolent beings do not exist at all.
> The actual nature of the mind is pure.
> One's own mind is called Māra.

> The actual nature of malevolent beings is also one's own mind.
> Dispel all conceptualization.
> From conceptualization, all malevolent beings arise.
> Lay hold of the mind, which is difficult to subdue,
> and eliminate all desires.

Nāgārjuna states,

> The buddhas have said that what authentically interrupts
> the flow of wholesome and unwholesome conceptualization
> is emptiness.

Śāntideva states,

> When the body, speech, and mind are in isolation,
> distraction does not occur.
> Therefore, the world is to be renounced,
> and conceptualization is to be thoroughly abandoned.

[Dignāga's] *Yogāvatāra* states,

> The mind that constantly eliminates
> the many conceptualizations called "saṃsāra"
> settles in meditative equipoise.

Saraha states,

> Śamatha depends upon its cause—ethical discipline.
> Its essential nature is isolation from mental afflictions and conceptualization.
> Its cooperative condition is reliance upon the unique features of the stages of mental stillness.

> The benefit is that coarse mental afflictions and suffering are suppressed.

[436] Now, here in this context, this is the time for cultivating śamatha by itself. Do your best to keep your mind still, without being scattered anywhere. With the body imbued with the vital points, rest your body and mind in a state of comfort and relaxation. If the mind becomes scattered, rest it upon stillness without letting it become diffused. Settling the mind in stillness,[121] having calmed[122] the scattering of conceptualization, is śamatha.

In this regard, there is (A) flawed and (B) flawless meditation.

A. Flawed Śamatha

Once the mind has entered śamatha, even if you are called, you do not hear, so it is as if you were in deep sleep, but you have not actually fallen asleep. At that time, the eyes do not see anything. The mind being unclear, you do not recall or think anything. Even though you are in such a state for a long time, you are unaware of the passage of time. When you are aroused from that samādhi, it is like waking up from sleep or being restored to consciousness after fainting, and you think, "Now what's happened to me?" A person who experiences such things is bewildered about śamatha.

At first if that happens only momentarily, that is not a problem, for it is an indication that the meditative state is about to arise. There are also accounts of this in the stories of previous masters, such as Düsum Khyenpa [the First Karmapa] and others. But it is inappropriate to continue in that, thinking it is meditation, for if you cultivate that alone, [437] it acts as a cause for rebirth as an animal.

Alternatively, if you focus the mind in the center of your heart, and remain without bringing any thoughts to mind, the mind will remain still

121. This again glosses the second syllable, *gnas*, of the Tibetan term for śamatha.

122. This again glosses the first syllable, *zhi*, of the Tibetan term for śamatha.

without any memories or thoughts arising. Thus, due to the absence of memories and thoughts, the eight configurations of outer consciousness are unclear. There are no other memories or thoughts in the mind; there is simply the discernment that the mind is remaining single-pointedly. But there is no observation of the essential nature of stillness. When you meditate in that way, you will not sense where the sun has moved, and this is said to be similar in some respects to śrāvaka cessation. Since this is flawless śamatha,[123] if at first it happens for a short time, this is no problem, but it is inappropriate to meditate continually in that way.

B. Flawless Śamatha

Well then, what is it like to have flawless śamatha? Wherever the mind is directed, it remains vividly still and luminously clear. When meditating in that way, the eight configurations of consciousness, including the eyes, ears, and so on, are not impeded; rather each one is clear.[124] The body and mind are pervaded by bliss, with no irritation. Meditation manifests in this way whenever you are meditating. When you are not meditating, without needing to arouse yourself, you have a great sense of autonomy, and that is śamatha alone, which is the foundation of meditation.

Moreover, by cultivating śamatha, physical and mental bliss arise. [438] When great attachment and craving for that bliss arise, by holding it to be supreme, you will be reborn as a god in the desire realm. If you sustain it without attachment or craving, it leads to the path.

In that śamatha, by applying yourself to investigation and analysis as

123. The text reads *zhi gnas skyon med yin pas* ("Since this is flawless śamatha"), but by context perhaps it should be read as *zhi gnas skyon can yin pas* ("Since this is flawed śamatha").

124. Whereas in the flawed meditation the senses are totally withdrawn, in flawless meditation sensory objects do appear to the senses, but they are not apprehended. This corresponds to the full achievement of śamatha, or access to the first dhyāna, which entails crossing over from the desire realm to the form realm. Although the five physical senses are "clear" in this state of samādhi, one is unaware of one's body and physical environment, for the mind has dissolved into its own self-illuminating, essential nature—the substrate consciousness.

antidotes to prevent the mind from scattering, you will be imbued with mental joy and well-being, and your mind will remain single-pointedly. That is the first dhyāna. Without need for investigation or analysis to ward off mental scattering, when there is an inner lucidity to the single-pointed mind, that is the second dhyāna. Remaining single-pointedly without investigation or analysis and without a sense of either well-being or sorrow, but with mindfulness and introspection, constitutes the third dhyāna. Pure mindfulness, with unwavering mental equanimity, and without investigation, analysis, well-being, or sorrow, with neither mental happiness nor unhappiness, and without respiration, is the fourth dhyāna. The bodhisattva Rangjung Dorjé states,

> With the antidotes of investigation and analysis, if you apply yourself to single-pointedness, the result of joy and well-being fully arise. That is the first dhyāna.
> Single-pointedness without investigation or analysis, with the joy and well-being of inwardly directed lucidity, is the second.
> Single-pointedness with mindfulness and introspection, free of investigation, analysis, well-being, or suffering, is called the third dhyāna.
> Pure mindfulness, [439] with unwavering equanimity, devoid of the eight faults of investigation and analysis, well-being and suffering, the suffering of mental happiness and unhappiness, and the mental pleasure or pain of inhalation and exhalation, is called the fourth dhyāna.

Moreover, when such fine śamatha arises, if it is sustained without attachment or craving, it leads to the path. If you respond with attachment and craving, holding it to be supreme, and practice while thinking, "This alone is meditation," in the short-term you may achieve tainted extrasensory perception and paranormal abilities—but you will not transcend saṃsāra.

By cultivating the first dhyāna, you are born in one of the three Brahmā worlds of Brahmākāyika, Brahmāpurohita, or Mahābrahmā. By cultivating the second dhyāna, you are born in one of the three worlds of Parīttābhā, Apramāṇābhā, or Ābhāsvara. By cultivating the third dhyāna, you are born in one of the three worlds of Śubha, Parīttaśubha, or Apramāṇaśubha. And by cultivating the fourth dhyāna, you are born in one of the three worlds of Anabhrakābhā, Puṇyaprasava, or Bṛhatphala. You are born in those due to śamatha alone, [440] and non-Buddhists, Bönpos, and so on are reborn there, too. Non-Buddhists assert the attainment of just that as being the ultimate fruition.

Avṛha, Atapa, Sudṛṣṭa, Sudṛśa, and Akaniṣṭha are called the five abodes of the āryas. Śamatha by itself does not result in birth there, and ordinary beings do not take birth there, for they are solely the abodes of āryas.

By stopping the discernment that grasps to the characteristics of luminosity and nonconceptuality, there is the samāpatti devoid of discernment. By blocking all appearances and obtaining causes, cultivating consciousness like space, there is [the samāpatti of] boundless consciousness. By meditating without determining either an object or a subject, and without determining anything whatever, there arises [the samāpatti of] nothingness. Upon stopping the coarse discernment of nothingness, by meditating with the thought that subtle discernment is not nonexistent either, one takes birth as a god in [the samāpatti of] neither the presence nor absence of discernment.

Those individuals regard śamatha alone as supreme, but since the mind is bound by subtle grasping, there is the flaw of not seeing one's own nature with vipaśyanā. Saraha states,

> Childish people are deceived by mistakes
> with respect to the indwelling mind,
> and all beings without exception become thoroughly
> disenchanted.

> Due to the fault of pride, [441] reality cannot be shown.
> The whole world is becoming bewildered by dhyāna.

Thus, once you have cultivated śamatha by itself, then the greater the śamatha, the greater the creative power and fine qualities of vipaśyanā. If śamatha is weak, the power of vipaśyanā will be weak, just as little rain falls from a small cloud or a small flame burns from a small piece of wood. Therefore, I beg you now to dispense with recitations and other virtuous practices, and do your best to still your mind single-pointedly!

Thus I have described the objects of śamatha held in common [between the Sūtrayāna and Mantrayāna]. With the thought of dedicating this virtue, and the virtue of meditating upon these objects, to all sentient beings, recite after me three times: "I dedicate this virtue to all beings in the six classes of existence, who have been my old mother."

This concludes the fifteenth chapter, on the cultivation of śamatha.

15. The Analytical Cultivation of Vipaśyanā According to the Pith Instructions Held in Common

FROM *THE GREAT COMMENTARY TO MINGYUR DORJÉ'S BUDDHAHOOD IN THE PALM OF YOUR HAND*, CHAPTER 16

Karma Chakmé

Whatever you think, whatever you recall,
whatever you see, and whatever you are aware of,
observe its essential nature and penetratingly see it as
empty.

...

However and whatever you may think, however and whatever you may recall, whatever [209] you see and whatever you are aware of, observe its essential nature, and thus penetratingly see it as empty.

Then, for the explanation of vipaśyanā: vipaśyanā is wisdom, for which there are the two divisions of (I) common and (II) uncommon.[125]

125. The section on "uncommon vipaśyanā" is not translated here, for it is treated separately in the following chapter of Karma Chakmé's *Great Commentary*.

I. Wisdom Held in Common

The intelligence that investigates and analyzes all outer and inner phenomena is, in some sūtra traditions, explained to be "wisdom." In the *Śatasāhasrikāprajñāpāramitā Sūtra* it is said,

> Those blind ones who have listened to few [teachings] do not know how to meditate—
> Without [having listened], then with such [meditation], on what are you to [442] reflect?
> Therefore, apply yourself to listening, and from that cause
> the vast wisdom of meditation in accordance with reflection will arise.

This refers to the wisdom of emptiness. Moreover, according to both the scriptures and pith instructions, drawing from the tantras and scriptural explanations you should first establish the view. If you do not do so, it is said to be pointless, like shooting an arrow without seeing the target. In this context, however, if you initially realize the view by way of the practice of meditation—as can be found in the pith instructions of the earlier *vidyādharas*[126]—then this is profound. In this regard, though you may have accumulated a vast store of merit, the collection of skillful means, if you do

126. The Sanskrit term *vidyādhara* (Tib. *rig 'dzin*), can have a variety of precise meanings within Buddhist Vajrayāna, but in the context of Dzokchen it refers specifically to someone who has not only identified pristine awareness but is also able to dwell in a direct, unmediated realization of pristine awareness. There are typically four levels of vidyādhara (which can be correlated with the five paths in various ways): the matured vidyādhara, the vidyādhara with mastery over lifespan, the Mahāmudrā vidyādhara, and the spontaneously actualized vidyādhara. According to the eleventh-century Tibetan translator and master of both Old and New Translation School traditions, Rongzom Chökyi Sangpo (in his commentary to the Dzokchen *Guhyagarbha Tantra*), the Sanskrit word *vidyā* (Tib. *rig pa*) refers to the "knowledge mantra" whose nature is that of wisdom and primordial consciousness. *Dhara* (Tib. *'dzin pa*) means "to hold," which refers to cases in which such wisdom and primordial consciousness are manifestly present within someone's mindstream.

not realize the referent of the wisdom of emptiness, you will not be liberated from saṃsāra. In the *Prajñāpāramitāsaṃcayagāthā* it is said,

> An assembly of a quadrillion blind men without guides
> do not even know the path, so how could they ever enter the city?
> Just so, if you lack wisdom, you have no eyes, and
> without the guide for the other five transcendences
> you lack the ability to reach enlightenment.

Enlightenment is attained when the store of merit, the collection of skillful means, is imbued with the wisdom of emptiness. In [Candrakīrti's] *Madhyamakāvatāra* it is said,

> Just as an entire assembly of blind men is easily led [443] to its desired destination
> by a single individual endowed with sight,
> so the mind of wisdom adopts the excellent qualities—which have no eyes—
> and proceeds to the very state of the jinas.

The *Prajñāpāramitāsaṃcayagāthā* states,

> With wisdom you thoroughly understand the nature of phenomena,
> And you perfectly transcend all three realms of existence.

The *Śatasāhasrikāprajñāpāramitā Sūtra* states,

> The root of all these seeing and unseeing
> excellent qualities is wisdom.
> Therefore, in order to accomplish both,

fully embrace wisdom.

. . .

If darkness is not dispelled by the light of wisdom,
you will not become endowed with pure ethical discipline.
For the most part, pure ethical discipline without wisdom
will be defiled with mental afflictions due to faulty knowledge.

If the mind is defiled with the faults of perverse intelligence,[127]
the virtue of patience will not be inclined to abide there.
You adopt the behavior of one uninterested in knowing right and wrong,
like the famous king who is without excellent qualities.

In the *Prajñāpāramitāsaṃcayagāthā* it is said,

If there is no wisdom, these five sightless transcendences
cannot reach enlightenment, for they lack a guide.
When they are [444] fully imbued with wisdom,
then they gain sight, and they acquire their name [of transcendences].

The *Bodhicaryāvatāra* states,

The Muni taught this entire system for the sake of wisdom.
Therefore, with the desire to ward off suffering, one should develop wisdom.

Although "wisdom" may refer to mundane wisdom, including the knowledge of medicine, sound, logic, and fine arts and architecture, in this con-

127. Reading *shes rab log pa'i skyon* in place of *shes rab legs pa'i skyon*.

text it does not refer to the wisdom of knowing those things. Nor is it the wisdom of the śrāvakas and pratyekabuddhas, by which one understands that one's own aggregates are impure, unsatisfying, impermanent, and identityless. The wisdom referred to here is the wisdom that realizes the emptiness of all phenomena. In the *Saptaśatikāprajñāpāramitā Sūtra* it is said,

> The knowledge that all phenomena are unborn is transcendent wisdom.

And the *Prajñāpāramitāsaṃcayagāthā* states,

> One who thoroughly knows that phenomena are without
> inherent nature
> is one who practices supreme transcendent wisdom.

And the *Bodhipathapradīpa* states,

> Knowledge of the emptiness of inherent nature, [445]
> which realizes that the aggregates, elements, and sense-bases
> are unborn,
> is thoroughly explained to be "wisdom."

Regarding the benefits of cultivating the wisdom of emptiness, the *Pañcaviṃśatisāhasrikāprajñāpāramitā Sūtra* states,

> Even if one cultivates transcendent wisdom for as brief a time as the duration of a finger snap, the merit of a bodhisattva, a *mahāsattva*, increases enormously. It is not equaled by meeting the needs of all the sentient beings dwelling in a billionfold world system through the practice of generosity, nor establishing them in ethical discipline, nor establishing them in samādhi, nor

establishing them in wisdom, nor establishing them in liberation, nor establishing them in the vision of liberating, primordial wisdom, nor establishing them in the fruit of stream-entry, nor establishing them in the fruit of a once-returner, nor in the fruit of a non-returner, nor establishing them in the state of an arhat, nor establishing them in the enlightenment of a pratyekabuddha. The merit of one who cultivates this profound transcendent wisdom [446] for just the duration of a finger snap increases far more.

The *Sarvatathāgatatattvasaṃgraha Tantra* states,

> Śāriputra, there is a greater increase of merit from cultivating the samādhi of suchness for the duration of just one finger snap than there is from listening [to the Dharma] for one eon. Śāriputra, therefore, by all means teach this samādhi of suchness to others. Śāriputra, all bodhisattvas whose enlightenment has been prophesied, without exception, abide in this samādhi.

And the *Sūtra on the Complete Blossoming of Great Realization*[128] states,

> Entering a session of dhyāna for one instant
> is more meaningful than sacrificing one's life
> for all the people of the three realms.

And the *Mahoṣṇīṣa Sūtra* states,

> There is greater merit from meditating on the meaning of the Dharma for one day than there is in hearing and reflecting [on

128. Tib. *Phags pa rtogs pa chen po yongs su rgyas pa'i mdo.*

> the teachings] for many eons. Why? Because it distances you from the way of birth and death.

And the *Sūtra on Generating the Power of Faith* states,

> The merit for a yogin [447] to meditate on emptiness for one session is greater than the store of merit from providing the necessities of life for all the sentient beings in the three realms for as long as they live.

And the *Ten Wheels of Kṣitigarbha Sūtra* states,

> It is more powerful to meditate for one day than to write, read, listen to, teach, and recite Dharma for an eon.

Furthermore, if you meditate on this meaning of emptiness, then the purpose of meditating on a deity, reciting mantras, making burnt offerings, and so on is fulfilled. It is the fulfillment of all ethical discipline, samayas, the triad of hearing, reflecting, and meditating, the six transcendences, and so on. The *Hevajra Tantra* states,

> There is no meditation, nor a meditator.
> There is no deity, nor any mantra.
> In the nature that is devoid of conceptual elaboration
> the deities and the mantras are perfectly present:
> Vairocana, Akṣobhya, Amoghasiddhi,
> Ratnasambhava, Amitābha, and the bodhisattvas.

The *Sarvabuddhasamayogaḍākinījālaśambara Nāma Uttara Tantra* states,

> You do not become a yogin
> with paintings, statues, cast images, and the like.

> But if you apply yourself to bodhicitta,
> there the yogin becomes divine.

[448] The *Tantra of the Ocean of Secret Ambrosia*[129] states,

> What is the purpose of burnt offerings?
> They bestow sublime siddhis and
> overcome conceptualization.
> But burnt offerings do not come from burning wood and so forth.

The *Vajrasamādhi Sūtra* states,

> If you do not waver from emptiness,
> the six transcendences are encompassed.

The *Ārya Brahmaviśeṣacintiparipṛcchā Sūtra* states,

> Not thinking is generosity; not dwelling as separate is ethical discipline; not categorizing is patience; neither accepting nor rejecting is enthusiasm; nonattachment is dhyāna; not conceptualizing is wisdom.

The *Kṣitigarbha Sūtra* states,

> The wise meditate on the reality of emptiness,
> living without reliance upon anything mundane.
> Not dwelling anywhere in the whole of existence,
> they guard virtuous ethical discipline.

129. Tib. *Gsang ba bdud rtsi rgya mtsho'i rgyud.*

The *Devaputraparipṛcchā Sūtra* states,

> Whether or not you have precepts, the absence of conceit is the ethical discipline of nirvāṇa, and that is pure ethical discipline.

The *Tantra of Complete Non-Abiding*[130] states,

> If one eats [449] the one food that is unfabricated and natural,
> then one is also satisfied by all philosophical tenets.
> The childish, without realization, rely upon conventional words.
> Everything is a sign of one's own mind.

Saraha states,

> Reading is that; memorization and meditation are that;
> bearing the scriptures in one's heart is also that.

The *Tantra of the Ocean of Secret Ambrosia* states,

> It is certain that when you discover
> the actual nature of the mind,
> the whole variety of deeds and activities,
> such as making offerings, *tormas*, and so on,
> will all be encompassed by this.

The *Prajñāpāramitāsaṃcayagāthā* states,

> As many qualities of joy and happiness as there may be in

130. Tib. *Rab tu mi gnas pa'i rgyud.*

buddhas, bodhisattvas, śrāvakas, pratyekabuddhas,
devas, and all sentient beings,
all of them arise from supreme transcendent wisdom.

In terms of the ways that such wisdom establishes emptiness, there is the analytical meditation of learned paṇḍitas, which cuts through conceptual elaborations from the outside, and the stabilizing meditation of *kusali* yogins, which cuts through conceptual elaborations from within. The paṇḍita tradition first establishes externally appearing objects as emptiness with the discerning wisdom of mentation, by way of scriptures and reasoning. [450] Then, as for meditating on inner, personal identitylessness, one establishes this by logical investigation in reliance on scriptures and reasoning, and then meditates on its referent.

In that regard, there are reasonings to undermine the four extreme views of eternalism and nihilism among non-Buddhists, and within Buddhism there are reasonings to undermine the views of the Vaibhāṣikas and Sautrāntikas and there are ways in which the Mādhyamikas undermine the Cittamātrins and set forth their own Middle Way system. Then, the Mādhyamika Prāsaṅgikas refute the Svātantrikas, while maintaining that their own view is free of philosophical assertions, and they maintain that there is no other view higher than this Madhyamaka Prāsaṅgika view. Sakya Paṇḍita states,

If there were a view superior
to the view of the transcendences,
that view would have to be one
that *has* conceptual elaborations.

Now, although most spiritual friends agree that there is no difference between the Mantrayāna and [Sūtrayāna] philosophy with respect to the view, if one lacks the profound methods of the unsurpassed, secret Mantrayāna, one needs to accumulate merit for one countless eon in order to realize the view of our tradition. With the profound methods of secret Mantrayāna, [451] one's wisdom becomes the direct realization of emptiness right now, so this is a great and profound distinction: one is not left with a mere aspiration for the view.

Now in this secret Mantrayāna tradition, conceptual elaborations are cut off from within. If one establishes the nature of the inner apprehending mind, this proclaims of its own accord the nature of outer apprehended objects, for appearances are the luminosity of the mind. Therefore, the root of all the Dharma of the Mantrayāna tradition is one's own mind. The *Laṅkāvatāra Sūtra* states,

> The mind that is stirred up by habitual propensities
> emerges as appearances that seem to be real.
> But they are not real, for they are the mind itself.
> To see external objects is a mistake.

The *Sampuṭa Tantra* states,

> All phenomena are identityless,
> so regard them authentically.
> Examine all these things, which have the nature of
> being external and internal, as being the mind.
> Apart from the mind itself,
> nothing else exists at all.

The *Laṅkāvatāra Sūtra* states,

> The nature of the mind is clear light,
> the pure tathāgatagarbha.

The *Vairocanābhisambodhi Tantra* states,

> Whatever is of the nature of space is of the nature of the mind. [452] Whatever is of the nature of the mind is of the nature of enlightenment. O Vajrapāṇi, thus, the mind and the domain of space and enlightenment are nondual.

The *Vajrapañjara Tantra* states,

> The world, just as it is, is the Buddha,
> and likewise phenomena are without concepts.
> In this way, the worlds of sentient beings are explained
> to be stainless, like space.
>
> The nature of the mind is contaminated
> by conceptual fabrications and conceptualizations that are not ultimate.
> By purifying the mind, it becomes pure.
> It is like indestructible space.

The *Uttaratantra* states,

> What is the clear light nature of the mind
> is immutable like space:
> Since the attachment and so on
> that arise from inauthentic conceptualizations
> are adventitious contaminations,
> that [clear light nature] does not become the afflictions.

The *Mahāparinirvāṇa Sūtra* states,

> That which is called "the nature of the Buddha" is the clear light nature of the mind. Empty, ultimate reality is primordial

wisdom. In that regard, what is called "empty" sees neither empty nor not empty.

The *Atyayajñāna Sūtra* states,

> If the mind is realized, that is primordial wisdom, but you should fully cultivate [453] the discernment that does not seek the Buddha elsewhere.

The *Abhidhānottara Tantra* states,

> The abode of all the tathāgatas
> knows everything and enacts everything.
> Great bliss is all-pervasive.
> The Protector, the Buddha, is Lord of All,
> dwelling in the hearts of all sentient beings.

The *Tantra of Inconceivable Coemergence*[131] states,

> The coemergent, actual nature of the mind is the dharmakāya,
> coemergent appearances are the light of the dharmakāya,
> and the indivisibility of appearances and mindsets is coemergent.

The *Vajrapañjara Tantra* states,

> Apart from the jewel of the mind,
> there are no external buddhas and no sentient beings outside.
> There are neither referential objects nor modes of
> consciousness
> that are external.

131. Tib. *Lhan cig skyes pa bsam gyis mi khyab pa'i rgyud.*

> . . .
>
> The Muni never declared forms, feelings, discernment,
> mental formations, or consciousness—any of them—
> to be anything other than the reality of the mind.

The *Mahāmudrātilaka Tantra* states,

> Recall that you and Lord Vajrasattva
> are of the nature of the mind.
> There is no reality of the deity that is not the mind—
> none that is something else outside.

[454] The *Vajracatuḥpīṭha Tantra* states,

> The mind and primordial consciousness are indivisible.
> Due to the special quality of their being equally nondual,
> form and the empty center of emptiness are unreal,
> just as real things are unreal.

The *Kurukullā Tantra* states,

> The actual nature of the mind is all buddhas,
> and one is liberated by the actual nature of the mind.

The *Tantra of the Synthesis of the Mysteries of the Great Compassionate One*[132] states,

> The referent of the tantras is your singular pristine awareness.
> It is the unmistaken, unmodified dharmakāya,
> the sambhogakāya imbued with the two purities,

132. Tib. *Thugs rje chen po gsang 'dus rgyud.*

and the nirmāṇakāya of unimpeded compassion.
Its essential nature is devoid of arising, cessation, and abiding.
It is unconditioned and primordial,
and it is naturally present within yourself.

The *Padmavikrīḍita Sūtra* states,

> "Devaputra, these external objects were not made by a Creator. They appear due to fortification of the habitual propensities for not fathoming the mind."
>
> Devaputra replied, "How can it be that due to the fortification of habitual propensities, mountains, oceans, the sun and moon, and so forth are firm and dense?"
>
> He replied, "It is reasonable for them to appear due to the fortification of conceptualization. In the city of Vārāṇasī, the brahmin woman named Bhadramukha [455] meditated on her body as a tiger, such that the inhabitants saw her as a tigress, and they all fled, leaving the city empty. If something can appear in that way for a short time, how could it be logical for something *not* to appear due to the fortification of habitual propensities since beginningless time?

The *Saṃdhivyākaraṇa Tantra* states,

From the clear light comes great emptiness.
From there skillful means emerges perfectly.
From that wisdom is born.
From that air comes to emerge.
From air, fire emerges perfectly.
From fire, water thoroughly emerges.
From water, earth comes to arise.
This is how sentient beings arise.

The *Vajracatuḥpīṭha Tantra* states,

> Water emerges from the mind,
> so consciousness is the element of water.
> If water were other than that,
> after dying, how would water emerge?
> Consciousness emerges as fire,
> ascertained in the body as heat.
> In a transmigrating body of primordial consciousness
> why wouldn't heat appear?
> Consciousness is exhaled and inhaled as air,
> like smoke, in bodies of vital energy.
> In a body of primordial consciousness that is transmigrating,
> however, there is no breath.
> The mind emerges as earth, [456]
> so it appears as something heavy.
> Bodies of primordial consciousness that are transmigrating
> float on the face of water.
> The valid cognition of the body comes in five ways,
> but the five are of a single essential nature.
> Upon recognizing them as one,
> one observes the abode of a yogin.

The *Mahāmudrātilaka Tantra* states,

> The absolute space of phenomena is revealed as the *bhaga*,
> and you should understand absolute space as the mind.

The *Tantra of the Great Perfection, the View that Thoroughly Dispels Ignorance, Primordial Consciousness Perfectly Complete from Its Depths*[133] states,

133. Tib. *Rdzogs pa chen po ma rig pa rab tu sel ba lta ba ye shes gting nas rdzogs pa'i rgyud.*

Saṃsāra and nirvāṇa dwell in the ground, so they are spontaneously actualized.
The essence of one's own mind is the enlightened dharmakāya.
Because it is naturally present in everything, it is the primordial buddha.
Neither realized nor unrealized, it is the ground of everything.

The Sūtra in High Praise of Realizing the Mind[134] states,

> If the nature of the mind is known, the nature of all phenomena will be known. The mind will not become attached to appearing objects, and without attachment, mental afflictions will not arise. If mental afflictions do not arise, one will not revolve in saṃsāra....
>
> Child of the family, if the nature of the mind is not known, however much one exerts physical and verbal effort for the accumulation of merit by generosity and so on, the dharmakāya [457] will not be achieved. If it is not achieved, the two rūpakāyas will not appear to disciples.

Thus, all the sūtras, tantras, and pith instructions declare that the root of the whole of saṃsāra and nirvāṇa is the mind, and it is also said that the root of all phenomena is the mind. So one must strive in methods to realize the mind. Moreover, all the miseries of the realms of the mundane worlds, as well as endless wandering in saṃsāra, come as a result of not realizing the mind. The three hundred and sixty false views of extremists come about due to misapprehending the mind. The slight superiority of the successively higher over the lower in terms of śrāvaka arhats, pratyekabuddhas, Vaibhāṣika, Sautrāntika, Cittamātra, and so on corresponds to their varying degrees of realization of the mind. By more and more accurately realizing

134. Tib. *Sems rtogs pa mngon par bsngags pa'i mdo.*

the essential nature of the mind, the excellent qualities of the grounds and paths increase more and more. Once the mind has been finally and completely realized, this is enlightenment.

Therefore, you should determine with certainty how it is that the fundamental meaning is just this mind. If that is not determined, this is like shooting an arrow without seeing the target, and the root of meditation will be mistaken. So it is important that each of you seek out your own mind. [458] The *Sarvatathāgatatattvasaṃgraha Tantra* states,

> Child of the family, discerningly realize your own mind through meditative equipoise.

Āryadeva states,

> Since it is asserted that by dwelling in the Vajrayāna, you will achieve buddhahood itself, once you have pleased your spiritual friend, seek out the essential nature of your mind.

The *Ratnakūṭa Sūtra* states,

> Thoroughly seek out the mind in this way, thinking, "What is the mind that becomes attached, hateful, or deluded? Is it something that emerged in the past, will emerge in the future, or emerges in the present? Whatever mind was in the past has ceased, whatever is in the future hasn't occurred, and the mind that emerges in the present has no location."

And the *Bodhisattvapiṭaka Sūtra* states,

> Śāriputra, for what is transcendent meditation a preliminary? It is a preliminary for the definite realization of the mind.

The *Tantra of Inconceivable Coemergence* states,

> The culmination of all phenomena
> is absolute space, which does not abide
> with any nature of its own.
> A mind devoid of views [459]
> observes Mahāmudrā.
> Everything is of the nature of the mind.

The *Treasury of Mysteries Tantra*[135] states,

> If the elephant of the mind is not subdued,
> and if one dwells in distraction, one is deluded.
> . . .
> If one does not see one's own mind,
> and if one speaks with great pride, one is deluded.
> Without experiencing one's own awareness,
> if one teaches what is right and wrong, one is deluded.
> . . .
> In order to repudiate the wrong views of
> those who seek a view of the self,
> and who set opposite to every view another view,
> and who ultimately assert their view to be the Middle Way,
> I will definitively explain the actual nature of the mind itself.
> . . .
> Deluded away from one's own awareness,
> awareness of other phenomena appears.
> Deluded away from the actual nature of the mind,
> habitual propensities emerge.

135. The full Tibetan title of this Nyingma tantra is *De bzhin gshegs pa thams cad kyi gsang ba gsang ba'i mdzod chen po mi zad pa gter gyi sgron ma brtul zhugs chen po bsgrub pa'i rgyud ye shes rngam pa glog gi 'khor lo zhes bya ba theg pa chen po'i mdo.*

Then, those delusions about one's own mind
arise fully, appearing as objects,
and though devoid of arising, they are mistaken as arising.

The ground of red-hot iron is one's own mind,
and that which creates this mass of fire is nowhere else.
The sufferings of hunger and thirst are one's own mind,
and that which obstructs food and drink is nowhere else.
The beating and slaughtering are one's own mind,
and the murderous butcher is nowhere else.

Therefore, [460] if beings of all kinds
do not recognize the six collections of objects and subjects
as the dependently related mind,
they abandon buddhahood.

Apart from the actual nature of the mind,
not even the buddhas see a buddha,
and apart from the mind, not even the buddhas see any other phenomenon,
nor did they speak, nor will they speak of anything else.

Therefore, this mystery of the mind of all sentient beings
is the supreme mystery,
and it is the mystery of the enlightened body, speech, and mind.
This treasury of the mind is the treasury of mysteries.
One's own pristine awareness, primordial consciousness,
is the treasury of fire.

So those who wish for siddhis,
do not abandon even at the cost of your life

this—your thoroughly pure, great mystery of the mind—
nor the buddhas, nor the gurus,
but constantly dwell upon them without distraction.

The *People's Dohas* [of Saraha] states,

The actual nature of the mind alone is the seed of everything,
from which both mundane existence and nirvāṇa issue forth.
Homage to the mind that is like a wish-fulfilling jewel,
which fully grants the fruition of your desires.
If the mind is bound, you will be bound,
but if it is released, there will be no doubt.

The *Dharmadhātustava* [of Nāgārjuna] states,

The mind is seen in two aspects: [461]
mundane and supramundane.
Grasping to a self is saṃsāra,
but if one is discerningly aware, that is suchness.

The *Avalokiteśvaravikrīḍita Sūtra* states,

Everyone travels upon the great highway,
including kings and paupers.
In the same way, along the great highway of the mind,
all sentient beings and all buddhas
travel along that highway.
So, practitioners of yoga,
ardently follow the path of the mind!

[Tilopa's] *Gangāma* (*Mahāmudropadeśa*) states,

> As an analogy, by cutting one tree trunk, a billion branches
> dry up.
> Likewise, if the root of the mind is cut, the leaves of saṃsāra
> wither.

And from the lips of Orgyen Rinpoché:

> Now that which is called "the mind" has the appearance of luminosity, but it is not determined as having the characteristic of being "this." Investigate carefully the beginning, end, and interim, as well as the origin, location, and destination of this [that is not determined as having the characteristic of being "this"]. From where and how does it first emerge? Properly establish its form and color, its defining characteristics, its nature of existence, its essential nature and qualities: encircle and observe it. If you cherish the advice on its empty aspect, it is even more important to exert yourself here. . . .
>
> Then it is very important that you carefully examine where it is located in the interim [462] and where its final destination may be, and that you immerse yourself in observing its essential nature.

The meaning of all these [quotations] is stated in the verse of vajra words:

> **Whatever you think, whatever you recall,**
> **whatever you see, and whatever you are aware of,**
> **observe its essential nature . . .**

The Great Compassionate One [Avalokiteśvara] states in his commentary to this:

> **However and whatever you may think, however and whatever you may recall, whatever you see and whatever you are aware of, observe its essential nature . . .**

That is the meaning, so from now until tomorrow's Dharma teaching session, it is very important that each of you carefully seek out your own mind. Is your mind located inside or outside of your body? If it is inside, from your brain at the crown of your head down to the soles of your feet, where does it reside among your five solid organs and six hollow organs?[136] Think about this and then search!

If you think your mind is located inside your heart, where is it—in the epicardium, in the pericardial fat, in the flesh, or in the blood? If it is located on the exterior of the body, where is it—on the upper or lower region, or at the front or on the back? Moreover, if the mind exists outside, where is it located—in the east, south, west, north, above, or below? [463]

What kind of color does the mind have? Is it white, yellow, red, green, blue, or the like? What sort of shape does it have? Is it round, square, semi-circular, triangular, or the like? Is the form of the mind beautiful or ugly, large or small? Is its sound pleasant or unpleasant? Is its smell fragrant or putrid? Is its taste bitter or sweet? Is it soft or rough to the touch?

What is the actual nature of the mind? Are the body and mind one or are they distinct? If the body and mind are one, when the body dies, does the mind die? And if they are distinct, when the body is in pain, why is the mind distressed?

If you think the mind does not exist, who is it that gives rise to hatred, pride, envy, anger, faith, and pure vision? If you think the mind does exist, what kind of thing is it? If you think it is both existent and nonexistent, since existence and nonexistence are mutually exclusive, that is impossible.

136. The five solid organs are the heart, lungs, kidneys, liver, and the spleen; the six hollow organs are the stomach, gallbladder, small intestine, urinary bladder, the large intestine, and the "vesicle of regenerative substances" (Tib. *bsam se'u*; Skt. *śukrāśaya ḍimbāśaya*), which refers to the seminal vesicle in men and to the ovaries in women.

From where did this mind first emerge, where is it now, and finally, when it has ceased, where will it go?

When each of you says, "I," is that the body? Or is it the mind? [464] If it is the body, when the body dies, since its parts disperse, once that which is called "I" and "myself" has died, you would become nonexistent.

If the mind is that which is called "I" or "myself," it must have a form and color. If it doesn't, that which is called "I" and "myself" would have no objective referent. This name of yours was designated by your parents, teacher, and so on. If you exchange your name for another, would you and yourself be exchanged for another?

Is the mind just one, or is it many? If it were one, how could there be eight configurations of consciousness, beginning with visual consciousness? If it were many, one person would have many minds, but that is impossible.

Is the mind permanent, unchanging, and unitary? If it were, how could any mind remember not just one thing but many, and how could it change and move? If the mind is impermanent, then is the mind impermanent in the sense of being formed and destroyed, and does it then become nonexistent?

If the mind is a single appearance, you should be able to see it and point to it. If the mind is invisible, nothing at all could appear. If the mind arises, from where does it arise? If the mind stays somewhere, on what basis does it stay? If the mind [465] ceases, where does it cease?

If you think the mind recalls all kinds of things and issues forth in all manner of ways, from where do the memories and thoughts of this mind first emerge? Right now, what sort of essential nature do they have? In the end, where do they appear to go and cease? If you think the mind is empty like space, how do various memories and thoughts appear in emptiness?

Now if the mind is dispatched to the space in the east, is there a dispatcher and a mover or not? If there is, what kind of an entity is it that moves? If it has gone, how far did it go? Just in the time it takes to return, it would have made a circle. Likewise, when you dispatch your mind to each of the four cardinal directions, the eight intermediate directions, above and below, totaling ten directions, how does it move? What is it that moves? How does it circle back? Please think about it!

As for the eyes seeing various forms, is it the eyes that see, or is it mental vision? If the eyes see, does a corpse also see? If the mind sees, does it have eyes? If the mind sees forms without having eyes, do the blind also see forms? Likewise, carefully examine how the ears hear sounds, [466] how the nose detects smells, the tongue experiences tastes, and how bodily sensations are felt.

When hatred, pride, envy, attachment, and delusion arise, do they arise in the body or the mind? If they arise in the body, would they arise in a corpse as well? If they arise in the mind, how and from where do they first arise? In what way does the mind in which hatred and so on arise exist right now? Are the mind and hatred the same or distinct? Finally, where do hatred and so on cease and vanish?

Regarding what are known as the mind's "conceptualizations," or its "movements," from where do the appearances of these various memories and thoughts first emerge? Do they exist? If they exist, where do the conceptualizations that will arise tomorrow come from today, and where are they? Where did the conceptualizations from yesterday up until now go? Where are these conceptualizations of the present located?

Think about these questions carefully, then analyze and investigate! This is important, so don't be pretentious! You are not allowed to respond after asking others. This is something to be known for yourself, so you must see this yourself. If you don't, it's not okay to bluff your way through by following after what others say. Bluffing your way through meditation is said not even to be worthy of a dog. [467]

If you lack decisive, definite knowledge of your own, and you offer explanations by way of analogies and anecdotes just by knowing the words, while pretending to have your own realization, that is unacceptable. That is a case of a crude scoundrel who is familiar with Dharma turning the Dharma into misery. Therefore, do not explain out of a dry understanding, thinking, "It is like this," based on analogies and anecdotes, for this will lead to your covering your own head. A dry rope needs to be cut in water. Now seek complete and conclusive knowledge that reaches down into your bones, and you will have something to say.

If you think, "I have searched, but I have not found," don't lose heart. You have acquired a precious human body replete with leisure and endowments. When such profound advice, from which the moist breath of the ḍākinīs has not yet evaporated, is taught, if you do not find, will you do so when you are born as an animal and so on? Or "If I don't find my mind, I won't have to experience suffering again." Report on this way of not finding! Even if you see a form, color, and so on, there is no need to be afraid to report on that. The ten signs and so on[137] can appear at any time to those of fine intelligence whose channels are in excellent condition.

Therefore, from tomorrow morning onward, all of you who have not received the instruction previously, explain without reservation what you have seen for yourselves to the stewards for these instructions. Even if you have received this guidance in the past, if you have not yet identified your mind, [468] explain what you have seen to a steward for these instructions.

From now until tomorrow morning, seek with a sense of personal responsibility, and that will suffice. You don't need to seek continually. But if you don't search decisively through tomorrow morning, there will be no benefit if you put it off until later. If you have previously gained certainty about the essential nature of your own mind, there is no need to report this to a steward.

Since this guidance has the crucial point of being complete in all respects, you must seek. If you don't come to a conclusion by tomorrow morning, you won't be purified to receive the teaching at tomorrow's Dharma session. So remain in solitude, adopt the qualities of the vital points of the posture,

137. This appears to be a reference to the ten signs that occur when the energy-mind enters the central channel. While the enumeration of these signs differs somewhat according to specific contexts, a classic list within Mahāyoga explains that these signs arise as appearances like those of (1) smoke, (2) a mirage, (3) clouds, (4) fireflies, (5) the sun, (6) the moon, (7) blazing jewels, (8) Rāhu, (9) stars, and (10) light rays.

and ask in what way your mind exists. Then you will have something to say tomorrow morning. This is very important. If you carefully seek out the mind, you will come to a decisive conclusion in the time it takes to drink a cup of tea. So, for those of you who have something to say, then starting this evening you should speak to a steward.

Thus, to dedicate the roots of virtue from offering this Dharma session on the vipaśyanā held in common, which cuts through conceptual elaborations from within, so that all sentient beings of the six classes of existence may swiftly realize coemergent primordial consciousness, please recite three times after me, "I dedicate this virtue to all beings in the six classes of existence, who have been my old mother."

This concludes the sixteenth chapter, on the analytical cultivation of vipaśyanā, according to the tradition of the pith instructions held in common [between the Sūtrayāna and Mantrayāna].

Translated by B. Alan Wallace
under the guidance of the Venerable Gyatrul Rinpoché,
with the assistance of Khenpo Chöying Namgyal and Eva Natanya

Śamatha, Vipaśyanā, and Guru Yoga in the Teachings of Düdjom Lingpa and Sera Khandro

Düdjom Lingpa

To read Düdjom Lingpa's autobiography, *A Clear Mirror*,[138] is to be drawn into a drama of personal experience in which the boundaries between our mundane world and the many pure worlds of buddhas, bodhisattvas, and ḍākinīs are gossamer and easily traversed—at least for a being of such enormous karmic momentum as Düdjom Lingpa himself. It is essential to understand the teachings transmitted by Düdjom Lingpa—regarding the empty nature of all phenomena and the way that they arise as one's own appearances within a web of dependent relationships—before one could actually fathom or even believe the extraordinary accounts he offers regarding the transcendent episodes of his own life.

Born in the Serta Valley, southwest of Golok, Tibet, in 1835, Düdjom Lingpa became a renowned *tertön*, or treasure revealer, and master of Dzokchen, and was said to be an incarnation of the great translator Khyeuchung Lotsāwa, who was one of Guru Padmasambhava's twenty-five closest

138. This stunning autobiography is translated in Traktung Dudjom Lingpa, *A Clear Mirror: The Visionary Autobiography of a Tibetan Master*, trans. Chönyi Drolma (Rangjung Yeshe Publications, 2011).

disciples in the eighth century. Apart from two lamas he knew during childhood—one who taught him to read and write, and the other who guided him in preliminary practices—Düdjom Lingpa's direct knowledge of the Dharma came not from human gurus, but instead was transmitted through visionary experiences in which he encountered various deities. Most important among these was the Lake-Born Vajra, a manifestation of Padmasambhava, who was his primary guru, as well as Avalokiteśvara, Mañjuśrī, Vajrapāṇi, Vajravārāhī, and Dorjé Drolö. He also had visionary encounters with numerous great masters of the past, including Śrī Siṃha, Yeshé Tsogyal, Saraha, and Longchenpa Drimé Öser, from whom he received consummate teachings and empowerments. It was through such visions that he even ventured to Guru Rinpoché's pure land of Zangdok Palri, the Glorious Copper-Colored Mountain, and received teachings directly from Guru Rinpoché himself.

At the age of twenty-two, Düdjom Lingpa journeyed from the Serta Valley eastward to the Mar Valley of Golok, under the patronage of the family of Gili Wangli. It was there among the rocks at Ba Treasure Cliff that, at the age of twenty-four, he revealed a prophetic guide that led to his uncovering twenty volumes of earth and mind treasures (*sa ter* and *gong ter*) that would, along with the treasures revelations of his successor Düdjom Rinpoché, become known collectively as the *Düdjom Tersar*, or *The New Treasure Teachings of Düdjom*. This new lineage contains a complete path to awakening, including its own set of preliminary practices, myriad sādhanas of the stage of generation, and specific practices of the stage of completion, all of which culminate in the path of Dzokchen, the Great Perfection.

Düdjom Lingpa's most extensive teaching on this complete path of Dzokchen is *The Vajra Essence*, which was revealed to him by the Lake-Born Vajra during an extensive pure vision that took place early in 1862. This text is a comprehensive guide through all the essential phases of practice, including tögal, the path of the direct crossing over, which can lead to the achievement of the great transference rainbow body.

Just months before the visionary experience in which *The Vajra Essence* was revealed, Düdjom Lingpa acknowledged that he had come to a point in his realization of the consummate totality of all phenomena within absolute space that "merely by focusing my mind's intent on any subject, whatever teachings I needed would flow forth [in the space of awareness] as if a precise copy had been made."[139] Such was the source of his ability to write down, much later, hundreds of pages of text revealed to him within the matrix of pure appearances and primordial consciousness, when his ordinary senses and physical faculties as a human being had been suspended for the long duration of the pure vision.

Amid his mature life of immense Dharma activity as a teacher and treasure revealer, Düdjom Lingpa had eight sons, all of whom were recognized as important incarnations of great lamas, and most of whom went on to become important teachers themselves.

Before Düdjom Lingpa had even passed away in 1904, his immediate incarnation was conceived in the prophesied region of Pemakö. This renowned tertön and prolific scholar and writer, Düdjom Rinpoché Jikdral Yeshé Dorjé, was recognized as the enlightened mind emanation of Düdjom Lingpa and became the principal lineage holder of the Düdjom Tersar. Düdjom Lingpa's other incarnations were Sonam Deutsen (the enlightened body emanation), Dzongter Kunsang Nyima (the enlightened speech emanation), Tulku Pednam (the enlightened qualities emanation), and Tulku Natsok Rangdrol (the enlightened activity emanation), who was the root lama of the Venerable Domang Gyatrul Rinpoché.

Of Düdjom Lingpa's disciples, thirteen attained rainbow bodies in accordance with a prophecy Düdjom Lingpa had received from a ḍākinī when only twenty-two years old. Further, among the many prophecies granted to him, he was told that an astonishing one hundred disciples would achieve the great transference rainbow body.[140] His teachings and literary works

139. Traktung Dudjom Lingpa, 74.

140. Traktung Dudjom Lingpa, 181. The term "great transference rainbow body" (Tib. *'ja' lus 'pho ba chen po'i sku*) can be explained as follows: The "great transference" refers to the indestructible vajra body in which pristine awareness has ripened as the vital essences of the

remain highly regarded and influential in the Nyingma tradition in the present day, as his authenticity as a treasure revealer has long been vindicated, and his teachings were so clearly prophesied to be of great benefit, particularly in the West, in a time of great darkness and degeneration.

The two texts by Düdjom Lingpa excerpted here focus succinctly on two phases of practice that are indispensable for ordinary individuals who are determined to reach and enter the path of Dzokchen. These are none other than śamatha and vipaśyanā. The first text, "Taking the Aspect of the Mind as the Path," is drawn from the detailed commentary to one of Düdjom Lingpa's visionary revelations, the *Sharp Vajra of Conscious Awareness Tantra*,[141] titled *The Essence of Clear Meaning*. This commentary was written down by Pema Tashi based on a series of teachings Düdjom Lingpa had offered to just a few of his close disciples near the hermitage of Drak Yangzong. Pema Tashi is known for being preeminent among Düdjom Lingpa's disciples[142] and is regarded by Düdjom lineage holders as one of the thirteen who achieved rainbow body.

The practice of "taking the mind as the path" taught here is a method for achieving śamatha that is, in its early stages, distinct from either the "śamatha with a sign" (focused on a visualization) or the "śamatha without a sign" (purely resting in awareness of awareness) as taught by Karma Chak-

elements yet appears in the form of one's former body. One has indeed reached the fifth path of no more training, meaning that one is an actual buddha, and by arising in a form such as that of Avalokiteśvara or Mañjuśrī, one is able to bring extraordinary benefit to others. One's form, then, is perfected as a display of the mahāmudrā form of the deity, which is the natural radiance of the dharmakāya, in whom clinging to outer appearances has never arisen; one's speech is purified as the natural radiance of the unborn mantra of the speech maṇḍala of great bliss; and the appearances of all ordinary thoughts are ripened in the manifest nature of the dharmakāya, clear light. On this basis, the yogin's body transcends substantial physicality and the rainbow body of great transference is achieved; the yogin's mind remains in the realization of nonobjective, unimpeded pristine awareness; and one is liberated in primordial purity. See the Grand Monlam Tibetan Dictionary entries for *'pho chen* and *'ja' lus 'pho ba chen po'i sku*: https://monlamdictionary.com.

141. This tantra, also revealed to Düdjom Lingpa in a pure vision, is a highly condensed verse presentation of most of the essential material taught extensively in *The Vajra Essence*.

142. Traktung Dudjom Lingpa, *A Clear Mirror*, 133–34.

mé above. Here, the key method is to identify the stillness of awareness and, simultaneously, the motion of all that arises in the mind when its creative displays (that is, thoughts, images, memories, and so forth) are allowed to manifest unimpededly but without being grasped or followed. By remaining motionlessly in the stillness of awareness and relentlessly observing the movements of the mind, gradually the movements of the mind slow down and fade out of themselves, even as the awareness of them becomes sharper, clearer, and gradually more effortless. Thus one progresses through the four kinds of mindfulness described here: single-pointed mindfulness, manifest mindfulness, the absence of mindfulness, and self-illuminating mindfulness. Once one reaches the culmination of those four, self-illuminating mindfulness, this experience of the bliss, luminosity, and nonconceptuality of the substrate consciousness should be equivalent to the "flawless meditation" of "śamatha without a sign" as described by Karma Chakmé.

Then, it is crucial to recognize that the "mere nonconceptuality" that arises in the course of the last two kinds of mindfulness described below refers specifically to the meditative experience (*nyam*) of nonconceptuality that arises from directly experiencing the substrate and the substrate consciousness. This experience is indispensable, but if not yet imbued with the wisdom of vipaśyanā, this "mere nonconceptuality" does not in itself lead to the path. In this and many other points Düdjom Lingpa's presentation here is exactly in accord with Tsongkhapa's explanation of nonconceptuality in the context of śamatha alone versus the *absolute* nonconceptuality that arises only as a result of realizing emptiness—as complete freedom from the eight extremes of conceptual elaboration.[143] Thus these two monumental teachers speak as if with one voice when they declare that unless śamatha is united with authentic vipaśyanā, it will not lead to the path. As stated by Düdjom Lingpa in the text that follows:

143. See Wallace, *Balancing the Mind*, 207–13, and Jinpa, *Tsongkhapa*, 286–88, as mentioned regarding *The Concise Presentation of the Stages on the Path to Enlightenment*, in the chapter on "The Words of Mañjuśrī and Vajrapāṇi: View, Meditation, and Conduct as Taught to Tsongkhapa," above.

> This is the actual path praised by the jinas for realizing the meaning of effortlessness, but as a method for this to occur, you must first familiarize yourself with [358] the union of the pair of śamatha with a focal object and vipaśyanā involving investigation and analysis. Novices should practice śamatha from the phase of single-pointedness until the point of making conscious awareness manifest, and also practice vipaśyanā, which is implicitly taught here, without ever being separated from them. So here they are taught sequentially.

In the context of Düdjom Lingpa's revelations, one does not fully enter the Dzokchen path—nor is one ready to engage in the truly effortless practice of "cutting through" (*trekchö*)—until one "establishes the ground of being by way of the view." As an introduction to this method for teaching vipaśyanā within Düdjom Lingpa's revelations and teachings, the second text included here is taken from *The Essence of Profound Mysteries: Guidance for Revealing One's Own Face as the Nature of Reality, the Great Perfection*, a teaching offered by Düdjom Lingpa at the request of another of his preeminent disciples, Pema Lungtok Gyatso (who served as a principal editor of Düdjom Lingpa's writings and is also said to have achieved rainbow body), as well as at the request of Khyenrap Gyatso. It is clear that the structure of this text bears a close connection with that of Düdjom Lingpa's autobiographical teaching, *Buddhahood Without Meditation*, and serves as a guide to it. Here we are taught the initial stages of analysis for establishing the Dzokchen view, by first establishing the view of emptiness that is held in common with the Sūtrayāna.

Sera Khandro

The extraordinary woman who would come to be known as Sera Khandro, Kunsang Dekyong Wangmo, Dewé Dorjé, or simply Uza Khandro, was born in 1892, and displayed an intense and prodigious inclination toward

Dharma in her youth. She revealed her first treasure at the age of seven by partially pulling out a ritual dagger from a rock at the meditation site of Drak Yerpa. Throughout her life, she had many visionary experiences in buddhafields and encounters with ḍākinīs and siddhas, becoming a widely recognized and revered treasure revealer.

However, Sera Khandro faced severe challenges and adversities from a young age and through the rest of her life. Her father tenaciously tried to groom her to follow in his footsteps as part of the political elite. Also, when she was only ten years old, he arranged for her to marry a Chinese leader's son. She became so distraught at the possibility of not having the opportunity to practice Dharma that she attempted suicide by drinking a nearly lethal amount of alcohol and opium. She was saved only by her father, who forced her to drink a bowl of seed oil and vomit out the poison. Further, when Sera Khandro was twelve, her mother died, the trauma of which led to a vision of Vajravārāhī, a form of Vajrayoginī. Vajravārāhī bestowed upon her an empowerment into the two treasure cycles that she would later reveal through the rest of her life: *The Secret Treasury of the Ḍākinīs of the Actual Nature of Reality* and *The Heart Essence of the Ḍākinīs*.

The ḍākinī's prophecies gave her the courage, when she was fourteen years old, to abscond from her home in Lhasa and her father's uncompromising demands in order to join a group of Golok pilgrims from eastern Tibet, never to return home again. When the group had temporarily taken shelter in her brother's house in Lhasa, she saw the lama, Tulku Drimé Öser—the fifth son of Düdjom Lingpa—and was instantaneously overcome by great faith, reverence, and devotion. Yet, despite her dangerous escape and determination to seek company with these pilgrims as a follower of Dharma, she encountered enormous hardship en route to Golok. Her wealthy, sheltered, aristocratic upbringing did not prepare her for the harsh, subzero temperatures she encountered, and she nearly starved and died of hypothermia. Moreover, upon the group's arrival at Dartsang Kalsang Monastery—Düdjom Lingpa's monastery—knowledge and fear of jealousy from Akyongza, the spiritual partner of Drimé Öser, forced her to live elsewhere. She thus became a servant in a nomadic household so that she could attend the winter teachings with Drimé Öser and his associates, which included both preliminary practices and advanced teachings passed down from Düdjom Lingpa. After a few years, a series of circumstances led her to become the "life partner" of Gara Gyelsé, son of the prominent treasure revealer Gara Terchen. Sera Khandro had three children while with Gara Gyelsé: a daughter, a son who was stillborn, and another son whom she knew to have been miraculously conceived, but who died in childhood. Life with Gara Gyelsé became increasingly difficult, as he disapproved of her being a treasure revealer and did not regard her as his prophesied spiritual partner. To make matters worse, she became afflicted by an arthritic condition in her legs, the complications of which almost caused her death. All the while, her reverence and devotion for her root lama, Drimé Öser, deepened, and Gara Gyelsé repeatedly expressed his intention to send her back to live with him.

After years of enduring complex conditions of illness, tensions within Gyelsé's community, and political violence in the region, Sera Khandro and Drimé Öser were finally reunited in an enduring way when she was twenty-nine. She credits the healing of her illnesses to their sublime reunion and wrote that this was one of the happiest times of her life. Together, they crossed an extraordinary threshold of realization at the culmination of the path, and revealed many great treasures as the outer sign of such realization. Due to an epidemic in 1924, however, Sera Khandro's young son and then Drimé Öser himself passed away—a mere three years after their reunion. One of Drimé Öser's disciples then invited her to live at his nonsectarian monastery in Golok named Sera Tekchen Chökhor Ling, the institution from which she thus came to be known as "Sera Khandro." She then traveled for much of the next fifteen years throughout eastern Tibet, teaching the treasures of Düdjom Lingpa and Drimé Öser, as well as her own, at monasteries of diverse lineages. Among her students were many of the most important reincarnate lamas of her generation, to whom she transmitted the empowerments, reading transmissions, and guidance associated with the treasures revealed by Düdjom Lingpa, Drimé Öser, and herself. She wrote extensively, and her authored works include commentaries on major works of Düdjom Lingpa, a biography of Drimé Öser, two autobiographies, and many shorter works, including letters, pith instructions, and poetry. She also completed a project of collecting, editing, and transcribing the complete collected works of Düdjom Lingpa from their original manuscripts.

In 1940, she passed away at the age of forty-eight, displaying signs of great realization as her body dissolved into light, diminishing to the size of a young child's body, before cremation.[144]

Among Düdjom Lingpa's most advanced instructions for actually achieving the great transference rainbow body in one lifetime, we find a text by the title *Buddhahood Without Meditation: Guidance Along the Swift Path to the Great Transference, from the Dharma Cycle of Mahā-Ati Yoga.* (This is not to be confused with his more famous text by the oft-repeated title of *Buddhahood Without Meditation.*) Sera Khandro wrote a commentary to this text on the practice of the direct crossing over, called *Pith Instructions on Liberation as a Body of Light*, based upon the oral transmission and teachings she received from Drimé Öser. We have chosen the following excerpts from this text because they highlight the core elements of practice that are preliminary to every stage of the path—from śamatha and vipaśyanā, to the stages of generation and completion, to the uniquely Dzokchen paths of cutting through and the direct crossing over.

We see here a succinct overview of the four revolutions in outlook (often translated as the "four thoughts that turn the mind to the Dharma"), how to generate the vast motivation of bodhicitta in the context of the Dzokchen

144. For further biographical details see Sarah H. Jacoby, *Love and Liberation: Autobiographical Writings of the Tibetan Buddhist Visionary Sera Khandro* (New York, NY: Columbia University Press, 2014), Sera Khandro Dewai Dorje, *A Dakini's Counsel: Sera Khandro's Spiritual Advice and Dzogchen Instructions*, trans. Christina Lee Monson (Boulder, CO: Shambhala Publications, 2024), and https://treasuryoflives.org/biographies/view/Sera-Khandro-Kunzang-Dekyong-Wangmo/10083.

view, and then how to practice guru yoga as the source of all blessings. The practice of guru yoga is an immense topic, which cannot be treated fully here, but we point the reader to the extensive commentary offered in *The Vital Essence of Dzogchen: A Commentary on Düdjom Rinpoché's Advice for a Mountain Retreat*[145] for a thorough presentation of this topic as it can be understood by contemporary practitioners who may not have grown up in a culture where devotional practices are imbibed "with mother's milk," as it were.

Suffice to say that deep admiration and reverence for the spiritual mentor—viewed as an emissary of all the buddhas and the presence of the all-pervasive dharmakāya—is necessary to thrive even on the Mahāyanā path in a Sūtrayāna context. In the context of Vajrayāna and Dzokchen, moreover, an authentic practice of guru yoga is simply indispensable to making any progress at all. In order to practice such guru yoga, one must simultaneously be developing a deeper and deeper understanding of emptiness; in order to see one's guru as an actual buddha, one must be able (at least temporarily) to dissolve one's conceptions of the obscurative realities of the guru's human qualities so that one can recognize the buddha nature—the pristine awareness primordially indivisible from emptiness—that is always already present where the guru is.

To do so effectively, one must already have encountered a qualified guru: one whose lineage and expression of the teachings are authentic and whose behavior and practice are in accord with the high ethical standards of what he or she teaches. Furthermore, one must have begun to find that this particular teacher's teachings strike a chord in one's heart and inspire one to practice in ways that bring tangible benefit, even in the short term. With these criteria in place, one may then have the confidence to look straight through ordinary appearances and concepts, and engage as directly as possible with the pristine awareness, primordial consciousness that is the source

145. B. Alan Wallace, *The Vital Essence of Dzogchen: A Commentary on Düdjom Rinpoché's Advice for a Mountain Retreat* (Boulder, CO: Shambhala Publications, 2025).

of all authentic Dharma teachings in the first place. This is the level of divine encounter at which the prayers for blessings and empowerments described by Sera Khandro must eventually take place. But we also learn precisely by practicing. Thus, we can often vividly recognize our own shortcomings right there amid the yearning to see the ultimate purity of the divine guru appear in the space in front of us. This clarified vision is what gradually and sometimes suddenly purifies our hearts, and so the very yearning and seeking can be an authentic practice of guru yoga even long before we can acknowledge that we have actually perceived our qualified guru as an embodiment of the living buddha.

16. Taking the Aspect of the Mind as the Path

Düdjom Lingpa

This section has three parts: the teaching, the explanation, and the synthesis.

The Teaching

> **Those of the class with inferior faculties**
> **are introduced to the two—stillness and movement—**
> **and, by taking the mind as the path, they are led to the**
> **domain of pristine awareness.**

Those of the class with inferior faculties, not having the fortune to identify [primordial consciousness] in that way,[146] should first **be introduced to** the difference between **the two**: (1) **stillness** with respect to consciousness and (2) the **movement** of thoughts. **And, by** first **taking** the aspect of **the mind as the path,** finally **they are led to the domain of pristine awareness.**

The Elaborate Explanation of How This Occurs

This section has four parts: (1) mindfulness, the essential nature of the path, [354] (2) that which is to be purified: the classes of meditative experiences,

146. That is, those who have not been able to "see with the eye of wisdom the primordial nature of existence" after sustaining attention on three different types of objects and thus remaining in meditative equipoise for a period of three weeks.

(3) the essential nature of that which is to be abandoned and its remedy, and (4) how never to be separated from the illumination of the practical instructions.

Mindfulness, the Essential Nature of the Path

First, from the two comes unification into a single point.
Then, by resting without observing, natural creative displays manifest.
Abide loosely devoid of mindfulness in a vacuous, wide-open clarity;
then, resting in a luminous vacuity is called self-illuminating mindfulness.

The former two make manifest whatever arises,
while in the latter two, apart from there being solely a mode of cognition,
since thoughts cease, there is nonconceptuality.

According to this teaching, there are four types of mindfulness, which are the essential nature of the path. The **first** entails distinguishing between the **two** of stillness and movement, and by the power of familiarizing yourself with what seem to be their differences, insofar as they **unify** as one, **from** that **comes** ***single-pointed mindfulness.*** **Then,** even while **resting without** strenuously **observing** as before, insofar as **natural creative displays manifest**, there is *manifest mindfulness*. **Abiding loosely** without **mindfulness in a vacuous, wide-open clarity**, a spacious vacuity, constitutes lying down on a bed that is devoid of mindfulness, which is the *substrate*.[147] Once coarse mindfulness has subsided, **resting in a luminous vacuity is called self-illuminating mindfulness**, or the *substrate consciousness*.

147. Tib. *kun gzhi*; Skt. *ālaya*. The vacuous space of the mind as it is directly perceived by the substrate consciousness (Tib. *kun gzhi rnam shes*; Skt. *ālayavijñāna*).

The **former two** kinds of mindfulness [single-pointed mindfulness and manifest mindfulness] **make** directly **manifest whatever** creative displays **arise**, while during the **latter two** [the absence of mindfulness and self-illuminating mindfulness], **apart from** abiding **solely** in dependence upon a subtle **mode of cognition**, all appearances that are its radiance and **thoughts** that are its creative displays **cease**, so there is mere **nonconceptuality**. Since these [four kinds of mindfulness] are aroused through the contributing conditions of the path, and since they descend upon the two types of substrate,[148] those are called the *substrates of descent*. [355] Some teachers regard the first as the "one taste" and the second as "freedom from conceptual elaboration."[149] Others claim it is ethically unspecified, but whatever they say, one has arrived at the essential nature of the mind.

That Which Is to Be Purified: The Classes of Meditative Experiences

> **For all, the various experiences of bliss, vacuity, and luminosity**
> **become objects of craving and attachment,**

148. The two types of substrate are the actual substrate (experienced during the absence of mindfulness) and the temporarily luminous substrate (made manifest during self-illuminating mindfulness). The former is a blank vacuity, like a cloudless sky covered over by darkness at dusk, while the latter makes it possible for thoughts to appear, just as a polished mirror reflects a face.

149. Here the "first" refers to the experience of the actual substrate, and the "second" refers to the temporarily luminous substrate. The four sequential yogas of the Mahāmudrā tradition are single-pointedness, freedom from conceptual elaboration, one taste, and nonmeditation. The dissolution of the coarse mind into the substrate consciousness, culminating in the experience of self-illuminating mindfulness, signifies the achievement of śamatha, or the threshold (Tib. *nyer bsdogs*; Skt. *sāmantaka*) of the first dhyāna. But some teachers mistake these two experiences of the actual substrate and the temporarily luminous substrate for the much deeper realizations of pristine awareness that occur in the third and second yogas of Mahāmudrā, respectively. For a detailed explanation of how the four yogas of Mahāmudrā relate to the stages of practice of Dzokchen, see chapters 10 and 11 of Karma Chagmé, *Naked Awareness: Practical Teachings on the Union of Mahāmudrā and Dzogchen*, commentary by Gyatrul Rinpoché, trans. B. Alan Wallace (Ithaca, NY: Snow Lion Publications, 2000).

and meditative experiences of illnesses and discomfort in
the body, speech, and mind
arise sporadically over time.

At **all** times on this path, due to being bound by the coarse and subtle modes of cognition associated with mindfulness, there can arise, indeterminately, **various experiences**, such as **bliss** like the warmth of a fire, **luminosity** like the breaking of the dawn, and **vacuity**, or nonconceptuality, like an ocean without waves. However, if you don't know that these deceptive meditative experiences are not to be believed or trusted, and if you fixate on them as the ultimate sublime qualities such that they **become objects of craving and attachment**, they will become nothing more than causes for rebirth in the three realms of mundane existence. Therefore, even if you cultivate them for a long time, you will not rise above saṃsāra. Moreover, from your guru's spoken teachings, you must thoroughly understand how outer upheavals involving conjured apparitions of gods and demons, inner upheavals of physical illnesses, and secret upheavals of various mental joys and sorrows, and so on, **arise sporadically over time** as various **meditative experiences of illnesses and discomfort in the body, speech, and mind.** [356]

Recognizing the Essential Nature of That Which Is to Be Abandoned and Its Direct Remedy as the Foremost Path

Whenever you presume to hope for good things and
intensely cling to them,
and fear bad things and view inflictors of harm as being
autonomous,
you have stumbled upon a dangerous juncture that can lead
you astray
into pitfalls, deviations, and mistakes.

Whenever you have fallen under the influence of **presuming to hope for and** thus **intensely clinging to things** that seem to be **good**, such as material gain, respect, and renown—passing your human life in this way—**and fearing** all **things** that seem to be **bad**, such as being misunderstood, abused, and slandered by your enemies, this makes for misery and suffering. In short, insofar as you **view as being autonomous** all gods and **inflictors of harm**, as well as all joys and sorrows, **you have stumbled upon a dangerous**, obstructive **juncture that can lead you astray** in the three ways of **pitfalls, deviations, and mistakes.** Thinking, "In that case, I will be unable to ascend to the supreme city of great liberation," take this to heart. Whatever good and bad experiences, joys and sorrows, and so on seem to arise, there is no need to counteract them, for mere appearances cannot bind you, as Ācārya Āryadeva wrote:

> These are mere appearances and are not to be blocked.
> Instead, stop reifying them.

The real root of the thing to be terminated is the mind that reifies appearances. Outwardly, everything that appears as demons, malevolent spirits, and deceptive māras arises from nothing other than this root. [357] Consequently, until you have subdued that root, there will be no end to subduing all the outward demons and malevolent spirits, one by one.

> **The general synthesis, the sole, crucial point of the path,**
> **is ascertaining all experiences of pleasure, pain, and**
> **indifference**
> **as false impressions of unreal meditative experiences.**
> **By releasing them, without blocking or embracing them,**
> **you bring an end to pitfalls and deviations, and this is the**
> **one eye of wisdom.**

The general synthesis that is the remedy of all that is to be abandoned and **the sole,** essential, **crucial point of** all **paths is ascertaining** that even though **all** good and bad **experiences of pleasure, pain, and indifference** appear, they are **unreal,** delusive appearances, nothing more than **false impressions of meditative experiences. By releasing them** as being of one taste, **without blocking** the bad **or embracing** the good, adverse circumstances will arise as the path and obstructive conditions will arise as aids. In so doing, **you bring an end to** the adversities of **pitfalls, deviations,** and mistakes. The conducive condition of the **wisdom** of infallibly seeing the referent of *the profound nature of existence* is indispensable for all entrances to the path, so **this is** like **the one eye.** You must come to understand this from the more elaborate explanation that will be presented later,[150] on the manner in which everything that appears consists of delusive appearances that are not determined as real.

This is the actual path praised by the jinas for realizing the meaning of effortlessness, but as a method for this to occur, you must first familiarize yourself with [358] the union of the pair of śamatha with a focal object and vipaśyanā involving investigation and analysis. Novices should practice śamatha from the phase of single-pointedness until the point of making conscious awareness manifest, and also practice vipaśyanā, which is implicitly taught here, without ever being separated from them. So here they are taught sequentially.

How Never to Be Separated from the Illumination of the Practical Instructions

> **Some, once they have become distant from sublime spiritual mentors,**
> **cherish the five topics as the sublime path.**

150. This refers to the *Essence of Clear Meaning* commentary to phase 3 of the *Sharp Vajra of Conscious Awareness Tantra*, not included here. See Düdjom Lingpa, *Düdjom Lingpa's Visions of the Great Perfection*, vol. 1, *Heart of the Great Perfection* (New York, NY: Wisdom Publications, forthcoming).

> **If they strive too hard in practicing single-pointedness,**
> **the power of their minds will decline, and with stagnant mindfulness,**
> **although their body is human, their mind becomes that of an animal.**
> **Some people stray into delirium,**
> **so devote yourself to a spiritual mentor, without ever being separated from him.**

Some, once they have become distant from sublime spiritual mentors who reveal the path, may not know how to distinguish between what is and is not the path or how to cut through their uncertainties and false assumptions. Therefore, since the previously presented **five topics** on the dyad of stillness and movement and the four kinds of mindfulness[151] are **the sublime path**—that is, by understanding that they are indispensable when first venturing into practice—you should **cherish** them by way of gaining the firm certainty of proper understanding.

Some, however, regard this practice that is merely preliminary as being the ultimate nature of existence and strive only **in** the **practice** of **single-pointedness**. Or, without knowing how to rely upon the appropriate degree of concentration and relaxation, in accordance with the state of their own mindstreams, like blocking a water canal, they regard the mere single-pointed consciousness in which thoughts are blocked as the [359] highest view and meditation. Then, **if they strive** much **too hard** in the practice, the functioning of the channels and elements—for those people who are dominant in the water element or earth element—causes the analytical **power of their minds to decline.** Their **mindfulness then becomes stagnant**, and **though their body is human, their mind becomes that of**

151. These five topics are the ability to recognize the difference between stillness with respect to consciousness and the movement of thoughts, followed by the four kinds of mindfulness.

an animal, by becoming stupid and turgid. With this in mind, Mañjughoṣa Sakya Paṇchen[152] wrote:

> Striving only in meditation, without study,
> leads to taking rebirth as an animal.

Some people with a dominant fire constitution or a dominant air constitution may **stray** off the path as their minds become muddled due to **delirium**, fainting, and so on. **So** cut through your false assumptions by **devoting yourself to a** sublime **spiritual mentor** who knows how to draw forth the crucial points of this path correctly, **without ever being separated from him**. Even if you lack such good fortune [of meeting a qualified spiritual mentor], it is indispensable that you, without falling into indolence, properly read, realize, and familiarize yourself with the pith instructions of the vidyādharas of the past who have achieved siddhis by way of this path.

The Synthesis

> **In short, even if you strive diligently in the phase of these**
> **practices for a long time,**
> **taking the mind as the path**
> **does not bring you even a hair's breadth closer to the paths**
> **of liberation and omniscience,**
> **and your life will certainly have been spent in vain!**
> **So understand this, O fortunate ones!**

In short [360], **these** practices taught previously, from śamatha to clear, cognizant consciousness and the substrate consciousness, constitute the **phase of taking** the aspect of **the mind as the path**. But as long as it is divorced from the vipaśyanā of knowing the nature of existence, this **does not bring**

152. This refers to the Sakya Paṇḍita Kunga Gyaltsen.

you even a hair's breadth closer to the path of liberation from the suffering of mundane existence **and** the path of **omniscience** that liberates from the two extremes.[153] Thus, **even if you strive diligently in these practices for a long time,** this does nothing more than perpetuate saṃsāra. **So understand** how **your life will certainly have been spent in vain!** With these words he offered loving advice to **fortunate ones** who are following this path.

However, those who have not yet identified pristine awareness within themselves, or else those who have identified pristine awareness, but have fallen into dissipated confusion due to distraction and sloth, should for a little while do as follows. First, since the conceptual mind is like a cripple that rides upon the vital energy[154]—which is like a blind, wild stallion—you should tether its mount with the stake of meditative experience and sustained attention. Then, little by little, you will be able to meditate uninterruptedly, and eventually an experience will arise in which all coarse and subtle thoughts have been cleared away—and the domain of unstructured, unmodified, ever-present consciousness will naturally manifest. Then, when it is time to alight upon the great nonmeditation of pristine awareness, [361] it is easy for the guru's pointing-out instruction to strike home. For this reason, and because it is so important for disciples not to stray onto false paths, it was implicitly stated that this point is taught clearly here.

This concludes the synthesis of this phase, revealed in the *Sharp Vajra of Conscious Awareness Tantra*.

Translated by B. Alan Wallace and Eva Natanya

153. In this context the two extremes are the extreme of mundane existence, or saṃsāra, and of peace, or nirvāṇa.

154. The Tibetan term here is *rlung*, which may refer to the vital energies or to the air element. Within the body, the air element primarily refers to the breath, and one way for your mind to ride the steed of the vital energies on the pathways of the channels is the practice of gentle vase breathing. Alternatively, this passage may be interpreted as referring simply to mindfulness of breathing, which is an especially effective method for cultivating sustained attention, leading to the subsiding of all coarse and subtle obsessive thoughts.

17. How to Establish the Ground of Being by Way of the View

Düdjom Lingpa

In this presentation there are four sections: (I) nonexistence, (II) singularity, [362] (III) pervasive symmetry, and (IV) the manner of spontaneous actualization.[155]

I. For the first explanation, regarding the manner in which all phenomena of saṃsāra and nirvāṇa do not exist by any inherent nature, there are two sections: (A) establishing the identitylessness of a person and (B) establishing the identitylessness of phenomena.

A. Establishing the identitylessness of a person

Here, there are two sections: (1) the manner of clinging to a personal identity and (2) how to establish identitylessness with your intellect.

1. The manner of clinging to a personal identity

So-called personal identity is this very sense of "I am" that appears to be real, which we experience on all occasions during the day and night, in

155. Only the initial part of the first of these four topics is addressed in this excerpt.

dreams, during the intermediate period, and in future lives. [363] Moreover, from the very beginning, there is an "I"-grasping consciousness that exists in latent form, and then on occasion a subsequent consciousness and conceptualization bring this to mind, stabilize it and fortify it, and in this manner cling to it, and that is self-grasping.

2. How to establish identitylessness with your intellect

Here there are four sections: (a) investigating the origin from which [personal identity] emerges, (b) seeking the essential nature of an identity that remains in the interim, (c) how there is no way it could have anywhere to which it finally goes, and (d) teaching analogies for how it appears and can be described, even though it does not exist.

a. Investigating the origin from which it emerges

If that identity exists, from what outer or inner phenomena of the physical world [364] or its sentient inhabitants does it emerge? Or in particular, from what part of your own body and mind does it emerge? Upon investigating what kind of an agent it is that emerges and so on, you will come to the conclusion that it has no origin.

b. Seeking the essential nature of an identity that remains in the interim

Regarding the search for the essential nature of an identity that remains in the interim, if that identity were to exist, there should be something that can be determined as a real, substantial entity for which its location and that which is located there can be identified as distinctly different. So investigate whether or not that is so in the following way. What is that so-called identity? The head is called a *head*, so it is not your identity. The parts of the head, including the scalp, skull, eyes, ears, nose, tongue, teeth, brain, flesh, blood, lymph, nerves, and sinews are also not your identity. Likewise, the arms and their parts—shoulder blades, upper arms, forearms, and fingers—as well as the spine, ribs, chest, lungs, heart, diaphragm, liver, intestines, kidneys, urine, and feces, the legs and their parts—thighs, calves, upper feet, and toes—and in general, the outer skin of the body, the intervening flesh and fat, the inner bones, and the innermost collections of marrow are also not your identity. [365] Moreover, consciousness is not your identity, for it is called *consciousness*, but it is not called *identity*. Therefore, your so-called identity is not determined to exist, and since its location is also not to be found, it has no location and there is no agent who stays anywhere; so recognize it as being empty of any inherent nature.

c. How there is no way it could have anywhere to which it finally goes

Likewise, upon investigating the essential nature of the place to which your so-called identity goes and the essential nature of the one who goes, you will come to the conclusion that there is no way there could be any place for it to go or anyone who goes.

d. Teaching analogies for how it appears and can be described, even though it does not exist

Therefore, if you are wondering what it is that appears as your so-called identity, in fact it appears while being nonexistent, like a hallucination. Know as well that even though an *identity* may be described with words, the referent of that description is not determined to exist, even as one speaks about it. This is like speaking about the horns of a hare.

Although at all times there is strong clinging to the "I,"
if it is sought among the phenomena of the aggregates, it is not observed;
and it is utterly without origin, location, or destination,

like the appearance of a hallucination and talk about the horns of a hare.

That is a verse in the interim that summarizes the points of this passage.

B. Establishing the identitylessness of phenomena

[366] Here there are four sections: (1) seeking the basis of designation of names, (2) destroying clinging to things as permanent and real, (3) combating the faults of benefit and harm, and (4) collapsing the false cave of hopes and fears.[156]

1. Seeking the basis of designation of names

Here there are two sections: (a) seeking the referents that are designated by names and the manner in which you actually establish them as empty and (b) the manner in which the aspect of appearances arises from emptiness as dependently related displays.

a. Seeking the referents that are designated by names and the manner in which you actually establish them as empty

Here there are three sections: (i) how to establish the phenomena that are subsumed within your own continuum as being empty, (ii) applying that reasoning to other phenomena that are not so subsumed, and (iii) the manner in which phenomena are also empty of inherent existence due to transitions in names and their referents.

156. The latter three sections are not included in this excerpt, but extensive parallel explanations of these four topics can be found in the *Sharp Vajra of Conscious Awareness Tantra* and its commentary, *The Essence of Clear Meaning,* in *Buddhahood Without Meditation* and its commentary *Garland for the Delight of the Fortunate* and in *The Vajra Essence,* in Düdjom Lingpa, *Düdjom Lingpa's Visions of the Great Perfection,* vols. 1–3.

i. How to establish the phenomena that are subsumed within your own continuum as being empty

If any phenomenon such as your head were to exist in the manner in which you cling to it—thinking, "this and this," while holding that and that as being real entities—this would be called the *identity of a phenomenon*. If it were to exist, when you search for the referent of the name by which it is designated upon the object, it should be found. So here is how this should be investigated: Why do you designate the word *head* upon anything? Because it was the first part of the body to be formed during gestation, or because it is round, or do you call something a *head* because it appears to be on top? The head [367] was not the first thing to arise in the body during gestation; everything that is round is not called a *head*; and if you investigate and analyze that which is said to be on top and below, that is indeterminate. Hair is not a head; the scalp, skull, and brain are not a head, nor are the eyes, ears, nose, and tongue. If you think that each of those things separately is not a head, but that the assembly of them is called a *head*, if the head of a creature were cut off and then ground into coarse particles and then down to very fine particles, and if this were subsequently shown to all the people living in the world, no one would call it a *head*. Moreover, even if those particles were moistened and kneaded into a round lump, it would not be called a *head*. Thus, a so-called head is nothing more than an appellation and designation, so recognize how the basis of that appellation has no objective existence.

Likewise the eyes, too, exist as a pair of fluid spheres, and if the eyelids, tears, veins, blood, and so forth were separated, they would not individually be an eye, nor would their assembly. Moreover, that which sees forms is not an eye, for that which sees forms is ever-present consciousness, not those moist spheres that are currently designated as eyes, which is known by the fact there is vision in dreams and during the intermediate period. [368] The ears, as well, are not the ear canals, nor the flesh or skin, and so on, either individually or collectively, nor are they that which hears sounds. The nose, too, is not the nostrils, skin, and so on, either individually or collectively, nor is it that which detects smells. The tongue is also not the flesh or skin and so on, either individually or collectively, nor is it that which experiences tastes. This is to be understood by applying the parallel reasoning in each case.

Similarly, that which is called the *body* is not, outwardly, the spine, ribs, and so on; nor the limbs, such as the arms; nor is it, inwardly, the lungs, heart, liver, gallbladder, stomach, spleen, kidneys, or intestines. Moreover, the arm is not the upper arm, shoulder, forearm, finger joints, flesh, skin, bones, marrow, and so on. Likewise, regarding the parts of the arm—including the upper arm, shoulder, and forearm—and also regarding a leg—with its hip, thigh, calf, and so on—when their flesh, skin, bones, and so forth are separated into their individual parts, by reflecting on the way in which those parts individually or collectively are not a leg and so on, realize that each of these is empty in nature.

ii. Applying that reasoning to other phenomena that are not so subsumed

Investigate outer mountains, houses, and so on [369] by differentiating their individual constituents, including earth, stones, grass, and trees. Do the same with regard to other people, as well as horses and so on, all of whom have their own mental continua. Moreover, among physical things, the term *drum* does not refer to the wood or the leather, to its exterior or interior, and so on. By applying the preceding reasoning to all phenomena, you will recognize them to be empty of real existence.

iii. The manner in which phenomena are also empty of inherent existence due to transitions in names and their referents

To illustrate this with an example, turning a knife into an awl entails that which was called a *knife* transitioning into an awl; again, when that is made into a needle, that changes and is then called a *needle*. Therefore, what is called a *knife* and an *awl* is simply designated as such, but you should understand how it is not determined to exist from its own side. Thus, this set of teachings on seeking out the self of a person and seeking the bases of designation of names constitute exceptional practical instructions spoken directly by the Supreme Ārya, the Great Compassionate One (Avalokiteśvara).[157]

b. The manner in which the aspect of appearances arises from emptiness as dependently related displays

These are practical instructions granted by the Lake-Born Vajra of Oḍḍiyāna when I directly encountered his illusory body of primordial consciousness.[158] Thus, he explained that because they are empty of an essential nature, appearing phenomena [370] emerge simply from the dependent relationships that consist of the confluence of their respective causes and contributing conditions. In dependence upon the confluence of the cause—the lucid, luminous ground space of awareness, which has the capacity to give rise to all manner of appearances—and the contributing condition—subtle consciousness that grasps to an "I"—appearances emerge in the manner of illusions. Thus, because (1) the ground, absolute space, (2) the mind that arises from its creative power, and (3) all outer and inner phenomena that are the appearing aspects of this mind are interrelated as a linked chain of events, like the sun and its rays, they are called *dependently related events*.

For example, this is (1) like the appearance of an illusion that occurs in dependence upon, and in relationship to, the convergence of a cause—namely, lucid, luminous space—and contributing conditions—namely, a magical substance, a mantra, and an emanating mind. In accordance

157. See Düdjom Lingpa, "Teachings of Avalokiteśvara" in *Düdjom Lingpa's Visions of the Great Perfection*, vol 2, *Buddhahood Without Meditation*.

158. See Düdjom Lingpa, "Teachings of the Lake-Born Vajra of Oḍḍiyāna," in *Düdjom Lingpa's Visions of the Great Perfection*, vol 2, *Buddhahood Without Meditation*.

with what was just explained, specifically, while all appearing phenomena ultimately do not exist, they manifest due to the power of grasping to an "I," which is (2) like a mirage. One becomes deluded due to the power of clinging to the reality of things that appear but do not exist, and one overtly clings to them as being objective. For example, when the environment and so on of (3) a dream appear, they are not determined as such, but this is like apprehending a realm created by dhyāna and then clinging to it. [Phenomena] merely appear to be something other than an internal, dominant condition, (4) like the appearance of a reflection before the eyes, due to the dominant condition of a face.

Due to the power of self-grasping, [371] the cities of the six classes of beings appear to arise one after the other. These are (5) like the appearances of a city of gandharvas[159] manifesting in an area such as a plain at sunset, which are solely visionary experiences of a focused mind. While sensory appearances have never been determined to be real, the various things that are seen, heard, experienced, and felt are your own appearances, but appear as if they were other, (6) like an echo. All appearances are not other than the ground and are of "one taste" with the ground itself, (7) just as the image of the moon reflected in the ocean is not other than the ocean but is of "one taste" with the water itself. Due to the power of grasping to the ground—absolute space—as "me," the appearance of self and others as truly existent is (8) like the welling forth of a bubble from water. The lucid, luminous aspect of the ground is subdued and converted into the mental consciousness of your own appearances, and in dependence upon that, manifests as various delusive appearances. This is (9) like the occurrence of a hallucination due to pressing the nerve of the eye or due to changes in the elements of the channels resulting from movements of the vital energies. From the perspec-

159. Tib. *dri za'i grong khyer,* Skt. *gandharvanagara*. An apparitional city of ethereal beings that was known to appear under certain conditions, such as along the horizon when the sky is filled with mist as the sun is rising. The appearances of the "city" vanish as the sun rises higher in the sky, thus revealing that there was never really any city at all, only an illusory apparition based on the confluence of certain conditions.

tive of the consciousness that grasps to an "I," various appearances from the ground appear to it, but they never waver from the ground or emerge from it. This is (10) like the case of someone who has mastered the samādhi of emanation and transformation; when that individual enters into samādhi, although various emanations appear, in fact, they are devoid of any basis or root and are not determined to be real.

If you wish to know how this applies to each of the causes and contributing conditions as related to the [ten] analogies of a mirage and so on, look to [372] *The Vajra Essence*. This is profound advice for training in [recognizing] appearances as illusions. When the Great Oḍḍiyāna [Guru Padmasambhava] himself was granting that advice, at the conclusion he said, "O, my unimaginable Khyeuchung, gradually meditate in this way, and once you have realized appearances as illusions, this will become the yoga of illusion," and he disappeared.

Regarding the referents of names, whoever may impute them—
including things that are and are not subsumed by one's mental continuum—
regardless of how one searches for them, they are not found, but are empty.
The dependent emergence of appearances is illustrated by the ten analogies.

That is a verse in the interim that summarizes the points of this passage.

Translated by B. Alan Wallace and Eva Natanya

18. Prerequisites for Practice of the Direct Crossing Over

FROM *PITH INSTRUCTIONS ON LIBERATION AS A BODY OF LIGHT*

Sera Khandro

1. The Preliminaries

In this section there is, first, taking hold of the ground with the view of cutting through (trekchö), then a general presentation of the common preliminaries, and finally, a specific explanation of the uncommon preliminaries.

First, there is taking hold of the ground with the view of cutting through.

> **Individuals who enter this door should have**
> **achieved stability in their mastery of saṃsāra and nirvāṇa**
> **as a great display of all-encompassing realization in great emptiness,**
> **and in making manifest the nature of existence, the mode of being,**
> **with the great wisdom that both knows reality as it is and the full range of phenomena.**

Individuals who wish to **enter** this profound **door** of the clear light, the direct crossing over (tögal), and who are endowed with karma and prayers should first establish

- the bases of designation for the identities of all the phenomena subsumed within the world of appearances—of both saṃsāra and nirvāṇa—even though they are without identity
- the bases for the appearances of the reality of things that are unreal, and
- the basis for the view that sees saṃsāra and nirvāṇa as autonomous and truly existent—even though they have no autonomous existence—which includes
- the two types of identity: both personal identity, which apprehends, and what emerges from that—namely, the identities of phenomena, which are apprehended.

Such individuals must establish that the nature of these two types of identity has never truly been determined as real, and is free of arising, cessation, and abiding. Thus, they establish them as the **emptiness** that is the very identity of the **Great** Madhyamaka. Then they should realize, just as it is, the equality of **saṃsāra and nirvāṇa**, the **nature of existence** that is fully **encompassed** and entirely **realized** in the sphere of the dharmakāya; and ascertain every single phenomenon of the world of appearances—of all the phenomenal worlds and their inhabitants, and of saṃsāra and nirvāṇa—as being none other than **displays** of pristine awareness and as being **great**, uniformly pervasive pristine awareness and emptiness. [477] By **mastering** the meaning of how these are perfectly complete in nondual equality, they alight upon the meaning of the view. Mastering the ground of the primordial consciousness that knows reality as it is constitutes the way to dwell in what is pure, the ground. Upon gaining mastery of the path of the primordial consciousness that perceives the full range of phenomena—that is, by the power of the **great wisdom** that simultaneously realizes the way to settle upon the path as well as all the stages of the grounds and paths—they

make manifest, just as it is, **the nature of existence**, which is **the mode of being** of the Great Perfection, by means of a samādhi that rests just as it is, primordially settled in its natural state. **After** they **have achieved stability** without wavering from this realization, if they follow this guidance along the very swift path of the direct crossing over, all obstacles and errors will automatically cease. This is the profound pith instruction for coming to the culmination of the path.

Second, regarding the common preliminaries, there is a general explanation and a specific explanation, and the first refers to the four revolutions in outlook. By contemplating the difficulty of obtaining a human rebirth with leisure and opportunity, you renounce all activities pertaining to this life—such as trying to control those who oppose you, trying to protect your friends and relatives, getting caught up in attachments, aversions, and so on—and devote your actions of body, speech, and mind solely to the sublime Dharma and utterly abstain from conduct that is contrary to the Dharma. [478] While bearing in mind the impermanent nature of all composite phenomena, it is crucial that you have only the thought of practicing Dharma without procrastination, and like a lovely woman whose head has caught fire, you take the essence of this life by applying yourself to the sublime Dharma without laziness or distraction.

Wherever you are born in the higher or lower realms of saṃsāra, nothing transcends the nature of suffering, and all actions and acting are a basis for saṃsāra and a seed of suffering. As an analogy, just as there are no pleasant fragrances in the midst of a filthy swamp, there is not even a moment's opportunity for joy in the abode of saṃsāra. With this in mind, now in dependence upon this fine human life of leisure and opportunity, earnestly strive for the omniscient state of a jina.

Once you have come to a firm conviction regarding actions and their karmic consequences, consider the reasons why you must unfailingly experience the fully ripened effects of your deeds if you do not precisely and meticulously guard your conduct, without mistake, in terms of those actions that are to be embraced and those to be avoided. Do not scornfully disregard the laws of karma with lofty words about your view and conceit about the vastness of your erudition, but rather correctly recognize without confusion the virtues to be embraced and the vices to be avoided.

Then [specifically], in order to cross the ocean of the miserable realms of saṃsāra, [479] bow at the feet of your glorious, sublime guru, and for the sake of achieving in this very lifetime and with this same body the eternal bliss of the precious, omniscient state of a jina, devote your whole life to Dharma, dedicate yourself to your guru and the Three Jewels, resort to a place of solitude that is suitable for practice, associate with pristine awareness, primordial consciousness, as your companion, clothe yourself just enough to protect you from the elements, and partake of food just for the sake of sustenance. On that basis, it is vitally important that you cast off the accretions of the eight mundane concerns, and don the sturdy armor of diligent practice—nothing less than this.

As for a specific explanation of the uncommon, inner preliminaries, you should engage in the practice of differentiating between saṃsāra and nirvāṇa. . . .

[482] . . . Regarding the performance of the outer differentiation . . . first, the distinction of the motivation is presented in the following passage:

> **Meditate upon your guru at the crown of your head and**
> **take the four empowerments;**
> **generate supreme bodhicitta for the sake of beings.**

[483] Thinking as follows, incite your mindstream toward the Dharma with the precious jewel of ultimate bodhicitta: "In this way I will clear away in absolute space the obscurations of ignorance borne by all sentient beings dwelling in saṃsāra, immediately destroy the bonds of delusional, dualistic grasping, and manifest naturally present, great primordial consciousness. Upon extinguishing all the appearances of phenomena into the expanse

of the actual nature of reality, I will then expand infinitely into the great, evenly pervasive absolute space of the three kāyas."

Then, it is of the utmost importance that you make efforts in cultivating guru yoga, which is the foremost principle of the profound path. As stated in the *Hevajra Tantra*:

> Coemergence—inexpressible by another
> and not to be found anywhere at all—
> is to be known when revealed by the guru,
> by means appropriate to the time,
> and it will be understood because of one's own merit.

And as it is said in the *Presentation of Samayas*:

> Meditating for a hundred thousand eons
> upon a deity endowed with the signs and symbols of
> enlightenment,
> is not one hundred-thousandth
> of what it means to recall your guru.
> To make supplication to your guru but a single time
> stands supreme over a million recitations of approach and
> accomplishment.

Therefore, since this sublime guru—who has taken you into his or her care by means of the three forms of kindness and reveals to you through ripening and liberation the swift, profound path of the two stages—is himself or herself of the essential nature of the Three Jewels and the Three Roots [484] all combined as one; since the degree to which the facets of primordial consciousness and sublime qualities of the profound path of the Mantrayāna will grow in you depends on the degree to which you are able to properly devote yourself to the guru; and since all the siddhis of the two stages, moreover, arise in dependence upon your gurus, *The Great Presentation of Ati[yoga]* states,

> Whosoever meditates upon the guru, Vajradhara,
> within the maṇḍala of their heart,
> upon the crown of their head,
> upon their limbs, their palms, and so on,
> will come to possess
> the sublime qualities of a thousand buddhas.

This being the case, here is how to **meditate upon** the guru, who is the ground for your supplication. See the place where the guru naturally dwells to be the pure land of Khecara: vast, expansive, and replete in all perfectly pure, celestial displays. In the space directly in front of the **crown of your head**, see an orb formed from masses of light and rainbows—the natural glow of the five facets of primordial consciousness. At its center, see your own root guru, whose complexion, hand implements, and so on appear according to the traditional descriptions of that particular form of the guru. Meditating thus, abandon all negative states of mind by which you might conceive of your guru as ordinary, and see that his or her holy body is adorned with the excellent signs and symbols of enlightenment, dwelling in radiant glory amid an expanse of light and blazing rays of light. The guru's holy speech [485] proclaims the inconceivable sounds of the Dharma in their sixty forms of melodious song. The guru's holy mind dwells within the meditative equipoise of the many hundreds of doors of samādhi. Visualize your guru thus as the archetypal form of all the jinas, whose very identity is enlightened knowledge, love, and power.

While recalling the kindness and sublime qualities of your guru, and at the same time bringing forth an immense and fiercely powerful sense of admiration and reverence, express that reverence with your body by making prostrations. In order to express that reverence with your speech, focus your whole being on making supplications. Expressing the reverence of your mind, let your own mind and the holy mind of your guru be unified in a single taste, and then **take the four empowerments**. To do so, pray as follows:

"Please, O guru, by reaching myself and all sentient beings as far as space itself, may all the blessings of your holy mind—which is great, utterly nonconceptual primordial consciousness—ripen and then liberate our mindstreams with a river of the primordial consciousness of the four empowerments."

Thinking thus, see that rays of light—colored white, red, and deep blue, respectively—are emitted from each of the three sacred places of the guru's form. Imagine that "as they dissolve into my own three places, the karma, mental afflictions, negative deeds, and obscurations related to my body, speech, and mind, along with their habitual propensities, are purified, and all at once I receive all the empowerments and achieve the ability to perform every siddhi without exception. Then I make manifest the four kāyas and the five facets of primordial consciousness."

The guru himself or herself then turns into a sphere of five-colored light. Then remain for as long as you can in the meditative equipoise where your body, speech, and mind, [486] and the guru's holy body, speech, and mind—the three vajras—are inseparable: a state of great bliss, complete equality, free of conceptual elaboration.

As a result of this, all the blessings of the actual continuum[160] of the sublime guru endowed with the lineage will directly descend upon you as the blessings of your guru's lineage of the enlightened view. At best, this will occur in the manner of a vase being filled to the brim; middling, like a clay *sātsa* image emerging from its mold; and at the very least, like a color being

160. Tib. *don rgyud*. This term could alternatively be translated as the "actual tantra," or the "tantra of definitive meaning," but according to Longchen Rabjampa, writing in the *Treasury of the Supreme Yāna*, the referent is "the actual nature of the mind, which is by nature clear light, free of the stains of conceptualization, and which dwells continuously within everyone. Thus, it is a *continuum*, and since it is also buddha nature, it is a *continuum*, and since it bears the defining characteristic of a buddha, it is also set forth as a *continuum*," where *continuum* is the same word as *tantra*. See the Grand Monlam Tibetan Dictionary entry for *don gyi rgyud*: https://monlamdictionary.com.

transformed by pigments. Without need for effort or striving, all the sublime qualities of meditative experiences and realizations will implicitly arise and grow within your mindstream as realizations, solely in dependence upon your supplications to a sublime guru endowed with the lineage, and because of your admiration and reverence. All obstacles to reaching the grounds and paths, as well as all potential errors, will, moreover, naturally release themselves. You will be blessed by all the *sugatas*, all the vidyādharas and hosts of ḍākinīs will grant you prophecies, and this will become the basis for many extraordinary qualities to come forth, such as finding relief [in a pure land], and so on. Therefore, the Precious Lord (Jetsun Rinpoché) himself said,

> When you develop intense devotion for the guru,
> it is certain that meditative experiences and blessings will
> come.

It is also stated,

> Those who constantly rely upon the guru
> will come to see every form of the ḍākinī
> [487] and partake of her blessings.
> They will reveal prophecies about
> the past, present, and future,
> and gain mastery over life and death.

In brief, the guru, the spiritual mentor, is the heir to every buddha of the past, the origin of every jina who will come in the future, and the very embodiment of the sacred deeds of all the buddhas of the present, synthesized in a single being. Since the guru serves as the sublime origin for every maṇḍala and all the buddha families, a sūtra states,

> The Tathāgata does not appear fully to sentient beings, but since

> the spiritual mentor does appear fully and teaches the Dharma, you should regard the spiritual mentor as superior even to the Tathāgata.

Therefore, whatever Dharma from the paths of the two stages, and so on, that you may take up for practice, since at the beginning guru yoga is like the central pillar of every path, you must practice it properly in this way. So, without hiding anything with respect to your samayas, single-pointedly supplicate your guru, and request him or her, "Please, take me and all the limitless numbers of **beings**, all sentient beings, to the bodhisattva ground of total liberation!" Then, utterly abandoning any negative thought of benefiting only yourself, [488] think, "**For the sake of** all sentient beings I will practice the differentiation between saṃsāra and nirvāṇa, and from this moment forward, neither I nor others will ever enter saṃsāra again." Thus you **generate** in an authentic way the precious jewel of **supreme bodhicitta**, and this is a sublimely important point.

Translated by Eva Natanya and B. Alan Wallace

Contemporary Masters of Dzokchen and Mahāmudrā

Domang Yangthang Rinpoché

Domang Yangthang Rinpoché was born on January 10, 1930, as Kunsang Jikmé Dechen Ösel Dorjé. He was born in the region of Yangthang in western Sikkim, which is now a state in northeastern India, bordered by Tibet. At a young age, he was recognized as a *tulku*, being one of two reincarnations of Tertön Dorjé Dechen Lingpa (1857–1928) of Domang Monastery in the eastern Tibetan region of Kham. Tertön Dorjé Dechen Lingpa was himself an incarnation of Lhatsün Namkha Jikmé (1597–1653), a mahāsiddha who was regarded as an incarnation of both the ninth-century Dzokchen master Vimalamitra and the great Nyingma master Longchenpa (1308–1364).

After being identified, the boy was known as Yangthang Tulku, and in 1942 he was taken to Domang Monastery where he began studying scriptures, learned the Tibetan language, and was educated in various subjects. There he became close friends with his contemporary tulku Domang Gyatrul Rinpoché (1925–2023), with whom he would be reunited many decades later. By 1957, after the Chinese communist invasion of Tibet in 1950, Yangthang Tulku had moved to a remote mountainside in Kham. When Tibet eventually surrendered in defeat, Yangthang Tulku felt he would no longer be able to remain in Kham, but one of his root gurus, Drupchen Lingtrul, firmly told him not to flee. Whatever the Chinese might do to him, he should let them do it, and if he had to experience great suffering he would do so, in prison, but he should not flee.

Consequently, Yangthang Tulku was captured by Chinese communists in 1959, and he was incarcerated in concentration camps for more than twenty years. Those who were close to him recall that he was never angry or resentful about the beatings he received from Chinese soldiers—rather, he would simply practice Dharma continuously through beatings, secretly reciting sacred texts until it was over. This was done with great risk; if prison guards noticed even a vibration in the throat when a prisoner was reciting mantra or texts, the practitioner would be tortured. They had to recite without any sound or movement being detectable at all. Yangthang Rinpoché told others later that whenever he saw Chinese soldiers, or even Tibetans who were secretly assisting the Chinese, he felt only compassion for them.

When prisoners were starving, it was reported by his fellow inmates that Yangthang Rinpoché would sometimes manifest—seemingly out of nowhere—ritual *tsok* offerings and distribute these to fellow prisoners for food. Others reported that they occasionally saw him walking through the wall of the prison. On one occasion when he saved the lives of three prisoners by teaching them mantras to recite day and night to avert their scheduled execution, he was punished severely for it. While in prison, he also took the enormous risk of secretly teaching Dharma both to Tibetan prisoners and Chinese guards, even helping many prisoners die peacefully by performing *phowa*, the ritual for transferring consciousness. Yangthang Rinpoché later stated that because of the Dharma, his mind was freer in prison than many people's minds who were in the best of circumstances but who had no authentic Dharma.

In 1979, he was released from prison after the death of the Chinese leader Mao Zedong and returned to Domang Monastery, only to discover that it had been demolished. In 1981, after correspondence with his family in Sikkim, he traveled back to his birthplace. He then wandered throughout India, receiving empowerments and transmissions from Dilgo Khyentsé Rinpoché, Düdjom Rinpoché, Dodrupchen Rinpoché, and Penor

Rinpoché. In 1985, Domang Gyatrul Rinpoché and his interpreter Sangye Khandro were staying in Boudhanath, Nepal, and were told that Yangthang Rinpoché was performing circumambulations at the great stupa. They ran to meet him there, inaugurating a joyful reunion between childhood friends, which directly and indirectly led to the burgeoning of Yangthang Rinpoché's teaching activity around the world. Over the course of the next thirty years, Yangthang Rinpoché shared the wisdom of the Dharma worldwide—in Taiwan, Hong Kong, Nepal, Tibet, India, Malaysia, France, Switzerland, and the United States—during which time he granted about two thousand empowerments and innumerable oral transmissions.

As a renowned Dzokchen master of the Nyingma tradition, Yangthang Rinpoché's teachings embraced the heart essence of the Dharma and pith instructions of the Great Perfection. Profound and to the point, his teachings encompassed mind training, bodhicitta, guru yoga, and the four revolutions in outlook, among many other sublime instructions for reaching the path and beyond. His teaching style was direct, spontaneous, detailed, and without excess. His disciples recall that he did not teach as if reading from a book; instead, he taught from the depths of his heart. He was gentle, humble, and easy to approach, all the while having all the signs of great realization. He is remembered for practicing Dharma continuously; he would recite mantras whenever he was not in formal sessions of meditation, even when he appeared to be asleep—which was only from 9 p.m. to midnight, after which he would rise again for waking practice through the rest of the night. He was also renowned for his indomitable stamina as a teacher. He performed empowerments and ceremonies with exquisite precision, and he expected that level of conscientiousness from his attendants and disciples in preparing the ritual maṇḍalas and offerings.

On October 15, 2016, Yangthang Rinpoché passed into *parinirvāṇa* in Hyderabad, India. He is remembered as being a great lama who immersed every moment of his life in the Dharma, had unshakable faith, and had a profound way of transmitting the Dharma, leaving in his wake boundless inspiration and a vast spiritual legacy.

Many lamas place restrictions on who is allowed to read Dzokchen texts, and here is what Yangthang Rinpoché said prior to granting his oral commentary on his own composition, *A Summary of the View, Meditation, and Conduct*, which follows below: "In times past when people had leisure, one might take as long as three years for the lama to examine carefully the students to see whether they were truly qualified for any given teachings. Also, it was up to the students to examine the lama to see whether the lama is also a suitable lama for the teachings. But now in this present occasion, and these days, we don't really have that opportunity. We don't have so much leisure. And so in terms of the qualifications for the disciples, what is most important here is really faith."

19. A Summary of the View, Meditation, and Conduct

Domang Yangthang Rinpoché

[2] Sole bindu, timeless, eternal protector, all-pervasive lord of all the families of buddhas, Guru Vajradhara, you know all.
Should I earnestly and single-pointedly pray to you, please grant your blessings that the lineage of the enlightened view may strike my heart!

You have obtained a human life, which is difficult to find,
have aroused the intention of a spirit of emergence, which is difficult to arouse,
have met a qualified guru, who is difficult to meet, [3]
and you have encountered the sublime Dharma, which is difficult to encounter.

Reflect again and again on the difficulty of obtaining such a fine human life.
If you do not make this meaningful, it will be like a butter lamp
in the wind of impermanence.
Do not count on this lasting a long time.
At death, if you have no confidence that you will be liberated in the intermediate period,

ah, then how much will you fear the miseries of future lives!
Then you [4] will have to wander in endless saṃsāra.
When you contemplate the nature of this, you will be disillusioned.
If you can try your best to gain confidence in this life,
I would be most grateful—this is my hope for you.

The View

If you wish to look into the mirror of the actual nature of your mind,
do not look outward. Rather, look inward.
Looking outward involves the delusion of reification.
By looking inward, you observe your own mind. [5]

Do not follow after past thoughts or anticipate thoughts to come.
As for the wild agitation of the thoughts of the present moment,
as soon as you direct your mind inward upon itself,
loosely rest right there, without fixing or modifying anything in the slightest.
This natural settling of thoughts is a way of resting, but it is not the main practice.
But in that very way of resting [6] you are ready to encounter
pristine awareness, which is the main practice.

As soon as you rest in your natural state, thoughts spontaneously cease and depart.
The natural lucidity of thoughts, what remains when they disappear,
is the empty, transparent, essential nature of the mind.
An experience arises that is like space:
without anything on which to focus and
free of falling to any extreme.
This empty *essential nature* is the dharmakāya.

Right there in that emptiness is the clear and lucid *manifest nature* of the mind.
Devoid of any substantial characteristics of which you can say, "this,"
its own spacious and unimpeded luminosity, which is naturally clear,
is the sambhogakāya.

There is no other perceiver of this luminous, empty pristine awareness.
That which is perceived is the empty dharmakāya.
That which perceives is luminous primordial consciousness.
These two may be called emptiness and luminosity,
and they may also be called [7] absolute space and primordial consciousness.

These two are not separate.
The manifest nature of that emptiness is luminosity,
and the essential nature of that luminosity is emptiness.
So luminosity and emptiness are a unity.

They are not separate, and since they are of one taste
there is no duality of the perceived and the perceiver.
This is perceived nondually, so it is called discerning self-knowing awareness,
in which the mind sees itself.

That very sphere of the one taste of luminosity and emptiness
is the equal taste of the good and bad, of saṃsāra and nirvāṇa.
So there is no difference between "the two" of saṃsāra and nirvāṇa.
Just that is the Great Perfection.

In the mindstream of one who realizes this Great Perfection,
impartial compassion and impartial pure vision

emerge effortlessly and naturally. [8]
That *all-pervasive compassion* is the nirmāṇakāya.

The pristine awareness of the three kāyas is just that.
Recognize with certainty that it is nothing other than that.
As long as there is vague uncertainty,
realization of the nature of existence will never come.
So you must ascertain this from within.
This is the view of the Great Perfection.

Meditation

Among the three—the view, meditation, and conduct—the view is primary.
So it is crucial to realize the unmistaken view.
Without realizing the view, there is no basis for meditation.
Once you have directly realized the unmistaken view,
then comes the time to take it into practice by way of meditation.
Diligently applying yourself to dwell for a long time
in the sphere of the view that identifies your own essential nature
is meditation. There is nothing else on which to meditate.

Until your view turns into the expanse,
without counting the number of years and months, [9]
determine to devote your whole life to Dharma.
That is what the best of Dharma practitioners do.

From the very outset, if you give lip service
to the equality free of conceptual elaboration and so on,
while taking it easy, without practicing in formal sessions,
doing whatever you like—eating and lying about—

in the end, there will be no difference between
your freedom from conceptual elaboration and futility;
and there is a great danger that you will sink into oblivion
when you are about to die.

Empty talk and boasting are useless, so in accordance with sublime beings,
be a humble Dharma practitioner, letting your conduct accord with your speech.

Therefore, it is best if you retire to mountain solitude,
or at least stay in a place where there are few distractions.
Divide your time between formal sessions and post-meditative periods,
and during delineated sessions of meditative equipoise,
give up the nine kinds of activity.[161]
Without being distracted outwardly and without grasping inwardly,
rest evenly [10] in your naturally settled, indwelling nature.

All appearances that arise as objects of the five senses
are like reflections of planets and stars in the ocean.
Whatever arises, dwell in meditative equipoise in the expanse—without grasping.
The best of meditations does not have even the slightest object of attention.
Even though that is difficult for beginners, after a while,
with gradual effort, it will emerge.

161. Tib. *bya ba dgu phrugs*. The nine kinds of activity include the body's (1) outer activities, such as walking, sitting, and moving about, (2) inner activities of prostrations and circumambulations, and (3) secret activities of ritual dancing, performing mudrās, and so on; the speech's (4) outer activities, such as all kinds of delusional chatter, (5) inner activities, such as reciting liturgies, and (6) secret activities, such as counting the mantras of your personal deity; and the mind's (7) outer activities, such as thoughts aroused by the five poisons and the three poisons, (8) inner activities of mind training and cultivating positive thoughts, and (9) the secret activity of dwelling in mundane states of dhyāna.

During the post-meditative periods, train in emptiness, compassion,
and the skill of recognizing phenomena to be like illusions and dreams.
Strive as much as possible in Dharma practices and in purifying obscurations.
In particular, it is a crucial point to direct your thoughts after meditation
to the view that arose while in meditative equipoise,
so that your post-meditative experience
is integrated with your formal sessions.

Distinguish between the substrate and the dharmakāya
and between the mind and pristine awareness.
Once you have analyzed and recognized all the ways
of mixing things up, going astray, or getting things wrong,
as well as all faults and virtues,
treasure your efforts to adopt virtues and reject faults. [11]

Those are the practices for the post-meditative periods.
When you strive for a long time to practice in this way,
whatever meditative experiences and appearances arise,
such as bliss, luminosity, and nonconceptuality,
do not appropriate them or fixate on them,
but ascertain them with the view and sustain your practice of resting naturally.
Gradually, fine meditative experiences will increase and bad ones will cease.

At the outset of each session, arouse bodhicitta, practice guru yoga,
and take the four empowerments, and after each session,
seal it with prayers of dedication.
These comprise the framework of meditation, so they are indispensable.
In particular, until you have reached the culminating stage of practice,
the ground of nonmeditation,
and your own pristine awareness has actually arisen as the guru,

the crucial point to be embraced
is to regard training in guru yoga as the main practice.

If you can practice each day in the yoga of four sessions [12]
without being too tight or too loose,
without doubt you will take hold of the fortress of eternal rest
in the culmination of all five kinds of meditative experiences,[162]
and so on, taught by Vimalamitra.

Even if not, if there are some who apply
just a moderate degree of effort in this practice,
while mostly just engaging in hearing and reflection,
they will experience less clinging to the eight mundane concerns
and will spend their lives in a relaxed, cheerful manner.
They will have taken the first step of the path,
and before long they will surely be liberated
in the eternal ground of omniscience.

Conduct

Then, to give a partial account of the conduct:
During the times when you are dwelling in meditative equipoise in that way,
when fresh thoughts suddenly emerge or else crop up subliminally,
perceive their emergence from the sphere of your own pristine awareness. [13]
Do not follow after them, and whether they are good, bad,
pleasurable, miserable, and so forth, do not do anything.

162. These five meditative experiences are (1) turbulence, (2) attainment, (3) familiarity, (4) stability, and (5) culmination.

Rather, as soon as you see them arise, rest in the nature of just that which has arisen.
By resting naturally, thoughts will disappear by themselves,
and you will return to the pristine awareness you had experienced earlier.
Then sustain the practice of resting naturally as before.

Thus, whatever good and bad thoughts arise, do not fixate on them,
but let them arise and be released by themselves.
However thoughts are released, in any of the three ways,[163] there is no difference.
The one point is that they self-arise and self-release.
Even though thoughts occur, they arise from the expanse of the dharmakāya.
Even though thoughts stop, they cease in the expanse of pristine awareness.
If you know their arising does no harm and
you know how to let them release themselves,
you will receive a special enhancement of the view. [14]

When you make efforts in this way, thoughts will decrease,
even as it does no harm to the ground of being should they arise.
With this process the lowest, middling, and supreme
modes of release will gradually come.
But if the crucial points for the modes of release are missing,
liberation will never be attained in the end.
Knowing how thoughts are released is the best conduct.

163. The three ways thoughts are released are as follows: (1) Thoughts are released simply upon being recognized. (2) By the power of familiarization, thoughts release themselves, like a snake unraveling itself. (3) In the culminating phase, there is no way thoughts can help or harm you, like a thief who comes to an empty house, where there's nothing he can do. In this final phase, thoughts empower your realization of pristine awareness, serving as aids to your practice.

As for the results of practicing in that way,
mental afflictions and thoughts gradually thin out,
clinging to the eight mundane concerns diminishes, and
admiration, reverence, and pure vision gradually increase.
Dreams are apprehended, and the clear light appears.
Such are authentic fruitions of the path.

On the other hand, such things as visions of deities, receiving prophecies,
and the arising of extrasensory perception may or may not be fruitions of the path.
If we cannot tell the right ones from the wrong, we will be deceived by māras. [15]
Do not wait for such things—just let them go!

Finally, on the verge of death or in the transitional phase
of the actual nature of reality, recognize the appearances of the ground
and take hold of the fortress in that very ground.
Then you will certainly be liberated.

I have composed this summary of the view, meditation, and conduct
simply in order not to rebuff a request by a friend.
This is lip service about things I lack, so there are bound to be many errors.
Therefore, please inquire of others and investigate carefully.
If there are a few points that are correct,
I pray that this may enhance the practice of my friends
and simply serve as a contributing condition for
them to reach the culmination of the practice,
so they will simultaneously be liberated, all together,
in the expanse of the eternal ground
and accomplish the needs of themselves and others.

Simply in order not to rebuff the request by my noble Dharma friend Lama Tsewang, [16] who came from Riwoché in Kham, the one going by the name of Yangthang Tulku composed this with no head and no tail. May it be a cause that benefits the practice of my friends.

Translated by B. Alan Wallace, with the assistance of Tenzin Weigyal Chodrak (Pojen Tseng), and edited by Eva Natanya

Contemporary Masters of Dzokchen and Mahāmudrā

Drupön Lama Karma

Drupön Karma Jnana, also known as Tsampa Karma ("Retreatant Karma") or Drup-la Karma Yeshé Tharchin, was born in 1953 in the Tashi Yangtsé region of eastern Bhutan, near the site of Pemaling, a hidden land sacred to Padmasambhava. He began his formal education in Tibetan language and Buddhadharma at an early age, under the tutelage of his father, Lama Sönam Wangchuk. By the time he was thirteen, he was already serving as a scribe in a royally commissioned project to prepare an edition of the Kangyur in golden ink in Thimphu, the capital of Bhutan, far to the west of where he was born.

Later he returned to the region of his birth and began intensive training at Long Nying Chöling Monastery, practicing the five sets of one hundred thousand accumulations of the Longchen Nyingtik preliminaries and learning various aspects of ritual performance. By about 1979, the twenty-six-year-old Tsampa Karma had been introduced to the extraordinary Tibetan yogin who would become his root guru: Lama Naljorpa Sönam Druktop (1934–1994). By this time Lama Naljorpa was already an accomplished master of Mahāmudrā and Dzokchen, having spent nine years of intensive study and retreat under the tutelage of masters from all four traditions of Tibetan Buddhism (after his escape to India in 1961), followed by nine years of retreat in various sacred places throughout Bhutan. Lama

Naljorpa's root guru was Tokden Sönam Chölek, who had been the principal tutor to the Eighth Khamtrul Rinpoché, Dongyü Nyima.

Upon meeting Lama Naljorpa, Tsampa Karma became one of his closest disciples, following a strict regimen of instruction and retreat practice for about the next three years in the Durong Charnel Ground in the region of Tashi Yangtsé. With a few other young disciples, Tsampa Karma received transmission and instruction in several forms of *chöd* practice, in the yogic conduct of equal taste, and in the Six Yogas of Nāropa in the Drikung Kagyü lineage. He completed two three-month mantra retreats focused on Avalokiteśvara and Amitāyus, respectively, as well as a seven-month retreat on the *Rikdzin Düpa* (a Nyingma guru yoga sādhana of the Longchen Nyingtik) and a one-hundred-day retreat on the four revolutions in outlook.

He received extensive transmissions on the stages of the path of the Mahāyāna, including (among others) Śāntideva's *Guide to the Bodhisattva's Way of Life*, Patrul Rinpoché's *Words of My Perfect Teacher*, Sakya Paṇḍita's *Ascertaining the Three Sets of Vows*, Gyalsé Tokmé Zangpo's *Thirty-Seven Practices of a Bodhisattva*, the *Profound Instructions on the View of the Middle Way*, and Sachen Kunga Nyingpo's *Parting from the Four Types of Clinging*. He also received teachings from Lama Naljorpa on key practices in the Nyingma tradition, including *Liberation Upon Hearing in the Intermediate State* (*Bardo Thödröl*), revealed by Karma Lingpa, and Düdjom Rinpoché's *Extracting the Vital Essence of Accomplishment: Concise and Clear Advice for Practice in a Mountain Retreat*. We see in the teaching that follows here that Lama Karma quotes frequently from the *Spiritual Songs of Milarepa*, the *Three Phrases That Strike the Crucial Points* by Garab Dorjé, and the *Gangama Instructions on Mahāmudrā* by the Mahāsiddha Tilopa, all of which he learned at that time.

During this period in the Durong Charnel Ground, Tsampa Karma and his fellow retreatants also received detailed instructions from Lama Naljorpa on the nine stages of mental stillness—or the nine attentional states—that culminate in the achievement of śamatha, and they were instructed to put these into practice in short periods of retreat right away. Yet when Tsampa Karma expressed to Lama Naljorpa his yearning and intention to actually achieve śamatha, Lama Naljorpa was delighted, and began to take him through a strict regimen designed precisely as preparation for this path.

As we see in the account translated below, Tsampa Karma was first guided through a practice to purify the body, speech, and mind, and only after passing a test with respect to his proficiency in that practice was he granted instructions on how to investigate whether the mind truly has any origin, location, or destination. It was only after several months of this investigation that his guru taught him how to identify "the triad of stillness, movement, and awareness" (which is a practice very similar to "taking the mind as the path" as taught by Düdjom Lingpa). Following this, Lama Naljorpa introduced Tsampa Karma to the actual nature of mind so that he would be ready to engage in the core practice of śamatha without a sign, not simply as it is held in common with the Sūtrayāna, but as it is embedded deeply within the context of the teachings of Mahāmudrā and Dzokchen. Thus, such practice of śamatha without a sign prepares one for the requisite stability of *meditation* to sustain the *view* of cutting through.

Tsampa Karma then entered a period of six or seven months in extremely strict retreat within a "sealed hut"; that is, he only emerged in the middle of the night to fetch water, when he would not see anyone else. This retreat also took place at the Durong Charnel Ground.

As Drupön Lama Karma explains below, this sealed retreat was followed by about five years during which his challenge was to integrate into his conduct the meditative equipoise he had attained in strict, sealed retreat. In the first year or so following that retreat, he completed another six- or seven-month retreat focused on the Seven-Line Supplication to Guru Rinpoché at Delek Namkha Kyung Dzong, high in the snow-capped mountains near the sacred site of Pemaling, where he was staying in the same cave as Lama Naljorpa. Tsampa Karma would also wander in the sacred area of Pemaling and would practice in frightening places haunted by many spirits. He also spent many months focused solely on the Dzokchen practices of cutting through and the direct crossing over. Then Lama Naljorpa asked Tsampa Karma to serve as the scribe for the renowned treasure revealer Pegyal Lingpa (1924–1988), who was transmitting the *Kusum Gongdü* at Sengé Dzong in response to profound supplications and offerings made by Lama Naljorpa. Tsampa Karma spent these years of active Dharma service (1984–1988) in a constant practice of mindfulness but not in strict, closed retreat. He commented at the time that he was sad not to be in formal retreat, but Lama Naljorpa replied that it was indeed a kind of retreat since he was not engaged in mundane activities.

Even while Tertön Pegyal Lingpa was still alive, Lama Karma was the one to bestow the oral transmission of Pegyal Lingpa's *Kusum Gongdü* treasure to an assembly of tulkus, lamas, and practitioners, while Pegyal Lingpa granted the actual empowerments, soon before he passed away in 1988. Following this juncture, Lama Karma gradually became Drupön Lama Karma ("Retreat Master"), completing two three-year retreats at Lama Naljorpa's former seat in Phurpa Ling (near Dechen Phodrang, outside of Thimphu) and then guiding a three-year retreat at Pema Yangdzong Monastery in Paro, Bhutan, where Drup-la has continued to serve as retreat master. In all, he spent more than eighteen years devoted to a life of retreat.

Drupön Lama Karma has also received extensive teachings and transmissions from the great Kagyü and Nyingma lamas of the late-twentieth and early twenty-first century, including Düdjom Rinpoché, both the Sixteenth and Seventeenth Karmapas, and Dilgo Khyentsé Rinpoché. Drupön Lama Karma's wife and spiritual partner is Khandro Tsering Drölkar. He currently lives with his family near Paro, Bhutan, guiding disciples in retreat both in Bhutan and around the world.[164]

164. For further information about Drupön Lama Karma, including ongoing teachings, see: https://druponkarmajnana.com. See also the extensive biography of Lama Naljorpa: https://druponkarmajnana.com/index.php/about/.

20. Experiential Instructions on Śamatha

Drupön Lama Karma

Santa Barbara, California, October 20, 2019

I was asked to give an account of the stages of my practice when I was in retreat. In general, I don't like talking about my experiences, not even my dreams, and my lamas would not be pleased. They say that someone who does that is a "jaded practitioner who spills from the mouth," whose mind is incorrigible and untamed by the Dharma. There is no custom to talk about these things publicly. But Lama Alan asked me to talk about what teachings I requested of my lama when I was practicing śamatha, and what kinds of certainties arose through my practice, including the conjoined practices of śamatha and vipaśyanā.

So, today I will explain different methods of śamatha meditation, including śamatha with a sign, śamatha without a sign, and the śrāvakas' way of meditating. There are many different methods taught by the lamas of the past. I will first discuss the way of meditating that relies upon counting the breaths. Counting the breaths is said to be one of the ways to establish śamatha. Normally, we have never tried to take care of or control our minds with our minds, but we let our minds follow after whatever thoughts and appearances come up. That is how the ordinary mind operates. But if we are going to meditate, we have to take care of our minds, and a method for that is to count the breaths, which leads to good experiences, proper ascertainments, and clarity of mind.

The mind is like the king of the body, speech, and mind. It has great strength and tremendous ability, but it has very little ability to place limits on itself. Therefore, when the time comes to meditate, we must reach the point where we can bring the mind under control. When you are able to do this, then, gradually your mind turns inward, and does not follow freely after thoughts. Little by little, it is corralled within. So you must train your mind to be able to settle in its own place. When we practice counting the breaths, once we become well experienced in that, then with no need to continue counting the breaths, the mind naturally settles. Normally, in our daily lives, the mind becomes distracted by an amazing number of thoughts, but when we have cultivated śamatha, there is a state of mind with no thoughts at all, which, marvelously, you can experience with ease. Once you have achieved śamatha, you can go there, but it would be difficult to go there all at once. So as a method for going there we train in dependence upon the respiration; like ascending a staircase one step at a time, you cannot get to the second step without reaching the first step, and without reaching the second step, you cannot ascend to the third. So just like gradually ascending a staircase, you need to understand the stages of practice, and then the śamatha of those who have gone through the process of developing good habits will become stable. This is a special method for making progress in śamatha.

Count one breath for each full cycle of exhalation and inhalation. Don't count two for one exhalation and one inhalation. For example, if you exhale and then inhale, in a very relaxed way, that is called one cycle of respiration. So, in the beginning, count each of those up to seven cycles of the breath. Don't count a lot of breaths, for this will create obstacles from the conceptualization that arises in between. Although thoughts continue to arise, here is a method so that you do not fall under their domination: you merge the many thoughts into just one thought for each cycle of the respiration, like many streams merging into the one Ganges River. Then, in the course of counting one cycle of respiration, thoughts will still be there, but once you have channeled them together, you make them into one thought, and then gradually it will be easy to reach stability. If you continue to let your mind follow after all the various thoughts of the three times—past, present, and future—you will not be able to stabilize your śamatha.

For beginners, it is best to count just seven breaths, for the siddhas of the past have said that one should have short sessions and many of them. There is great value in this. I have much experience in this regard. When you think, "Now, I'm going to meditate," and then stay there meditating for a very long time, sometimes the mind wanders around in the past, present, and future; sometimes it doesn't. Sometimes it's clear and undistracted, but you cannot remain there. Rather, when counting the breaths, you should think, "I might make a mistake," and really focus as you exhale and then inhale, and when you make your mind remain on that, you gather all the thoughts together into a single thought. With the concern that you might lose count, when you sustain this mindfulness, then in this meditation there is the mindfulness of śamatha, which is without forgetfulness. Then with each exhalation and inhalation count once, maintaining your mindfulness with the constant concern that you might lose count. If you count more than seven, thoughts will infiltrate your mindfulness. But as a start, as one successfully counts from one to seven again and again, after becoming trained in this, without ever becoming distracted by infiltrating thoughts when counting from one to seven, then you can count up to twelve. Thus you lengthen it.

Normally, during the first moment we're thinking about one thing, then during the next moment, we're thinking about something else, and in the third moment yet another thought arises. Since the mind isn't under control, we don't recognize that these thoughts are arising, for they're like water that spreads all over a plain. But now, by counting the breaths, like draining all the water into one channel, thoughts are merged into the thoughts of counting, thus decreasing in number.

So you gather all the thoughts together and place them into the count. When one follows the explanation from experience, meditating for a long time in that way, the result will come. If one has experience in meditation, then one knows the meditative experiences. One understands. But if you just hear and talk a lot about meditation, you have no experience. A long time ago, I received from my lama the instructions on how to meditate. Then I meditated a great deal. Later, when I was meditating near a river gorge, at first, I would hear the sound of the river outside, but as my mind gradually calmed down and remained still, I would hear the sound of the river from within. I would hear all sounds within. Such experience arises through familiarization, and you need to know how far your meditation has progressed.

Normally, we don't notice tiny sounds, but when meditating, with familiarization over a long period of time, on occasion you'll very clearly experience momentary sounds like that of your own heart beating, which we don't normally hear when we are doing other things. When we do, this is a sign that conceptualization has subsided. Once it has subsided, various sensations and experiences continually arise.

Once you have brought your respiration to a pace that is slow and gentle, that is enough. You do not need to make the breath faster or slower. You do not need to breathe more quickly. Breathe gently, with your mind relaxed and happily settled. After you've practiced a lot in that way, when your practice of śamatha is going well, then sounds like that of the wind, cars, airplanes, and human voices will be experienced inside. When you focus outside, outer appearances will be unimpeded and luminous, like a drawing made of rainbows; then when you look at visual objects such as mountains, rivers, snow, sky, gardens, and forest, they will appear as though luminous and empty. Meanwhile, when you look inwardly, it will seem as though everything is of the nature of emptiness and luminosity, with nothing to be seen. When you meditate on the union of these two [outer and inner], all sounds will be experienced from within. This comes from a great deal of śamatha meditation. If you have not yet reached even just the single-pointed stage, you won't understand these things. From śamatha, you go to the single-pointed yoga, and you eventually progress to the yoga of one taste and the yoga of nonmeditation. This is the way to progress in Mahāmudrā.

So you have to get to the single-pointed yoga, right? This is a practice for arriving at śamatha, the single-pointed yoga. So we have to understand these things, which I explained earlier.

Another sign of progress is that you can remember events from previous lifetimes, or else from a long time ago in this lifetime, that you had completely forgotten. When you are cultivating śamatha, it is possible for the memory of them to return. There's a story of one great meditator who lent a book to his friend, and he forgot about it for many years, and then one day when he was meditating, the thought suddenly arose that "Oh, one day, years ago, I lent this book to so and so." He remembered this. This is good meditation! You can remember anything. This is what Milarepa says:[165]

> Please doubt the mistake of thinking
> self-emergent, spontaneous effulgence
> and many memories showing up directly
> are all just about the same, same, same.

Right now, for us, "self-emergent, spontaneous effulgence"[166] could mean memories from your many past lives—in this context. Being able to remember clearly things you did in an earlier part of this life, having that memory reawakened, is what having "many memories showing up directly" refers to. But this can happen even to those who have not yet practiced meditation. We can have all sorts of memories about things we did in the past, and those are not "self-emergent, spontaneous effulgences," but rather just "many memories showing up directly." "Self-emergent, spontaneous effulgence" means remembering distinct events from your past lives. Sometimes this

165. This verse is from the *Spiritual Songs of Milarepa* (*mi la'i gsung mgur mdzod nag ma*).

166. In general, this phrase refers only to that which arises spontaneously from realization of pristine awareness, not merely from the substrate consciousness, so that is the deeper distinction that is being referred to here, even though memories from past lives can indeed arise simply from the substrate consciousness.

can indeed happen. It is coming from the root of practice. But then there is also just the reawakening of memories from the earlier part of our lives.

Another method is to focus on an image, such as the form of a deity or the body of the Buddha, which is a kind of śamatha with a sign and is a practice for us Buddhists. For this you first prepare a painted scroll of the Buddha's body, not too large or too small, not larger than one cubit and not smaller than one handspan in height. It should be clear, but not shiny, and in a relaxed, joyful way, focus on that, not too close or far away—a distance of about the length of an ox yoke. If it's far away, thoughts will be more scattered, and if the image is too large, that will cause thoughts to scatter. Having a smaller object is a method for drawing thoughts inward. In stage of generation practice, in the samādhi of generating the deity, we focus on very tiny visualizations, such as the seed syllables inside the *samādhisattva*, but they must be very clear. These are powerful means to withdraw the mind inward. But if the [physical] visual object is too small, so that you cannot see it clearly, it's hard to focus on it, so this is not good. Also, the object of meditation should not be fluttering due to wind or moving about but should be stable. There are extensive explanations of the many benefits of practicing śamatha this way in the *Samādhirāja Sūtra*, but this is a rough account of the reasons for practicing in this way.

First, this method serves to calm the mind, and second, focusing on the body of the Buddha develops a state of mind with intense clarity, so it serves you well for both the practice of śamatha and the stage of generation. When you focus on the image of the Buddha's body, at the beginning focus your gaze on the coil of hair between the Buddha's eyebrows. When you get bored or dull, shift your gaze to different parts of the body, such as the eyes, nose, arms, legs, and implements. Then you can also focus on the whole body and again narrow in on specific parts of his body. At the beginning, when you are training, you should look with your eyes and focus your mind on what you see with your eyes. It is a method to tame your mind. Sometimes, when your mind becomes stable and thoughts have subsided, then even if you close your eyes, you will still see the image mentally.

There was a shepherd boy who became a disciple of Milarepa known as Lukdzi Repa (Cotton-Clad Shepherd), who later became a mahāsiddha. When he was looking after his flock of sheep, he encountered Milarepa and asked him to teach him meditation. Milarepa instructed him just to "visualize on the tip of your nose an image of the Buddha, remain there single-pointedly, and then come back to me." So he went away, found the wall of a ruin and, while leaning against it with his body straight and his hands in meditation posture, he meditated on a tiny image of the Buddha. But after some time, he forgot [all else] and seven days went by. He was a shepherd, and his parents and other relatives were worried that he had become lost. They looked for him everywhere and eventually came to Milarepa and asked him whether their boy had come here. Milarepa told them that their son had come to him to learn how to meditate, he had taught him to visualize the Buddha, and then he had left. They asked how long ago this had happened, and he replied it had been about seven days. Eventually they found him, but he seemed to be zoned out, with his eyes downcast. When they touched him, they aroused him and asked what he had been doing. He replied that he had been meditating. "Is that what meditation is about?" they asked, commenting that they hadn't seen him for seven days. He replied that he had just sat down to meditate. From his perspective only a moment had gone by, but his mindfulness had been lost and seven days had gone by.

This happened several times, so they told him they couldn't look after him anymore, for this had brought them much distress, so he should return to Milarepa. The shepherd reported back to Milarepa that he had focused on Śākaymuni's body, but he lost mindfulness, without any sense of the passage of time. Only afterward, when he saw how the sun had moved, did he recognize that time had passed. When he entered meditation, it was evening, and when the clarity of his mindfulness was restored, it was morning. Only in that way could he believe that time had passed. Milarepa told him, "This is called 'stagnant śamatha' and is not a sign of having achieved śamatha, nor a virtue of having reached the path, nor is it something that should or shouldn't happen. But if you revive this with vividness of attention, this will help you in the practice of vipaśyanā. As an analogy, just as the sun rises gradually, so do the signs of the path in meditation occur only gradually. You should not think they happen all of a sudden. When you meditate, signs of the qualities of the path arise, but you shouldn't think stagnant śamatha is something excellent.[167] Now if you can remain with me for twelve years devoted to the practice of vipaśyanā, then you can report on your progress in vipaśyanā. If you can't do that, then you won't be able to give such a report."

The shepherd then asked Milarepa to guide him, saying, "I enjoy meditating, and with thanks, please teach me." Later, he became a great mahāsiddha, but for the years in between, he had difficulty controlling his mind; whether for two or three days, or for five or six days, he would lose mindfulness. Later, he wrote in his autobiography how he practiced, what kind of experiences he had, and how Milarepa corrected him.

Those are examples of practices of śamatha with a sign, and the stages of practice on that basis are set forth definitively in the sūtras and treatises as the nine stages of mental stillness, or nine attentional states by which one engages samādhi, but we are not able to practice of all them now. For now, the first three stages of mental stillness are important, so they should be known. They are directed engagement, continual engagement, and resurgent engagement. For śamatha, these are extremely important.

When you begin practicing śamatha, conceptualization seems to increase. In fact, thoughts are always arising, but we don't take charge of them or recognize them. But when we practice śamatha, we can clearly recognize how many thoughts come up and how the mind works. As conceptualization increases, it seems to arise as unhappiness or as though we are being tossed about in a great storm. Everyone experiences many of these kinds of powerful thoughts—which are unlike anything they have expe-

167. This "stagnant śamatha" can be compared to the "flawed śamatha" described by Karma Chakmé, above.

rienced before—when they practice śamatha, and they may feel discouraged, thinking they're really poor at meditation and that they'll never make any progress. Then they should seek advice from a qualified lama who will tell them that this is a sign of experience; those thoughts were occurring all along, but they weren't recognized. The lama will tell them that this is the "meditative experience of recognizing thoughts" that comes once you are practicing. I personally have had a lot of experience with this. When I would meditate, thoughts would rise up strongly: I found it very difficult when I was practicing śamatha in retreat for six months while sealed inside a mud hut. That phase of the meditative experience of recognizing thoughts happened to me just like that. But if you don't meditate, you won't recognize thoughts.

When I came to Lama Naljorpa to request guidance in my meditative practice, he first gave me a practice to purify the body, speech, and mind. If one failed to pass the test related to that, then he would not grant the instructions on investigating the origin, location, and destination of the mind. When I did succeed in that, then he guided me for several months in inquiring into the origin, location, and destination of the mind. Then he taught me "the triad of stillness, movement, and awareness," after which he introduced me to pristine awareness, saying, "Now, your meditation is this." So he pointed it out precisely with his finger. Then during the six months in the sealed meditation hut, I solely practiced śamatha. For two of those months I didn't even recite my daily commitments.

After about seven days, I became extremely depressed with the amount of conceptualization that was coming up—one thought after another, relentlessly. When I recognized that, then all through the night, with my eyes wide open, the thoughts would arise constantly, and that was torture. I thought, "I'm making this suffering for myself. I can't handle it! If this is the kind of difficulty that arises if one meditates, it would be better just to try to enjoy myself! It would be better to do something else, to recite *maṇi* mantras, to offer the regular *gaṇacakras*, perform rituals, and meditate on the stage of generation."

Later, when my lama came to see me, he told me, "This was happening to you all along, but in the past, you weren't aware of it. Conceptualization is occurring constantly. Now due to your practice, as you've been cultivating śamatha, you are recognizing what's going on in your mind. This is called the 'meditative experience of recognizing thoughts.'[168] This is the first barrier to dhyāna. If you don't cross over this hurdle, if you try to avoid it, since you won't be able to recognize thoughts, your practice will develop only partially. Only about one out of a hundred can get through this. It's difficult. If you can meditate, then you will become adept in coping with these naturally arising feelings and experiences. If you don't meditate, or if you meditate for an hour or two each day, but then rest and become distracted, you won't progress. You have to meditate single-pointedly after you have sealed your hut. When you meditate single-pointedly, then the first meditative experience of dhyāna, 'the experience of movement,' occurs when conceptualization bursts forth like a cascading mountain brook. You will encounter its essential nature. In the Mahāmudrā instruction known as *The Ganges*, the Indian mahāsiddha Tilopa said that for novices, thoughts flow like a cascading mountain brook. These thoughts weren't absent previously, but you weren't aware of them. Once you cross over the first hurdle, then gradually, over time, you must reach the 'meditative experience of recovering from preceding thoughts.' Then, little by little, they gradually withdraw. Now you have recognized thoughts, and you must definitely cross over this hurdle; if you cannot cross this hurdle, then no matter what practices or rituals you perform, fine experiences will never come. So this is the first experience."

For six months I focused solely on śamatha in the sealed hut. Sometimes various thoughts would arise a bit more strongly, sometimes the practice would be pleasant, and I had all kinds of experiences. When I emerged from my meditation hut after six months, all appearances manifested as never before. Outer appearances of the grass, rocks, crops, trees, and mountains

168. This is also known as the "experience of movement."

arose, but when assessed with mindfulness and introspection, I saw them differently. I reported this to my lama, and because my lama had gained the realization that is "like space," he [understood immediately, and] quoted the saying from Jetsun [Milarepa]:[169]

> Please doubt the mistake of thinking that
> being affixed to the nectar of śamatha
> and meditation that has taken hold
> of the indwelling as one's own place
> is all just about the same, same, same.

So he told me that I had not yet taken hold of the eternal kingdom of the indwelling [mind], but that some say that meditation that takes hold of the eternal kingdom of the indwelling and being stuck to the nectar of śamatha are the same! Then, Lama Naljorpa said, "Right now, whatever you see and whatever you feel and whatever you look at is arising as an experience in the nature of clear luminosity and emptiness. So if, whatever you look upon, you remain without moving, with your mind completely unwavering, then whatever you see will have the aspect of clear luminosity, so you will see everything as having become empty, and a state of mind will arise that realizes things to be completely devoid of true existence."

Once he had said this, my lama laughed and said, "You've been practicing śamatha quite a lot, so you are affixed to the nectar of śamatha, but as for taking hold of the eternal kingdom of the indwelling, in the future, with respect to all of this, if you continue to meditate a great deal, then you will come upon something like that, and at that time, you will take hold of the eternal kingdom. Right now, your śamatha has become affixed to its nectar. You have achieved a partial degree of vipaśyanā, enough to recognize it, but it's not actual, definitive vipaśyanā, because, as it is said,[170]

169. This, too, is from the *Spiritual Songs of Milarepa*.

170. This verse is from *The Golden Key to the Essential Meaning of Mahāmudrā* (*Phyag rgya*

When you recognize
this self-cognizing awareness,
which is luminous and free of grasping,
as spontaneous actualization,
you have reached the end of the single-pointed yoga.

When your mind is clear and free of grasping, then from the perspective of your state of mind, it is not holding on to anything at all, and when you have actually seen that, this is an aspect of vipaśyanā, but at this point actual, definitive vipaśyanā has not yet arisen."

That was my way of meditating. I've been asked to speak about this, so I have.

My lama told me that from now on I should not let my mind wander at any time. I was to sustain my mindfulness and introspection without distraction twenty-four hours every day. From that point onward, for five years I didn't engage in any studies of obscurative dharmas but focused solely on sustaining the mindfulness and introspection I had developed earlier. For just five years of such practice, my mind would still become distracted at night, but I was able to maintain continuous mindfulness throughout the whole day. During this time, at a certain point, I served as the scribe for Pegyal Lingpa as he was narrating his mind treasures, and according to my lama's instructions I would examine how many lines I could go before my mind would wander, or how many pages I could go before being distracted. I would observe how long I could maintain mindfulness during one session with him without becoming distracted, and how many steps I could go before my mind would wander, after a session had finished and I was walking. I had a long way to walk home, for I lived up in the mountains. Sometimes I would go by car with my lama, and sometimes by foot. On all such occasions I had no other practice than to maintain undistracted mind-

chen po'i bsdus don gser gyi lde mig).

fulness, called *staring down the face of appearances*,[171] in reliance upon mindfulness and introspection. After about five years, from the time I awoke in the morning until I went to bed at night, I was able to sustain continuous mindfulness [of pristine awareness]. So this was probably the medium stage of the single-pointed [yoga]. It was not the great stage.

At that point, I was able to experience luminosity not only during the day but also through the night. Sometimes while dreaming at night, I would recognize dreams that had been aroused from afflictive habitual propensities. Dreams would arise as the clear light, and sometimes I would be able to observe the stages of dissolution. For us right now, when we fall asleep, our minds dissolve into the substrate consciousness, we dream, and apart from the time when we awake from sleep, we don't understand what is going on at all. When you practice śamatha a lot, you can recognize the stages of dissolution and re-emergence of the dark near-attainment, the white appearance, and the red emergence. And when I was about to wake up, I could observe all the dream appearances dissolving back into the substrate. Then when mindfulness was restored, and appearances of coarse mindfulness emerged, I could observe the gradual arising of daytime appearances. So, when śamatha is cultivated, it is useful for us in that way. That was my way of meditating.

For ordinary sentient beings, whenever appearances arise throughout the day, they don't recognize pristine awareness, so they are distracted to appearances; they're caught up in conceptualization, and habitual propensities are stored in their substrates. When they fall asleep, all the appearances to their eight configurations of consciousness dissolve inwardly, and then in the end they go into the dark near-attainment. This is the very same dark near-attainment that you will enter while on the path. It is what happens at death too. But right now, while we are practicing, after we've

171. Tib. *snang ba gdong 'ded*. This is a technical term that means embracing all appearances with single-pointed mindfulness and introspection, usually in the context of a single-pointed mindfulness that is immersed in pristine awareness, and not merely the mindfulness of śamatha.

crossed beyond the dark near-attainment of the substrate, then, from the reversal of that dark near-attainment, mindfulness is restored, and subtle consciousness and appearances emerge. Dreams emerge the whole night long, drawing on habitual propensities stored in the substrate, and one sees those dream appearances. Then, when they are worn out, and the duration of dream appearances is finished, they dissolve back into the dark near-attainment, and when the dark near-attainment reverses sequence, our current appearances arise from it again.

So this goes back and forth, such that we're deluded during the dream state, and if we don't recognize pristine awareness, we're deluded during the waking state. The buddhas realize that appearances in the dream state and waking state are both devoid of true existence, and they recognize that dreams and the waking state are equally delusional, so they realize this without delusion. We don't realize that. We may think we're deluded in the dream state and that nothing is truly existent, but during the waking state we think everything is real and truly existent. But buddhas know that all our currently appearing phenomena are deceptive. When you come to know that, then with the practices of the path, on the basis of your śamatha, you use the awareness of vipaśyanā, and then you'll be able to experience many objects of consciousness with pristine awareness.

Now we should probably abbreviate the presentation. Whenever we meditate, there are two very important instruments to be put to use: mindfulness and introspection. When we first focus our attention on an image such as that of the Buddha, when it appears in its entirety before the mind, and the mind quickly comes to it, this is called *directed mental engagement*. Maintaining our attention on that appearance without abandoning it is called *mindfulness*. There are two meanings of "mindfulness" (Tib. *dran pa*). On the one hand, it refers to recollecting past events, including actions we've done long, long ago. In that case we call it "remembering" (*dran pa*). But here we are not using that mental faculty. In the context of śamatha, mindfulness refers to sustaining our focus [for example,] on the image of the deity, which is appearing in its entirety, without letting it become distracted. In addition, it enables us to be aware of the vivid and empty aspects of the object, without slipping into laxity or excitation. This is "mindfulness."

When we are counting our breaths, it is with mindfulness that we sustain our attention as we count "one, two, three . . . ," taking extreme care not to lose count. When our attention strays, and we lose track of the count, this is due to the loss of mindfulness. Then, *mental engagement* means the object is appearing to the mind. When the object is appearing but our attention is once again distracted, the mental faculty by which we recognize this fault in mindfulness is called *introspection*. Mindfulness and introspection are our most important tools.

There are also two distinguishing qualities of our minds. The quality of mind by which we clearly distinguish the particular characteristics of the external objects to which we may direct our attention, such as identifying "that is a light, that is a painting," and so on, as well as using investigation and analysis to identify individual characteristics, such as "that is white, that is red, that is black," and so on, may be called *self-cognizing and self-illuminating* (Tib. *rang rig rang gsal*). Along with that, the part of the mind that experiences the onset of the thoughts that identify individual qualities such as color is called *introspection* (Tib. *shes bzhin*). This is the precise place where we point out the name [introspection]. Therefore, with a focus on experience, when you meditate, there will come an experience where there are no thoughts at all—where, amazingly, they have all been pacified. You can experience this! At the same time, in order to be able to remain in this peace, you need strong enthusiasm. Whether meditation goes well or not depends on mindfulness and introspection. If you are someone whose mindfulness is stable and introspection is sharp, and if you actually do meditate, then when you meditate, your meditation will go quite well. Even if mindfulness is present, if introspection lapses, then our mindfulness will not be restored to its object once it has been distracted elsewhere, so you will not be able to attain [the third attentional state of] resurgent engagement.

When, relying on mindfulness and introspection, you are able to sustain your attention for a while, that is called *continual engagement*, and with *resurgent engagement* you develop even greater continuity. At this [third] stage, even if you cannot remain engaged with the object continuously, you're immediately able to recognize when your mind has become distracted by a single conceptualization—such as drifting off into memories of going to India, visiting Bodh Gayā, and so on—that is, when conceptualization flows on and on, taking your mindfulness with it. But at this stage of resurgent engagement, you immediately recognize with introspection that your attention has strayed, and you can bring it right back to the object. Introspection is like a shepherd, for it looks after the mind to prevent it from being carried away by conceptualization. When the attention strays, introspection restores it again and again to the meditative object. If it is not restored, then conceptualization will flow continuously.

At the moment when the mind has settled well for a given session, it's important to stop the session. If you don't stop before there is scattering, before conceptualization has had a chance to arise in a stream, then stability will not arise. Right now, our practice of meditation is not stable. Until the mind is stabilized and conceptualization no longer infiltrates, you need to correct for scattering. Until conceptualization doesn't arise at all for five or ten minutes or even half an hour, you should have short sessions again and again, for if you do that, conceptualization won't as easily carry you away. "Many sessions of short duration"—that is what has been taught by supreme siddhas of the past, and it is important. One might think it's important to have long sessions, but unless one's meditation is inwardly stable, coarse or subtle undercurrents of conceptualization will continue to flow, like water moving beneath grass, hay, or husks of grain. Attention will stray as if it had been carried away by a thief. You need to recognize whether or not your mindfulness is stable, and when you restore it and you're able to stop conceptualization, it is like waves that subside back into the ocean. Or like a rainbow fading back into the sky. Once you have recognized the nature of your mind, it's best if conceptualization simply disappears into that fundamental character.

It's important to properly recognize stillness. If you don't, then the proximate enemies, laxity and dullness, will arise. You need to recognize movements of the mind. If you don't, then undercurrents of thoughts will flow. Likewise, you need to recognize awareness. If you don't, you will be lost in confusion.

Apart from staring down the face of appearances, there is no other practice.

> Whether walking, relaxing, standing, or lying down,
> Gather the mind.
> This is what it means to practice virtue,
> without sessions or in-between.

There is no period between sessions. There are neither sessions nor post-meditation sessions. When you are practicing staring down the face of appearances, during sessions you are "gluing yourself to meditative experience," so with regard to "post-meditation," it is not as though there is one and then a second. During both you are practicing *staring down the face of pristine awareness*[172] or staring down the face of appearances.

Teaching on How to Practice a Session of Meditation

Whether our meditation sessions are short or long, they should be comprised of three stages: preparation, the actual meditation, and the conclusion. The preparation is the generation of bodhicitta, the actual meditation is non-referential, and the conclusion is the dedication. The preparation—the generation of bodhicitta—is virtue, so your practice is imbued with skillful means. Regarding the non-referential actual meditation, neither

172. Tib. *rig pa gdong 'ded.*

thoughts, nor the roughness of thoughts, as it were, arise within the meditation. The mind settles in its own nature, or awareness settles in its own nature, which means that it's not sullied by thoughts of the past, future, and present, but is perfectly pure. The mind's essential nature is empty and its manifest nature is not simply vacuous but is luminous, so there is a union of emptiness and luminosity. When it arises vividly, it will not succumb to laxity and excitation. This is called the non-referential actual meditation.

Whatever roots of virtue you practice, the end of the session should not be obstructed with negative thoughts. After you've finished practicing, continue with authentic prayers of dedication of all your virtue for the sake of all sentient beings throughout space. This is like pouring a drop of water into the ocean, so that until the ocean dries up, your drop of water, being mixed with the ocean, will not be extinguished. Likewise, your roots of virtue will not be extinguished until enlightenment is achieved but will increase more and more. Longchenpa spoke of these three things to cherish as you traverse the path to liberation, and whether your sessions are long or short, they must be imbued with these three.

Within the triad of teaching, listening, and practicing meditation, we have finished teaching and listening, so now it's time to meditate. Arouse the aspiration "May all sentient beings throughout space achieve the precious state of enlightenment!" Then, to begin, engage in the ninefold cleansing of the stale winds. Then, there are some winds remaining that have not entered, so you want to take in the remaining winds. So those of you who are familiar with the vase breathing, you may proceed with that. If you are not familiar with the vase breathing, then you can simply release the remaining breath gently through the nose and mouth, with your hands on the knees. Relax your mind. Then, as it is said, "If you make the auspicious form with your body, then realizations will dawn in your mind," so adopt the seven-point posture of Vairocana, or if that is uncomfortable, then you can sit up straight in the bodhisattva posture. Your entire body and mind should be relaxed. Then offer prayers of supplication to the lineage of your lamas, finishing with this prayer:

> Come, my precious root guru, shining in glory,
> sit atop the lotus and moon upon my crown,
> and in your great kindness take me after you;
> please grant me the siddhis of body, speech, and mind.

Then, you can visualize the one whose essential nature is your root lama in the form of our teacher, Śākyamuni, coming to be seated upon the lotus and moon above the crown of your head. Then call for blessings that your meditation in this session will go well. Imagine that you receive blessings, and then your lama melts into light and as a ball of light enters your crown *cakra*, descends to the center of your heart, and finally dissolves into your heart. Then imagine that the Buddha's mind and your mind become inseparable, of one taste.

Once you have come to that point, you enter the actual meditation. View thoughts of the past as aspects of your mind and prevent them from entering. Do not usher in thoughts of the future; instead, stop them. This brings your consciousness to the present. Don't investigate or analyze this consciousness. When practicing śamatha, this consciousness that is the dominant condition, what you call your "mind," does not have any location where it can be determined. Therefore, when you observe the essential nature of your mind, when you can't point to it, you see that it's empty. But not only is it empty, the luminosity of visual, auditory, olfactory, gustatory, and tactile sensations remains unimpeded. As Milarepa said to Rechungpa, his spiritual son:

> May this wish-fulfilling jewel of the
> precious samādhi of luminosity and emptiness
> arise in your mindstream, Rechungpa, my son.

The mind has the two inseparable aspects of luminosity and emptiness. Its emptiness is devoid of laxity and its luminosity is devoid of dullness. Laxity and dullness are transcended. You will never quite arrive at the consciousness of the present moment that transcends origination, cessation, and abiding, which is empty awareness, but you remain right there for as long as you can. That is called *meditative equipoise.*

Whatever thoughts arise, simply release them. Don't try to block them, for you will never succeed. Also, don't fall under the influence of an autonomous stream of conceptualization, for that is delusional. With respect to these thoughts, we need to understand how to release them into their ground, their aspect of liberation. The ground, the mind that is unborn and unceasing, has an aspect that is utterly empty. Although all kinds of thoughts may arise from that, when thoughts have been turned around, they can be released once again, within that aspect of freedom. We need to be able to give rise to a strong conviction in the state that does not "identify" the essential nature.[173] Rechungpa said, "Thoughts of the past have ceased and disappeared. Those of the future have not yet arisen. Those of the present are unidentifiable." It is called "the transcendence of identification." The mind whose essential nature is free of identification finally leads to the Madhyamaka view, the Mahāmudrā view, and the view of the Great Perfection. When cultivating śamatha—depending on the level of your practice, be it great, middling, or small; on the qualities of your channels and elements; and the strength of your courage, or how far one has advanced—for some people, due to the purity of their karma, it is possible for them to recognize their own pristine awareness. The mind that is free of thoughts of the three times is the best.

When you hear the sound of the chime [that begins the meditation session] fading away, settle your mind in its natural state, and from that point onward, do your best not to become distracted.

Meditative equipoise is said to be *space-like,* for it is like empty space. When you arise from meditative equipoise with your space-like, luminous, empty mind, you might think, "Now my session is over, so I don't need to

173. This practice is said to be *free of identifying and of not identifying.*

meditate"—but don't think you're now on vacation. Between sessions you must sustain the mindfulness of meditative equipoise and blend it with your everyday activities. You should unify your meditative equipoise and post-meditative state.

When you're first practicing, you may practice for an hour of formal meditation and shorter periods of post-meditation, such as ten minutes, which you try to blend with your meditative state. As you are able to maintain your meditative mindfulness throughout your post-meditative periods, then you should extend the post-meditative practice to twenty minutes; eventually, your training would consist of one hour in meditative equipoise and one hour of post-meditation. Gradually, you decrease the time spent in formal meditation and increase the time in the post-meditative state. With the increase of pliancy, during all your activities of eating, washing, walking, and sleeping you can integrate the mindfulness of meditative equipoise with your post-meditative experience. When you can indivisibly merge the two so that they are unified, you will be able to arrive at high levels of meditation.

In his text *Three Phrases That Strike the Crucial Points*, which synthesizes all the crucial points of the Great Perfection, Garab Dorjé states that there should be no difference between meditative equipoise and the post-meditative state, and no separation between meditation sessions and between-session periods. Meditative equipoise occurs during your formal sessions, and between sessions the mind tends to wander. But if your meditative equipoise can enter into the times between meditation sessions, then meditation persists without distraction. When the mindfulness and introspection of your meditative equipoise enters into your activities, then you've made those two periods inseparable and no difference exists between meditative equipoise and the post-meditative state. For siddhas of the past, if in the beginning they were meditating in a mountain hermitage, and then practiced until they could successfully blend sessions and between-session periods, then, whether they were teaching disciples or wandering about in the town, it made no difference, for they had achieved stability within. If you practice gradually and reach a high level, then this will happen.

At the beginning you should not meditate with your eyes closed, nor should they be wide open; they should be partially open, looking out in front of you. If you familiarize yourself in that way, in the future you will be able to achieve clairvoyance, the "divine eye," the "eye of wisdom," and so forth. If you meditate with your eyes closed, for a while it seems better, but later you will fall toward sleep, because your meditation will not have attained stability. When you achieve quite a good degree of stability, then you will be just like Milarepa, who said,

> When I cover my head with my shawl,
> I see with the distant eye.
> I can clearly see all the worlds.

When you have taken hold of the eternal kingdom with undistracted mindfulness, then it won't make any difference whether your eyes are open or closed. But for us right now, keeping our eyes closed is not the way to practice śamatha.

Now that we have participated in teaching, listening, and practicing meditation, let us dedicate whatever roots of virtue we may have gained so that all sentient beings may achieve enlightenment simultaneously, as one.

It is written in the old textbooks that siddhas of the past have said that if you can maintain the stability of your mind, or samādhi, through the practice of śamatha, for as long as it takes for a louse to crawl from the top of your head to the tip of your nose—that is, for a few minutes—you will be able to purify instantly the negative karma accumulated over eighty thousand eons. This was declared by the Buddha himself. That's an analogy. The siddhas in the old days had a lot of lice, but now we can say this refers to a few minutes.

Translated by Khenpo Namchak Dorji, B. Alan Wallace,
Khenpo Sonam, and Eva Natanya

Part II

Pith Instructions for Aspiring Contemplatives in the Twenty-First Century

1. A Lamp for Dispelling the Five Obscurations: Pith Instructions for Achieving Śamatha in the Dzokchen Tradition

B. Alan Wallace, in collaboration with Eva Natanya

Homage to the Guru Samantabhadra, Embodiment of all Refuges.

In this degenerate era, cloaked by the darkness of ignorance and delusion
many are those who practice Vajrayāna, including Mahāmudrā and Dzokchen,
but rare are those who achieve the supreme and mundane siddhis.
Many are those who cultivate immeasurable loving-kindness and compassion,
but rare are those who reach the sublime path of the bodhisattvas.
Many are those who practice mindfulness and introspection,
but rare are those who truly achieve śamatha or vipaśyanā.
Since the mind resting in its natural state is the sound basis for the samādhis
of vipaśyanā, bodhicitta, and the Vajrayāna stages of generation and completion,
here I shall share pith instructions for achieving śamatha by a direct method.

View

We are all space-travelers, *ḍākas* and ḍākinīs. As human beings we move through what appears to be objective, physical space. But contemporary physicists are challenging this belief, maintaining instead that the three-dimensional reality we experience is actually a projection of a deeper dimension of reality, some maintaining that the latter is a realm of pure mathematical forms. This resonates with the Abhidharma view of our experienced world, which is called the "desire realm," for it is our desires that motivate us to move through this world. According to the Abhidharma, this dimension of existence emerges as a projection from the subtler, underlying form realm, from which archetypal forms (Skt. *nimitta*) of earth, water, fire, air, and space manifest in the desire realm as physical configurations of solidity, fluidity, heat, motility, and space. At an even deeper level, the form realm is said to emerge from the formless realm, the subtlest dimension of conditioned existence. The domain of reality that we perceive with mental consciousness (consisting of both physical and mental phenomena) is known as the space of phenomena (Skt. *dharmadhātu*), one of the eighteen elements of the phenomenal world. When analyzed ontologically by way of the Madhyamaka view, it is found that just as visual objects do not exist independently of visual perception, and visual perception does not exist independently of visual objects, so are the spaces of phenomena and mental consciousness mutually interdependent. Neither member of the pair, nor any of the remaining subject-object pairs among the eighteen elements, exists by any inherent nature of its own.

Physicists have concluded that space is not a flat field. Some modern theories, like loop quantum gravity theory and string theory, assert that it is rather composed of discrete, minute space quanta, and this parallels a view expressed in the *Kālacakra Tantra* that space is composed of space particles. But this immediately presents a problem if those particles are assumed to be truly existent. For if two adjacent space particles touched, they would merge into one, and that would no longer be the "smallest particle," but if they do not touch and are separated by an absolute vacuum, they could not interact in any way.

According to quantum cosmology, without introducing an observer, time would be frozen and the universe would be static. The universe can evolve and change only when one divides it into two parts: a subjective observer and the rest of the objective universe. Moreover, the wave function of the rest of the objective universe depends on the time measured by an observer. Thus, the nature of the myriad worlds is in the character of what each sentient being encounters every living moment; in actuality, it is neither inside nor outside, but prior to the very notion of a division between the two at all.

While space is believed to consist of quanta, their existence is only nominal—that is, in a manner of speaking—and not objectively real. If space has only a conventional existence, it might seem to be inert and impotent. However, according to modern physics, space has its own energy, called the zero-point energy, which is more primal and ubiquitous than the various forms of energy stored in matter. This energy is present throughout the universe, and some calculations estimate that it has an energy density of more than 10,110 times that of the radiant energy at the center of the sun, which corresponds to a mass density of about 10^{96} kilograms per cubic meter! So the energy of empty space is in fact the most powerful force in the physical universe.

Based on the teachings of the third turning of the wheel of Dharma, which have been corroborated by many accomplished contemplatives who have verifiably recalled their own and others' past-life experiences, Asaṅga affirmed the existence of a subtle continuum of individual mental consciousness called the *substrate consciousness* (Skt. *ālayavijñāna*), which carries over from one lifetime to the next. However, according to Nāgārjuna, while it appears as if this mental continuum truly moves through space in the course of one lifetime as well as multiple lifetimes, this is an illusion. Just as space is unreal, this substrate consciousness has no inherent identity of its own, so what appears to be movement in space is nothing more than a shifting of appearances, as in a magical illusion, or in modern times, a 3D movie.

In the context of Dzokchen, a distinction is made between the substrate (Skt. *ālaya*), in which all past-life memories, habitual propensities, and knowledge are stored, and the substrate consciousness, which is conscious of that substrate. It is into this subtle dimension of consciousness that the human mind repeatedly dissolves when one faints, falls into dreamless sleep, and dies. In those cases, one normally loses consciousness, but one can lucidly experience the substrate consciousness through the practice of śamatha. Moreover, in Dzokchen it is said that all phenomena of the three realms emerge from and dissolve back into one's individual substrate, which in turn has no inherent nature of its own. So instead of there being one objective universe experienced by myriad sentient beings, there is, so to speak, one universe for every sentient being. Yet all of these phenomenal worlds of existence are interrelated with those of others through countless past-life actions, the propensities from which are stored in each being's substrate.

All of the appearances that arise during the waking state, dreaming, and the transitional processes between one life and the next emerge from, are present in, and eventually dissolve back into the space of the substrate. Such is the creative power of the primal space of awareness.

Quantum field theory asserts that all physical phenomena consist of "excitations of the vacuum," much as surface waves in a pond are excitations of the pond's water. The vacuum in itself is shapeless, but it may assume specific shapes, and in so doing, it becomes a physical reality. Based on strong empirical evidence, many cosmologists have concluded that fluctuations in the quantum vacuum triggered the Big Bang. Such is the power of the zero-point energy of physical space, which is itself a projection from the space of the substrate.

Lest we reify either external or internal space, it is important to remember that a central tenet of quantum physics is that prior to and independent of the act of measurement or observation, all physical phenomena exist in a "superposition state," for which their ontological status is indeterminate—neither existent nor nonexistent. Only when a measurement is conducted is the measured phenomenon actualized as existent, relative to that empirical and conceptual system of measurement. Likewise, according to the Madhyamaka view, no phenomenon has any inherent nature of its own, but phenomena come into existence—relative to a cognitive frame of reference—only in dependence upon conceptual designations of them. They are literally conceived into existence.

Through the practice of śamatha, we penetrate through the highly configured, nonphysical human mind, which arises in dependence upon and in correlation with the functioning of a physical human brain, to the subtly configured, nonphysical substrate consciousness, from which this human mind emerges during the process of gestation. Through the practice of vipaśyanā, we penetrate through the substrate to the absolute space of phenomena, the ultimate dharmadhātu, or emptiness. Then, through the Dzokchen practice of cutting through to the original purity of pristine awareness, we penetrate through the substrate consciousness to utterly unconfigured primordial consciousness, or the dharmakāya, which naturally and timelessly illuminates the whole of reality.

When we become vidyādharas, with the direct perception of our own identity as the primordial nonduality of the dharmadhātu and dharmakāya, we perceive all phenomena as empty of inherent nature and as manifesting only as creative displays of primordial consciousness, indivisible from the absolute space of phenomena and permeated by the infinite energy of primordial consciousness (Skt. *jñāna-vāyu*), which is the ultimate source of all other derivative forms of energy. That is the primordial space in which the vidyādharas consciously dwell and through which they travel, and it is they who have fully realized their nature as ḍākas and ḍākinīs.

Meditation

The initial, indispensable preparation for the practices of both śamatha and vipaśyanā is to settle your body, speech, and mind in their natural states. For the body, the optimal meditation posture is to sit cross-legged, with your back straight, and your body relaxed, still, and vigilant. Nevertheless, at first, to learn how to fully settle your body in its natural state, motionlessly rest your body in the *śāvāsana*, like a corpse in a charnel ground, relaxing all the muscles in your body. In this posture there are three kinds of balance to be achieved: (1) relax more and more deeply without losing the initial clarity of your mind; (2) increase the stability of your mind, without losing the sense of ease and relaxation; and (3) enhance the vividness of your awareness without losing your inner stability.

On that basis, to settle the respiration in its natural rhythm and the inner voice of the mind in its natural state of effortless silence, with your eyes open, rest your awareness in the space in front of you while maintaining just a peripheral awareness of the rhythm of the respiration. With each inhalation, focus your attention on the nonconceptual experience of consciousness in the present moment, by which thoughts are naturally blocked, or arrested. With each exhalation, release any thoughts that arise into the space in front of you, thereby subduing the tendency for obsessive conceptualization. This is in accordance with the pith instructions of the Tibetan *yoginī* Machik Labdrön (1055–1149), who was believed to be a reincarnation of Yeshé Tsogyal, the divine partner of Padmasambhava (as quoted by Paṇchen Losang Chökyi Gyaltsen [1570–1662] in his *Highway of the Jinas: A Root Text on Mahāmudrā of the Precious Geden and Kagyü Lineages*):

> Tightly focus, then loosely release.
> There is the mind's place of rest.

In this way, maintain a continuous flow of nonconceptual, clear, and cognizant awareness, while allowing the respiration to flow naturally and effortlessly, thus relaxing your body more and more deeply with each exhalation.

To protect your body-mind system from having too much energy buildup in the upper body, keep in mind Asaṅga's physiological observation: "The movement of inhalation is downward and the movement of exhalation is upward." Once you gain experiential understanding of the referent of this statement, you will know how to maintain balance and stability within your *prāṇa* system, even as the vividness of awareness becomes more and more brilliant.

While being aware of them, do not primarily focus your attention on the tactile sensations correlated with the breath, for you will likely reify them, which may impede the uninhibited flow of the respiration. Allow the breath to flow as effortlessly as possible, so that you are not reinforcing the sense of being an inherently existent agent who is breathing. Make a point of relaxing more and more deeply with each exhalation, then allowing the next inhalation to occur effortlessly. In this way your respiration will gradually settle in its natural rhythm, thus enabling blockages in the flow of prāṇa through your *nāḍis* and cakras to release themselves. As Tertön Lerab Lingpa advises, "Train in calming the movements of your respiration just until you do not notice them, thereby settling your speech in its natural state."

As much as possible, continue to maintain this flow of nonconceptual awareness between sessions, mindfully allowing thoughts to arise, but not identifying with them or letting your awareness fuse with them. In this way, during formal sessions, your breathing will eventually become rhythmic, shallow, and virtually imperceptible, and the inner voice of your mind will come to rest in effortless silence, like a lute on which the strings are cut.

Then you will be ready to devote yourself single-pointedly to settling your mind in its natural state during formal sessions. For this, rest in the sheer clarity and lucidity of your mind—like the early morning sky in autumn, uncontaminated by dust, mist, or darkness. Allow thoughts to arise unimpededly, but without being distracted by them or identifying with them. This itself is a direct path to resting your mind in its natural state and thereby to achieving śamatha.

The first step on this path is to experientially distinguish between the stillness of awareness and the movements of the mind. Then you set out to accomplish the first of the four kinds of mindfulness—single-pointed mindfulness—in which you are continuously and simultaneously aware of this stillness and movement. As you deepen your familiarity with this union of stillness and movement, it becomes increasingly effortless, and the natural power of mindfulness manifests without your needing to observe strenuously as you did before. You thereby achieve the second mindfulness: manifest mindfulness.

If, however, you would prefer to take mindfulness of breathing itself as your path to achieving śamatha within a Dzokchen context, then, once you have simply settled your mind in its natural state in a preliminary way, then you may return to maintaining awareness of the rhythm of the respiration.

Now, especially during the inhalations, begin to recognize the emptiness of the mind—there is only luminosity and cognizance.

Then, once this is well established, especially during the exhalations, begin to realize the emptiness of the body—there is only space with tactile sensations appearing in it, like rainbows in the sky.

Consciousness is co-extensive with space, such that the nature of consciousness is space, and the nature of space is consciousness. (This is the perceivable space of the substrate, not physical space, which no one has ever seen directly.)

The appearances arising in that space are illuminated and known by themselves, so the inner space of the mind and the outer space of the body are actually nondual.

Thus, the actual nature of the mind and the actual nature of the body are indivisible and mutually pervasive.

Once you are at ease with understanding the nonduality of both types of emptiness, you may oscillate between emphasizing the emptiness of the mind (on the inhalations) and the emptiness of the body (on the exhalations) within each cycle of respiration. But the oscillation does not necessarily need to be correlated with every cycle of breath. Rather, establish a rhythm that naturally counteracts both laxity and excitation by alternately intensifying and relaxing the awareness, without that awareness ever losing its object of mindfulness: the rhythm of the respiration. Once the respiration has actually settled in its natural rhythm, the durations of the inhalations and exhalations will be quite brief, so by that time it would not be advisable to alternate between meditating on the emptiness of the mind and the emptiness of the body on every cycle of the respiration. Rather, one will have become so familiar with each that the experience of the emptiness of both the body and mind seamlessly merge as one gradually releases the oscillation.

In this Dzokchen approach to mindfulness of breathing, you effectively settle your mind in its natural state by taking as your path an approximation of the final two of the four modes of mindfulness: mindfulness devoid of mindfulness, corresponding to the substrate, and self-illuminating mindfulness, corresponding to the substrate consciousness. The actual stage of mindfulness devoid of mindfulness occurs once your physical senses have withdrawn into mental awareness, and with a subtle, nonconceptual mode of cognition, you are aware only of the substrate—the space of awareness—without bearing anything else in mind. This is the culmination of releasing your mind into space. The fourth and final phase of mindfulness in the Dzokchen practice of taking the mind as the path occurs when you then invert your awareness in upon itself and directly unveil the innate luminosity of your own substrate consciousness. This is the culmination of focusing your attention on the luminosity and cognizance of awareness itself.

Here, when taking an approximation of these as the path at an earlier stage of practice, you will continue to experience tactile sensations and so on while breathing, but this is because they are apprehended with your coarse mental consciousness, which functions simultaneously with, and temporarily veils, the nonconceptual knowing of the substrate consciousness. But through maintaining awareness of the ever-present vacuity of the substrate, nondual with the substrate consciousness, while still practicing mindfulness of breathing, conceptualization is naturally calmed. Continue with this oscillating inversion and release of attention until you can maintain a continuous flow of mindfulness with no incursion of coarse excitation (that is, excitation in which your attention completely disengages from the object of meditation).

At that point, you can then also release the concept of "duration" of the in- and out-breaths, and simply maintain an ongoing flow of homogenous mindfulness of the whole body of the respiration. Simultaneously, maintain a peripheral awareness of the energetic fluctuations corresponding to the rhythm of the respiration throughout the body. By this time, you can release the oscillation altogether. Eventually, your attention will become so single-pointedly withdrawn from the five sensory domains and focused on the mental domain of substrate / substrate consciousness that thoughts and appearances of the five physical sense fields will subside.

By progressing through the phases of śamatha—with its four modes of mindfulness, beginning with single-pointed mindfulness and then manifest mindfulness—the coarse mind eventually dissolves into the substrate consciousness and all six fields of perceptual experience dissolve into the substrate, which brings you to the third mindfulness, which is devoid of mindfulness in the sense of the coarse mental function that bears something in mind. When you then withdraw your awareness from this empty space of the substrate and invert it upon itself, this results in the fourth mindfulness, self-illuminating mindfulness. Here, the mind authentically rests in its natural state, śamatha is fully achieved, and you gain experiential access to the first dhyāna, or meditative stabilization, in the form realm.

Abiding in this state of samādhi, you simultaneously experience a sense of well-being, luminosity, and nonconceptuality, and your mind is imbued with the five dhyāna factors of (1) single-pointed attention, (2) well-being, (3) the faculty of coarse investigation, (4) joy, and (5) the faculty of subtle analysis. Consequently, from this point onward, for as long as you remain in meditative equipoise, your mind is free of the five obscurations: (1) fixation on the allures of the desire realm, (2) malevolence, (3) laxity and dullness, (4) excitation and anxiety, and (5) afflictive uncertainty. The five dhyāna factors, respectively, have progressively served as antidotes to the five obscurations along the path to śamatha, and now, upon achieving śamatha, they come into their full power.

While progressing through these four modes of mindfulness, the flow of nonconceptual knowing is to be sustained as much as possible between formal meditation sessions, so that the division between meditative equipoise and the post-meditative state begins to dissolve away. In general, the five obscurations are attenuated during periods of samādhi, but the key is to apply their antidotes in a steady flow, day and night, along the path to śamatha.

Through the practice of mindfulness of breathing, you sustain a flow of nonconceptual knowing throughout the entire course of each cycle of the respiration, which leaves no space for the intrusion of concepts. Thus, this śamatha method prepares you in a special way for the nonconceptual knowing of the unconditioned emptiness of inherent existence of the mind and the conditioned luminosity of the wisdom realizing emptiness that must come in vipaśyanā. Upon entering the Dzokchen practice of cutting through, this śamatha method, in turn, will have prepared you for the nonconceptual knowing of the unborn luminosity of pristine awareness and its unconditioned emptiness of inherent existence.

Conduct

Between formal meditation sessions, during the waking and dreaming states, waves of appearances constantly arise to our awareness, and habitually we appropriate them as "I" and "mine," and then reify them, thus planting and replanting the roots of our own suffering. But when we closely apply mindfulness to the various appearances of the body, we see that they are simply appearances with no owner, arising in the space of awareness, and nowhere among or apart from them do we perceive an objectively existent, substantial, physical body. Parallel to the Buddha's statement "The mind is not the mind; the nature of the mind is clear light," it may be said that the body is not the body. The nature of the body, which the Buddha likened to a clot of foam, is space. The same is true of mental appearances, both when we are awake and while dreaming: none of them has an owner, nor do they inherently exist from their own side. So while engaging in various activities off the cushion, "Between sessions, act as an illusory being," as Atiśa advised. You appear, you are a causal agent and are influenced by appearances manifesting to your awareness, but you are not really here. Hence you are an illusory being.

As for all the appearances of your surrounding environment—again, while awake or while dreaming—note that all these appearances, while seeming to be *really over there* in objective space, are in reality empty appearances arising in the space of your awareness: the substrate. This is equally true during the daytime and while dreaming, with the primary difference being that daytime appearances may be intersubjectively experienced by multiple sentient beings, while dream appearances are normally experienced by only one subject: the dreamer. As much as you can, rest your awareness in the intervening space in front of you—for this will help curb the tendency to reify the physical objects appearing in that space—and follow Atiśa's advice, "View all phenomena as dream-like."

The reification of ourselves, other people, and our environment throughout the course of the day and night is sustained by an obsessive, compulsive flow of conceptualization. In order to undermine the delusion of viewing oneself and all other phenomena as inherently existent, between meditation sessions rest as continuously as possible in a flow of perceptual awareness, without superimposing concepts or labels on external or internal appearances. As soon as a thought arises, simply note it, without diverting your attention to its referent and thereby appropriating or thinking it. In this way, thoughts arise and pass of their own accord, without being conflated with or superimposed on perceptual appearances. As Lerab Lingpa counsels in his teachings on resting the mind in its natural state, there arises "a nonconceptual sense that nothing can harm your mind, regardless of whether or not thoughts have ceased." In this way, as Atiśa again advises, "Constantly resort solely to a sense of mental well-being."

2. The Crucial Point of Settling Mental Speech in Its Natural State of Silence by Settling the Respiration in Its Natural Rhythm

B. Alan Wallace and Eva Natanya

In his *Great Treatise on the Stages of the Path to Enlightenment*, when beginning the pith instructions on achieving śamatha, Jé Tsongkhapa describes the seven-point physical posture of Vairocana, and as the eighth point, he writes, "Regarding your respiration, the movement of the in- and out-breath should not be audible, forceful, or agitated. By all means, its outward and inward movement should be imperceptible, ever so gentle, and effortless." After further describing the benefits of an upright, cross-legged posture, he adds, "In this way, at the outset, practice maintaining your body in the eight points of physical conduct just as I have explained. In particular, completely calm the prāṇa of your breathing until it settles in its own place."[174]

Later in the text, when describing the achievement of pliancy, Jé Tsongkhapa cites Ratnākaraśānti's *Pith Instructions on Transcendent Wisdom*:[175]

> Bodhisattvas, dwelling alone in solitude, direct their attention to their intended object. Having silenced mental speech, they

174. Cf. *The Great Treatise on the Stages of the Path to Enlightenment*, vol. 3, 31 (translation modified).

175. Cf. *The Great Treatise on the Stages of the Path to Enlightenment*, vol. 3, 81 (translation modified).

> repeatedly direct their attention to the actual nature of the mind, just as it appears. Until physical and mental pliancy arise, this mental engagement is a facsimile of śamatha, but when they do arise, that is śamatha.

Tsongkhapa later cites Ratnākaraśānti's vital point, "Upon focusing on the very mind that illuminates various appearances, silence mental speech and cultivate śamatha," and explains, "Mental speech is the conceptualization that 'This is this.'"[176]

Keeping in mind these crucial points from Jé Tsongkhapa, what follows is heart advice regarding these words from the Lake-Born Vajra found in phase 7 of *The Vajra Essence*,[177] revealed by Düdjom Lingpa: "In a similar progression, first you arrest and subdue the thoughts aroused by your energy-mind, and then you relax and let thoughts manifest." If one has been practicing śamatha diligently in retreat for some time but finds the stability of attention has still not improved, this is likely because one has not yet fully settled the body and respiration in their natural states. That is, there is the essential step of training the inner voice of the mind to stop talking, stop commenting, stop taking the microphone, which has to happen *before* we are truly ready to "relax and let thoughts manifest." Otherwise, the stories will keep overtaking us before we notice them.

So, first, go back to settling the body in its natural state. This should start in śāvāsana, the corpse position, whether that is a pose you like or not. Just surrender and lie down, since it is so very helpful to start there, and because you will find it a crucial preparation for times of sickness and when dying. In that posture of total ease, it is then essential to establish three kinds of balance: (1) totally relax every muscle in the body, without losing the mental clarity with which you began the session; (2) increase the stillness of the

176. Cf. *The Great Treatise on the Stages of the Path to Enlightenment*, vol. 3, 89 (translation modified).

177. See Düdjom Lingpa, *Düdjom Lingpa's Visions of the Great Perfection*, vol. 3.

body and stability of the mind without losing that sense of ease and relaxation; and (3) gently enhance the vividness of awareness without losing the inner stability.

Having thus settled the body, you are then ready to *rest* the body in its natural state, which means to stay there for longer and longer periods, without letting the three balances diminish in quality, but rather enabling them to deepen. This process takes such thorough attention that the mind will naturally become quite focused if you do it properly and fully. But you are not yet primarily concerned with the mind at this point.

Eventually, you will need to re-establish this same sense of ease, stillness, and vigilance within a properly balanced, upright seated posture. If you are having difficulties finding sustainable stillness in the body in either supine or seated posture, see the section on Asaṅga's method for mindfulness of breathing, below.

Then, for settling the speech in its natural state of effortless silence, there are two alternating steps, corresponding to "arrest and subdue."

Once the body is settled, the first step is to arrest/block/prevent (Tib. *dgag pa*) the arising of thoughts. As Yangthang Rinpoché states, "If you wish to look into the mirror of the actual nature of your mind, do not look outward. Rather, look inward." Likewise, even with the body, if you are looking at tactile sensations, they are "outward"; so simply rest your awareness in the space in front of you and peripherally notice the tactile sensations in your body. Be sure to keep your eyes at least partially open.

As you sense the breath flowing in, arouse and focus awareness on what is already there and of which you are already aware: the unmediated experience of being aware of being aware. This itself nudges aside any thoughts that might intrude. It is like a large man filling a small telephone booth; no one else can get in. This prevents the arising of conceptualization.

Then subdue your thoughts (Tib. *gcun pa*): As you exhale, that is when thoughts creep in very quickly. Deliberately release your awareness into the space in front of you; the thoughts will disperse into space and have no power to continue, just as though there were a strong wind from behind blowing away all the mosquitoes on a windy day—the breeze is stronger than the mosquitoes, so they cannot land on you.

At this point, you are not interested in looking *at* the thoughts and you are not telling them to stop, but according to another analogy, just as when you put your hand on your wallet as a pickpocket reaches out to grab it, just by "staring down the face of appearances" the thoughts cease automatically.

Thus, as you breathe in, by inverting your awareness in upon the sheer luminosity and cognizance of consciousness, you prevent thoughts from arising. As you breathe out, by releasing your awareness into the space in front of you, devoid of thoughts, you immediately subdue any thoughts that might arise so that they do not proliferate. By alternating these processes with each cycle of the breath, you are constantly reminding yourself how to practice at each moment. There isn't time to get carried away. Yet right here you are not explicitly practicing "mindfulness of breathing" either, because the sensations or even the rhythm of the breath are not the primary object of meditation. What you are doing is following the above pith instructions on each inhalation and exhalation while resting in the awareness of awareness, in order to settle the inner speech of the mind in its natural state of effortless silence. That itself is a full-time job.

Now, relax and let thoughts manifest. Only when the internal commentator has been silenced, only then can you allow thoughts to arise of their own accord and not be carried away by them. Then, because the respiration has actually settled in its natural, effortless rhythm, the inner sense of ease is sustained by the gentle flow of the prāṇa. Dwelling in the spaciousness of resting your awareness in the space in front of you, you are ready to develop confidence in increasingly longer periods of steady mindfulness, where thoughts will not disturb the stillness of awareness. Then you will actually have passed the threshold into "single-pointed mindfulness," the first of the four kinds of mindfulness taught by Düdjom Lingpa, in which you are simultaneously aware of the stillness of awareness and the movements of thoughts.

Even at that point, you may have sessions in which you feel as though you have never meditated before. There will be times of drought and flood. This is unpredictable, for progress is not linear. Without hope that the meditation will turn out one way or fear that it will turn out another way, remain in the present moment, and ask yourself, is this the way to achieve śamatha? If the answer is yes, then stop questioning and judging, and simply let it happen. Be satisfied with that and continue with confidence. That is how you achieve śamatha, rather than just hoping for it. We know that māras still showed up even *after* the Buddha's enlightenment, but they always went away disappointed. You can develop such confidence while training along the path.

You will see a clear emptying out of the sense of being the internal commentator, and later, with the second phase of mindfulness, manifest mindfulness, you will not even feel that you possess roaming thoughts; they occur but are not appropriated as your thoughts. Further along, even the sense of being a human being with a past, present, and future is emptied out as you overcome the tendency to appropriate and reify the movements of the mind. At that point, when you take the four empowerments in the context of guru yoga, the "telephone booth" of your body-mind is truly empty, and the guru or yidam can enter. More elegantly, you might say that you have cleared the shrine room and no one is sitting on the cushion.

To offer a further analogy, appropriated thoughts are like pets that live indoors, right where you are—you must constantly take care of them and clean up after their messes; while unappropriated thoughts are like the wildlife outside the retreat hut—they are not yours, but simply live in the vicinity. For the most part, the worst they can do to you is give you a mosquito bite. So, for now, train your mind diligently in settling the inner voice of the mind in natural silence and the respiration in its natural rhythm, so that you can later make stable progress in "taking the mind as the path," or any other śamatha practice.

Asaṅga's Method for Mindfulness of Breathing

For some individuals, especially those with a constitution that is dominant in the elements of fire and air, practicing such a method for arresting and subduing thoughts—or even taking the mind as the path or resting in the awareness of awareness—can catalyze imbalances in the body's system of the five *vāyus* and especially the prāṇa-vāyu. This can manifest in a variety of ways, from general discomfort, to physical shaking, to sudden and sharp exhalations of the breath or spontaneous jolts and twisting motions. This can happen especially if you focus primarily on the nature of space and awareness without remaining sufficiently grounded in the earth and water elements present in the body and without yet having fully and sustainably settled the body and respiration in their natural states. Such disturbances in the prāṇa system—which may have their roots in trauma or other imbalances that were there before you began meditating—can often develop or be revealed only after you have been practicing in retreat for some time. Moreover, these can emerge even when you have been properly following the instructions to rest your awareness in space and *not* to focus primarily on the tactile sensations correlated with the breath, in order not to reify them. Settling the body and respiration in their natural states, in particular, is not always a linear process, and some problems may seem to be catalyzed by the very practices designed to settle the body, speech, and mind in their natural states.

Initially, the proper response for an experienced meditator would be to treat such patterns of pranic movement as a meditative experience, or nyam, in which case you would simply be aware of those movements without appropriating or reifying them. However, if such disturbing patterns of movement persist for weeks or months without releasing themselves, then a different approach is called for. Regarding the practice of resting the mind in its natural state, Lerab Lingpa writes in *The Vital Essence of Primordial Consciousness*, "Excessive, imprisoning constriction of the mind, loss of lucidity due to lassitude, and excessive relaxation resulting in involuntary vocalization and eye movement are faults."[178] Thus, at a certain point, such involuntary movements of the body might, from one perspective, also need to be treated as "a fault," and therefore something that does need a remedy (just as lassitude or excitation does). Insofar as such pranic imbalances do pose an obstacle to one's ability to progress more deeply into the stillness of śamatha (and therefore higher practices as well), one does need to find a way to retrain the system of prāṇa and respiration so that it does not slip into vibrations or jolts as a default mode when resting in awareness. The foundational practice of mindfulness of breathing, whether taken purely as a śamatha practice, or in the vipaśyanā mode of inquiry of the close application of mindfulness to the body, is precisely such a foundational practice that can tangibly heal the body-mind system.

Specifically, the close application of mindfulness to the body may be extremely helpful in such cases. This practice, taught by the Buddha in the *Mahāsatipaṭṭhāna Sutta*, guides you to examine the "factors of arising and dissolution" of whatever is experienced in the body—in this case, the various spasms or vibrations themselves. This close attention to sensations, in a mode of inquiry, is a quite different technique than that of viewing the body from the perspective of space and vast awareness, as taught in a Dzokchen context. But it is a foundational practice, and may help you to notice, moment to moment, aspects of the way your prāṇa system is functioning that you would not be able to see when not paying direct and close attention to it in this way. As in the Buddha's discourse to Bāhiya, "In the tactilely sensed, let there be just the tactilely sensed." There is much that can release simply as a result of one's entering deeply into the experience of the many tactile sensations that arise with the subtle undulations of each breath cycle, no matter how varied the rhythm of the breathing may be.

Just as many psychological problems can release themselves through the practice of taking the mind as the path—simply by noting the arising of

178. B. Alan Wallace, *Open Mind: View and Meditation in the Lineage of Lerab Lingpa* (Somerville, MA: Wisdom Publications, 2017), 32.

mental afflictions, neuroses, and recollections of trauma without identifying with them or reifying them—so can many physical problems stemming from damage to the prāṇa system be healed through such close, mindful awareness of tactile sensations, specifically those associated with the respiration. When offering a classical presentation of "Mindfulness of the Inhalation and Exhalation" in his *Śrāvakabhūmi*, Ārya Asaṅga identifies precisely the types of problems that many practitioners encounter in our modern era:

> There are two kinds of faults with respect to one's exertion in inhalation and exhalation: excessively slack engagement and excessively tight engagement. Due to excessively slack engagement, the lazy mind is either veiled with dullness and drowsiness, or else it is distracted outward. Excessively tight engagement inflicts harm on the body or on the mind. How is the body harmed? By forcefully inhaling and exhaling the breath, imbalanced energies enter the afflicted body, and right at the start they pervade the major and minor limbs, so they are said to be *pervasive*. When those pervasive energies increase, these are said to be *afflictive*, and they produce illnesses in each of the major and minor limbs. That is called *harm to the body*. So how is harm brought about in the mind? With too much force, the mind is overwhelmed by becoming distracted, depressed, or disturbed. In those ways harm is done to the mind.[179]

Ārya Asaṅga begins his presentation by teaching how to count the breaths in various ways. This is a practice that the Tibetan tradition has maintained, but usually only as a preliminary, often counting one or more sets of seven,

179. Asaṅga, *Śrāvakabhūmi*, *Rnal 'byor spyod pa'i sa las nyan thos kyi sa*, *Bstan 'gyur* (*gser bris ma*), vol. 138, 223–46. An earlier version of this translation was published in B. Alan Wallace, *Minding Closely: The Four Applications of Mindfulness* (Boulder, CO: Shambhala Publications, 2021), 321–33.

ten, or twenty-one breaths at the beginning of a session to quiet the voice of the mind. Asaṅga himself acknowledges that "People with sharp faculties and clear minds take no pleasure in the practice of counting. Simply by receiving the instructions on counting, they very quickly comprehend it and are not attracted to it." As an alternative, he gives the core instruction for such individuals:

> By closely applying mindfulness to the object of inhalation and exhalation, they closely attend to, and thus comprehend and recognize, the location, duration, manner, and time of occurrence of the inhalations and exhalations. That is how they train. By devoting yourself to that practice and familiarizing yourself with it many times, physical pliancy and mental pliancy will arise, and upon reaching single-pointedness, you will take delight in the object.

Then, as commentary upon "thorough training by way of the sixteen aspects" along the path of meditation, the fourth of the five paths in the Śrāvakayāna as taught by the Buddha, Asaṅga offers these crucial details for training by way of the first five aspects:

1. Thus it is said, "When the breath is mindfully inhaled, one practices by mindfully noting the inhalation; when the breath is mindfully exhaled, one practices by mindfully noting the exhalation."
2. When focusing on the inhalation and exhalation, if a long inhalation occurs, one practices noting that a long breath is inhaled; if a long exhalation occurs, one practices noting that a long breath is exhaled.
3. When focusing on the interim inhalation and exhalation, if a short breath is inhaled, one practices noting the short inhalation; if a short breath is exhaled, one practices noting the short exhalation. One engages with inhalations and exhalations as being of long duration, while one engages with interim inhalations and

exhalations as being of short duration, so one characterizes and recognizes them accordingly.

By "interim inhalation and exhalation," Asaṅga may be referring to those shorter, partial breaths that can often be experienced in between the longer cycle of a full breath, when it seems as though an extra bit of air needs to be inhaled or released. Nonetheless, since we certainly experience variations in the length of the main part of the breath as well, one can understand this to mean that one maintains constant vigilance to notice the relative duration of each breath, and to notice when, over time, they may become shorter, as the entire system is calmed and one needs less and less air.

4. When one is intent upon and focuses on the passage of inhalations and exhalations through the minute cavities of the pores of the body, one authentically experiences the entire body; when a breath is inhaled, one practices by noting that "I authentically experience the entire body and the breath is inhaled." When one is authentically experiencing the entire body and the breath is exhaled, one practices by noting that "I authentically experience the entire body and the breath is exhaled."

At this stage, one is able to feel the entire body as a single whole, with a broad scope of awareness that encompasses the entire body in its stillness. The awareness is not moved in the slightest by "following" the sensations associated with inhalations or exhalations; rather, one witnesses the subtle movements of prāṇa throughout the body from the vantage point of a much more expansive stillness of awareness. Ideally, this has been the case all along, but at the earlier stages the awareness may find itself moved more often by noticing various sensations, as well as rhythms and sub-rhythms within the breath as it works through blockages in the prāṇa system.

5. When the inhalation and interim inhalation have ceased and there is an absence of inhalation and exhalation, one focuses on this occasion of the absence of inhalation and exhalation. When the exhalation and interim exhalation have ceased, and when the inhalation and interim inhalation have not yet occurred, there is an absence of exhalation and inhalation. When they are absent and one focuses on the occasion presented by their absence, if the breath is inhaled upon having achieved pliancy by utterly refining bodily formations, one practices by noting that, once having utterly refined bodily formations, the breath has been inhaled.

This refers not to the cessation of breathing but rather to the moment at the end of either the inhalation or the exhalation when air is neither moving inward nor outward. It can be a moment of sublime stillness in concentration, and as it naturally gets longer, there is more time to experience the healing of the "bodily formations," or the karmic energies that continuously shape the patterns and behavior of the physical body. Lingering in these moments—by the sheer stillness of attention, and not by "holding the breath"—is what leads to the crucial factor of pliancy, which Asaṅga describes further:

> When, upon achieving pliancy by utterly refining bodily formations, the breath is exhaled, one practices by noting that, once having utterly refined bodily formations, the breath has been exhaled. Moreover, as a result of completely devoting oneself to this practice, familiarizing oneself with it, and practicing it many times, when one senses the harsh inhalations and exhalations that have not already been thoroughly purified, whatever discomforts occur are utterly refined, and when one senses the gentle, thoroughly purified inhalations and exhalations, different kinds of bliss arise.

Thus, just as in the practice of taking the mind as the path—resting in the stillness of awareness while discerningly observing the entire space of the mind and the movements that occur within that space—here one rests in the stillness of awareness and observes the movements correlated with the respiration throughout the entire tactile field of the body. Just as the former practice can be deeply healing for the mind, so may this practice prove to be deeply healing for imbalances occurring within the body, as attested by generations of accomplished yogis.

Düdjom Lingpa, too, seems to make reference to a practice of focusing intently upon the movements of vital energy, or prāṇa, in order to tame them, as stated in his commentary to the *Sharp Vajra of Conscious Awareness Tantra*: "First, since the conceptual mind is like a cripple that rides upon the vital energy—which is like a blind, wild stallion—you should tether its mount with the stake of meditative experience and sustained attention."[180]

For those dealing with problems of excessively intense or active vital energies, it is especially important, as mentioned above in *A Lamp for Dispelling the Five Obscurations*, to keep in mind Asaṅga's statement that "The movement of inhalation is downward and the movement of exhalation is upward." Even while one can feel and potentially be aware of many upward movements of energies in the body during the inhalation, at a certain point it is essential to actively pay attention to the *downward* movement of air and its associated energies when inhaling. Then one may observe the air moving *upward* through the nose and mouth when exhaling, releasing the air and, with it, thoughts into space. This helps to calm and ground the many energies moving in the body, especially when catalyzed by systemic reactions to the environment, emotional upheavals, illnesses, and so on.

One can experiment with deliberately watching the flow of energy correlated with the inhaled air as it moves downward—like a wave of water washing through the interior of the body—and then watching the reverse flow as the energy correlated with the breath gently rises and releases in the

180. See Düdjom Lingpa, *Düdjom Lingpa's Visions of the Great Perfection*, vol. 1.

exhalation. This preliminary stage might be seen more as a method for "settling the body in its natural state" than a śamatha method per se, because the attention must actually move too much at the beginning, in following those many patterns of change, for it to stabilize in the stillness needed for a proper śamatha method. Even for an experienced meditator, however, when there are upheavals in the body, sometimes it is simply not possible to find sustainable stillness of awareness until one has "ridden the waves" of the downward and upward movements of the flow of the respiration for many hours over the course of days or weeks.

Nonetheless, settling the energies by actively watching the downward and upward movements associated with the respiration prepares one for the occasion when one knows one is ready to let the awareness expand once again to encompass the whole body. Then the awareness again remains perfectly still, while observing the sensations throughout the body in a single "gestalt," as it were. One then enters upon a true form of mindfulness of breathing as a method of śamatha.

It is especially important, in this method, to fully unite the nonconceptual mental awareness with the equally nonconceptual flow of tactile sensations, thus leaving no room for conceptualization to incur. One so completely fills the nonconceptual flow of awareness with the continuous rhythm and experience of the tactile sensations arising in the body that thoughts and images disperse of themselves. This, then, is another classical method for settling the speech of the mind in its natural state of effortless silence.

With discerning intelligence, one lays the nonconceptual flow of mindfulness—imbued with introspection, stability, clarity, and vividness—like a blanket upon the bed of the ebb and flow of tactile sensations corresponding to the rhythm of the respiration throughout the entire body, so that there is no "space," so to speak, between the mindfulness and its nonconceptual object. Like the horse whisperer taming the "blind, wild stallion" of the prāṇa, you gently and thoroughly calm all the wandering thoughts of the restless mind, so that a flow of deep, silent rest becomes the new default mode for the body and mind.

Once you have established that flow, you can notice areas of the body where energy starts to intensify, and then you can experiment to see if this soft, gentle breath can soothe that energy before it becomes explosive. Your mindfulness of the sensations is so vigilant that you might even notice when there is going to be a disturbance in the flow of prāṇa before it happens. Your sheer attention will not necessarily stop an involuntary movement from occurring, but as you become more sensitized to when it is about to happen, you can then deliberately relax at the root of the movement, and it may indeed release more gently.

As you allow this complete engagement of mindfulness to descend upon the imageless appearances of tactile sensations, you may also begin to gain insight into the lack of inherent nature of the body *as* a body. That is, you begin to notice that the visual images by which you usually identify "my body" are not present in the tactile sensations, nor are the tactile sensations present in the conceptualized images that are based on bits of various sensory data habitually pieced together to be called "my body." Thus you may take your raw experience of nonconceptual tactile sensations—in which no "body" is to be found anywhere—as an opportunity to recall the view that the body is a mere conceptual designation, empty of inherent existence. Furthermore, you will recognize that tactile sensations themselves are not even physical—they are simply appearances arising in the space of awareness. There is nothing physical there in the direct, nonconceptual experience of the basis of designation for what you call "a body." Thus, focusing single-pointedly on the experience of prāṇa can lead you to realize the nature of the body as being empty, like space.

Likewise, focusing single-pointedly on tactile sensations in the objective field, you do not get caught up in the subjective experience of feelings—pleasant, unpleasant, or neutral—that may be associated with those tactile appearances. Thus you release the mental story associated with whatever is happening in the body. As conceptualization naturally diminishes, this allows the flow of prāṇa (upon which the conceptual mind rides) likewise to soften and become subtler, which in turns soothes and heals the disturbing patterns of movement that may have been arising. Once the energetic system is deeply calmed, you may then, if you wish, continue with the Dzokchen approach to mindfulness of breathing, practicing the oscillation between empty space and awareness, as described above in *A Lamp for Dispelling the Five Obscurations*.

Thus, even if one does not follow Asaṅga's classical method of mindfulness of breathing all the way to its culmination in śamatha (which one may indeed choose to do), it can be a crucial preliminary method to "completely calm the prāṇa of your breathing until it settles in its own place," in preparation for taking the mind as the path or another śamatha method. After all, this is what Jé Tsongkhapa himself set forth as the final attribute of the eight-point posture by which one should properly *begin* any other form of śamatha meditation. So, whether one wishes to practice śamatha with a sign (such as focusing upon a visualized image), a Dzokchen approach to mindfulness of breathing, taking the mind as the path, or śamatha without a sign (culminating in the realization of the empty, actual nature of the mind through vipaśyanā), settling the respiration in its natural state is an indispensable preparation. It is a practice to which one may return again and again as a source of healing for various upheavals of the body and mind, especially while engaged in a long-term retreat designed to actually achieve śamatha and reach the path.

3. Taking Consciousness as the Path: A Synthesis of Pith Instructions from Our Lineage Gurus

B. Alan Wallace, in collaboration with Eva Natanya

"Of [the] ten *kasiṇa* bases, this is the foremost, namely, when one perceives the consciousness *kasiṇa* [i.e., the quintessence of consciousness] above, below, across, undivided, measureless. There are beings who are percipient in such a way. But even for beings who are percipient in such a way there is alteration; there is change. Seeing this thus, [61] bhikkhus, the instructed noble disciple becomes disenchanted with it; being disenchanted, he becomes dispassionate toward the foremost, not to speak of what is inferior."[181]

—Buddha Śākyamuni, *Kosala Sutta, Aṅguttara Nikāya*

"In this way, the mind is not the mind; the nature of the mind is clear light."

—Buddha Śākyamuni, *Aṣṭasāhasrikāprajñāpāramitā Sūtra*, chapter 1

"Examine the character of unborn awareness."[182]

—Atiśa Dīpaṃkara Śrījñāna, *The Seven-Point Mind Training*

181. Bhikku Bodhi, *The Numerical Discourses of the Buddha: A Translation of the Aṅguttara Nikāya* (Somerville, MA: Wisdom Publications, 2012), 1380.

182. Translated in B. Alan Wallace, *The Art of Transforming the Mind*, 243, translation slightly modified.

All of us "space-travelers" are directly or indirectly taking consciousness as our path to śamatha and beyond, to the identification of pristine awareness. In phase 1 of *The Vajra Essence*,[183] the Lake-Born Vajra teaches the practice of "taking the impure mind as the path" as the entryway to the Dzokchen path of cutting through to pristine awareness. This is directly parallel to the practice of "taking the aspect of the mind as the path" as taught in the *Sharp Vajra of Conscious Awareness Tantra* and its commentary, excerpted earlier in this volume. The Lake-Born Vajra describes the culmination of this particular practice for achieving śamatha as follows:

> O Vajra of Mind, the bonds of mindfulness and firmly maintained attention are gradually dissolved by the power of meditative experiences until finally—because the ordinary mind of an ordinary sentient being, as it were, disappears—thoughts go dormant, and roving concepts subside into the space of awareness. You then slip into the blank vacuity of the substrate, in which self, others, and objects disappear. The state that becomes manifest, in which the appearances of self, others, and objects have vanished, and in which there is an inwardly focused grasping to the experiences of vacuity and luminosity, is the *substrate consciousness*. [47]

This description corresponds closely with many other classical descriptions of the achievement of śamatha within the Buddhist tradition, wherein the five physical senses no longer perceive their objects, and the mind is completely focused within a domain of subtle mental consciousness. As Jé Tsongkhapa writes in his *Concise Presentation of the Stages on the Path to Enlightenment*, "Finally, when you settle in meditative equipoise, only the aspects of sheer cognizance, luminosity, and bliss of the mind appear,

183. See Düdjom Lingpa, *Düdjom Lingpa's Visions of the Great Perfection*, vol. 3, for all quotations from *The Vajra Essence*.

without the appearance of the signs of visual form, sound, and so on."[184] In the context of Dzokchen, this subtle dimension of brilliantly lucid, nonconceptual consciousness is simply called the substrate consciousness, but not in the philosophically reified sense typically associated with the Cittamātra school. There is consensus, then, from the Pāli Canon through Asaṅga's *Śrāvakabhūmi*, Kamalaśīla, Tsongkhapa, and many other authoritative sources within the Indian and Tibetan Buddhist tradition, that the achievement of śamatha—as the necessary basis for fully realizing the fruits of vipaśyanā—involves a withdrawal and implosion of the five physical senses. In the Dzokchen and Mahāmudrā traditions, however, if one continues to meditate diligently, one will pass beyond this phase of "an inwardly focused grasping to the experiences of vacuity and luminosity" to a phase where the creative power of consciousness that manifests as outer appearances is once again unimpeded, but in a transformed way, so that one may remain in flawless śamatha with the senses "clear."

In this vein, the Lake-Born Vajra goes on to describe a further stage of practice that is still within the domain of śamatha alone yet is more advanced than taking the impure mind as the path, because the meditator already has the capacity to rest consistently in the substrate and substrate consciousness, undisturbed by even subtle mentation or conceptualization. Here is just a partial account of this phase of meditation, which is not yet explicitly imbued with the wisdom of vipaśyanā, and thus is not yet the actual practice of cutting through to pristine awareness—though one may be very close:

> On the other hand, someone with enthusiastic perseverance may recognize that this is not the authentic path, and by continuing to meditate, all such experiences defiled by clinging to vacuity, or to vacuity and luminosity, are cleared away into the space of awareness, as if you were waking up. Subsequently, outer

184. Wallace, *Balancing the Mind*, 207, translation slightly modified.

> appearances are not impeded, and the inner rope of mindfulness and firmly maintained attention is cut. Then you are not bound by the constraints of good meditation, nor do you fall back to an ordinary state through pernicious ignorance. Rather, ever-present, translucent, luminous consciousness shines through, transcending the conventions of view, meditation, and conduct. Without dichotomizing self and object, such that you can say "this is consciousness" and "this is the object of consciousness," ever-present, self-emergent consciousness is free from clinging to the domain of experiences within mentation.

The Lake-Born Vajra then makes a crucial distinction between experiencing just this ever-present, self-emergent consciousness and actually identifying the ground dharmakāya, which is pristine awareness:

> Even though you practice in order to achieve stability in the profound path of this conscious awareness itself, free of conceptual elaboration, if the dharmakāya, primordial consciousness that is present as the ground of being, is not realized, as soon as you pass away from this life, you will have the power to be propelled to the form and formless realms. [49] But with that alone it is impossible to achieve the omniscient state of buddhahood. Once you have identified this path for the first time, if the dharmakāya—primordial consciousness that is present as the ground—is then identified through the power of intense meditation, this is the path wisdom and the creative power of primordial consciousness.

In a consistent theme, even such a marvelous meditation as flawless śamatha that abides with stability in the profound path of "consciousness awareness itself" is necessary but not sufficient for achieving the actual, liberating path of Dzokchen. For the latter, one must realize the great emptiness of all phenomena and then identify the ground dharmakāya, which completely transcends all extremes of conceptual elaboration.

As tantalizing as it may be to imagine such states of meditation, if one is an ordinary practitioner—and not a highly realized being even before taking birth in this lifetime—one must pass through the preliminary phases step by step. In phase 6 of *The Vajra Essence*, there is a passage that clearly distinguishes a more advanced phase of śamatha practice known as taking consciousness as the path—which "makes manifest unimpeded ordinary consciousness, which is the ground of the mind"—from the beginner's phase of taking the impure mind as the path. In the beginner's phase, "you observe thoughts with the conceptualization that the mind is observing the mind, you observe conceptualization with consciousness, and you seek the path that merely elicits the upheavals of pleasure and pain that are produced when you correct, modify, accept, and reject with cognition and mentation." By taking the impure mind as the path, you purify the mind, gradually subduing the five obscurations, but because you are still observing the movements of the mind dualistically, this elicits outer, inner, and secret upheavals, as mentioned by Düdjom Lingpa in the text "Taking the Aspect of the Mind as the Path," above. When, in phase 1 of *The Vajra Essence*, the bodhisattva Boundless Great Emptiness asks the Lake-Born Vajra why it is necessary to practice such meditation, which often arouses various painful and even frightening meditative experiences and is not sufficient by itself for reaching the path to omniscience, the Lake-Born Vajra responds:

> O Vajra of Mind, when individuals with coarse, dysfunctional minds agitated by conceptualization initially enter this path, by reducing the power of their thoughts, their minds become increasingly still, and they will achieve stability free of forgetfulness. On the other hand, even if people identify conscious awareness but do not continue practicing, they will succumb to the faults of spiritual sloth and distraction. Then, even if they do

practice, due to absent-mindedness they will become lost in endless delusion.

So it is necessary to practice meditation for all these reasons: The mind, which is like a cripple, and vital energy, which is like a blind, wild stallion, are subdued into service by tethering them to the stake of meditative experiences and firmly maintained attention. Once people of dull faculties have established the mind [as primary], they control it with the reins of mindfulness and introspection. Consequently, as a result of their meditative experiences and familiarization, they will have the sense that all subtle and coarse thoughts have vanished. Finally, a state of unstructured consciousness becomes manifest, devoid of anything on which to meditate. Then, when they come upon pristine awareness, the state of great nonmeditation, and their guru points this out, they will not go astray. [46]

For this to occur, first you undergo great struggles in seeking the path; you take the movements of thoughts as the path; and finally, when consciousness settles upon itself, this is identified as the path. Until path pristine awareness, or unstructured consciousness, manifests and rests in itself, due to the arousal of afflictive mentation, you must gradually go through rough experiences such as the ones discussed earlier.

Thus, one first dredges the impure mind from its depths in order to experience the bliss, luminosity, and nonconceptuality of the substrate consciousness directly. This is equivalent to the achievement of śamatha by other methods, whether in the form of śamatha with a sign or śamatha without a sign. Dwelling lucidly in the substrate consciousness alone, however, impedes outer appearances, and does not by itself constitute a path to enlightenment. Nevertheless, śamatha with all five dhyāna factors present is a necessary baseline from which to support the realizations pertaining to any of the Buddhist paths to enlightenment, from the Śrāvakayāna up to the

Dzokchen path as explained by the Lake-Born Vajra in Düdjom Lingpa's pure visions.

Once one has fully achieved śamatha and can thus dwell with ease in the substrate consciousness, if one then perseveres in this meditation while understanding that it must lead beyond itself, eventually, as described above, "all such experiences defiled by clinging to vacuity, or to vacuity and luminosity, are cleared away into the space of awareness, as if you were waking up. Subsequently, outer appearances are not impeded, and the inner rope of mindfulness and firmly maintained attention is cut." In the experience of "ever-present, translucent, luminous consciousness" that ensues, one then has the robust capacity to take consciousness itself as the path, because one has—at least while resting in formal śamatha meditation—transcended the vagaries of the coarse, impure mind. It appears, then, that this more advanced practice of taking consciousness as the path, as described by the Lake-Born Vajra, is closer to practicing and eventually remaining in flawless śamatha without a sign (as described by Karma Chakmé in the context of śamatha alone, not yet imbued with the wisdom of vipaśyanā), while taking the mind as the path is a natural preparation for this, a beginner's method for gradually dissolving the coarse mind into the subtle mind.

Of course, what is known as "śamatha without a sign," or sometimes "śamatha focused on the mind," is a classical method for achieving śamatha for the first time, so it is not as though you have to wait until you have fully achieved śamatha by another means to practice śamatha without a sign. This is the practice in which you rest in the stillness of awareness, ascertaining but not analyzing the sheer luminosity and sheer cognizance of awareness, free of grasping to thoughts regarding the past, present, or future, as described in different ways by both Karma Chakmé and Yangthang Rinpoché within this volume. Moreover, whether one is initially taking the impure mind as the path or eventually taking ever-present consciousness as the path, both of these methods involve settling the mind in its natural state, and an indispensable foundation for this, as I have emphasized before, is to have settled the respiration in its natural rhythm. But this does not mean you must have totally mastered settling the respiration in its natural rhythm before you can begin either of the above two practices, let alone śamatha in general!

Phase 7 of *The Vajra Essence* further comments on the early phases of the path whereby you first arrest and subdue the thoughts aroused by your energy-mind, and then "relax and let thoughts manifest." This is the phase of alternating between concentrating and releasing, whereby you tame the mind and vital energies, which are together likened to a cripple riding upon a blind, wild stallion. Settling the respiration in its natural rhythm thus corresponds to the phase of arresting and subduing thoughts, and a gentle but effective way for doing so is the familiar practice of mindfulness of breathing as a śamatha practice. In the *Mahāsatipaṭṭhāna Sutta* the Buddha explains, "And how, monks, does one abide regarding the body as a body? Here, gone to the forest, or to the root of a tree, or to an empty hut, one sits down, having folded one's legs crosswise, and positions one's body erect. One rests while directing one's mindfulness in front of one, and mindfully, one breathes in, mindfully, one breathes out."

Optimally, sitting with one's legs folded crosswise means sitting in the vajrāsana, or what has come to be known as the full-lotus posture. But for many people, this is not comfortable, as Gyatrul Rinpoché comments in his commentary to *Natural Liberation*:[185]

> Upon learning about the proper posture, with its seven attributes of Vairocana, including folding the legs in the full-lotus position, you may be thinking, "Well, that's not only excruciating, but it's simply impossible for me," or "I have a physical impairment that makes that posture impossible. So does that mean that the meditation is hopeless for me?" The answer is, "No, it is not hopeless." Go ahead and proceed. Have faith, do the best you can, and this can lead to perfectly good results. Don't quit simply because you

185. Padmasambhava, *Natural Liberation: Padmasambhava's Teachings on the Six Bardos*, trans. B. Alan Wallace (Somerville, MA: Wisdom Publications, 2008), 91.

> can't sit in that special posture. . . . In terms of the posture, it is generally best not to meditate lying down if you are prone to laxity and lethargy, because lying down makes you feel like falling asleep.

When I was training in hatha yoga in 1981 under B. K. S. Iyengar, he told me, "You're not ready to meditate until you've mastered the śāvāsana!" This was the culminating āsana of all those he taught, and I surmise that mastery of it also entails having settled both the body in its natural state and the respiration in its natural rhythm. Indeed, as Gyatrul Rinpoché commented, lying in the supine position for sustained periods can be challenging for people who are prone to laxity and lethargy. After all, we habitually associate this posture with spacing out, daydreaming, and falling asleep. But meditating in śāvāsana is a useful skill to develop, even during short sessions. In this posture, resting your body like a corpse in a charnel ground, you can relax all the muscles in your body, and this facilitates your ability to breathe effortlessly, with a deeper and deeper sense of relaxation, thus allowing the respiration to settle in its natural rhythm. This posture of utter ease can also help you to release grasping to the very notion of "having a body" more rapidly than in other postures. The great Dzokchen master Nubchen Sangyé Yeshé, who lived in the ninth and tenth centuries, says the following regarding posture in the context of *atiyoga*, or Dzokchen:[186]

> As for the physical posture, from the yoga of generating [the deity] onward, the body is fashioned as that of a deity, so no posture is specified. Since one is free of any notion of grasping to a body [as a body], there is no definitive posture. Now, suppose

186. Nubchen Sangyé Yeshé (Gnubs chen sang rgyas ye shes), *Sgom gyi gnad gsal bar phye ba bsam gtan mig sgron* (Leh: S. W. Tashigangpa, 1974), 403. (Our translation.) For an alternative translation and analysis of this entire work, see Dylan Esler, *The Lamp for the Eye of Contemplation: The* Samten Migdron *by Nubchen Sangye Yeshe, a 10th-century Tibetan Buddhist Text on Meditation* (New York, NY: Oxford, 2022), section 7.2.1.

> you wonder whether this refutes the cross-legged postures of the lower vehicles. Once you are no longer focusing on a body as a body, those postures are not refuted. If you are not deliberately taking up a posture, whether you are sitting in a cross-legged posture, or lying on your back or lying face down, there is no contradiction. An actual contemplative should do as is comfortable, but not because of laziness.

Moreover—returning to the *Mahāsatipaṭṭhāna Sutta* with the confidence that it is not at all contradictory to Dzokchen—the Buddha's instruction to direct your mindfulness in front of you is crucial, and it clearly indicates that you should practice with your eyes open, resting your awareness in the space in front of you, as taught so often in the Tibetan Buddhist tradition. Then, in the fivefold sequence to achieve śamatha, one (1) mindfully notes the inhalation and exhalation; (2) notes the long in- and out-breaths as long; (3) notes the short, interim in- and out-breaths as short; (4) authentically experiences the whole of the body while breathing in and out; and (5) notes that the formations of the body have been utterly refined while breathing in and out. In the śrāvaka context, authentically experiencing the whole of the body entails viewing it as impermanent, unsatisfying, and neither "I" nor "mine," while in the context of transcendent wisdom, one views it as empty of inherent existence, so the tactile sensations throughout the body are perceived as empty appearances arising in the space of awareness. Through the practice of mindfulness of breathing, during which the respiration settles ever more deeply into its natural rhythm, the formations of the body—namely, the tactile sensations throughout this space—become more and more refined until finally they dissolve into the space of awareness as one's mind dissolves into the substrate consciousness.

Long before that point, when the flow of the breath is rhythmic, shallow (breathing in short, breathing out short), and almost imperceptible, the thoughts aroused by your energy-mind will not be so obsessive and compulsive that you involuntarily appropriate them and can observe them only retrospectively, after your awareness has already been set in motion by them. By now, at least temporarily, the mind has been sufficiently tamed for you to be able to observe thoughts the moment they arise—without ever appropriating or thinking them—thus observing the movements of the mind from the perspective of the stillness of awareness. So, from session to session, I encourage you first to subdue thoughts by settling the respiration in its natural rhythm by means of mindfulness of breathing. Then, when the breathing has settled and the mind is relatively calmed, you may continue in mindfulness of breathing to the full achievement of śamatha, or else you may take either the mind as the path or consciousness as the path (that is, practice śamatha without a sign), as you wish. Even though the substrate consciousness will not become fully manifest until you first achieve śamatha, you may still take an approximation of making ever-present consciousness manifest as the path to actually doing so.

If you do decide to take either the mind or consciousness as the path to śamatha, whereby ever-present consciousness will become fully manifest as a result, the first step is in either case to clearly, experientially identify the nature of the consciousness of the present moment. As Padmasambhava writes in *Natural Liberation*, "Then, while steadily gazing into the space in front of you, without meditating on anything, steadily concentrate your consciousness, without wavering, in the space in front of you. Increase the stillness and then relax again. Occasionally seek out, 'What is that consciousness that is concentrating?' Steadily concentrate again, and then seek it out again. Do that in an alternating fashion."[187]

Consciousness can be identified only by way of its two defining characteristics: luminosity and cognizance. From moment to moment, its luminosity can be recognized by the manner in which it illuminates, or makes manifest, all experiences and appearances, including that of consciousness itself. This recognition is retrospective moment by moment, in that you identify the luminosity of the consciousness of the preceding moment, and

187. Padmasambhava, *Natural Liberation*, 105.

the same is true of recognizing the cognizance of the preceding moment of consciousness. So, in effect, you are continuously "looking in the rear-view mirror" at the previous moment of consciousness, rather than there being any single present moment of consciousness that is directly, reflexively aware of its own luminosity and cognizance. Experientially, however, you do not need to analyze this distinction while practicing śamatha alone, because the main point is to remain free of conceptualization regarding any of the "three times": past, present, or future.

Once you become deeply accustomed to this meditation, however, you may not be satisfied with observing the *effects* of consciousness—the experiences of knowing and perceiving appearances—and you may wish to peer right into the nature of consciousness itself, the consciousness *that* illuminates all appearances and knows all things. After all, we can say that we experience and know things only because we, as sentient beings, are imputed on the basis of individual streams of consciousness. But what is the nature of the consciousness that illuminates and knows? When we seek for the referent of the "consciousness" that has the attributes of luminosity and cognizance, it always eludes us. As in the case of the mind, which the buddhas of the past, present, and future never see, so is consciousness unfindable. That which is unfindable in principle, never witnessed even by the buddhas, cannot be said to exist—but that which makes manifest all appearances and knows all things can hardly be determined not to exist either. So we can only conclude that ultimately, consciousness is neither existent nor nonexistent; it is empty of both conceptual extremes.

To return to the recurrent theme of concentrating your consciousness in the space in front of you, it is important to note that this is not a confined space, like the space inside your room. Rather, during the daytime, it is all the space between you and the appearance of the sun and the clear blue sky, and during the nighttime, it is all the space between you and the night sky and the appearances of the moon, planets, and stars. The "space in front of you" includes all of external space in which physical objects appear. How does this external space relate to the internal space of your mind, in which all thoughts and mental images appear during the daytime and all dreams appear during the nighttime? In *The Vajra Essence*, phase 1, we read how the bodhisattva Boundless Great Emptiness declares his insight to the Lake-Born Vajra:

> The essential nature of my mind is, without doubt, definitely space. During the daytime, earth, water, fire, air, self, others, form, sound, smell, taste, touch, and mental objects proliferate in the domain of space, while the conceptual mind appropriates them. In dream appearances as well, the ground of the mind appears as space, and all physical worlds, their sentient inhabitants, and all sense objects proliferate as before. [29] In future lives, too, the essential nature of the mind appears as space, and in that domain all physical worlds, their sentient inhabitants, and all sense objects appear in the same way: the mind appropriates them, and one is deluded over and over again. Therefore space, self, others, and all sense objects are of one taste—they are certainly not separate. Moreover, it is the luminosity of space itself, and nothing else, that makes appearances manifest. The ground and essential nature of the mind is space itself.

Thus, the conclusion is that external and internal space are indivisible; there is no demarcation between them. The bodhisattva Boundless Great Emptiness clarifies this point further: "While space is not other than its luminosity and luminosity is not other than space, the actual nature of the mind, of the very essence of radiant luminosity, is experienced as self and others by the power of contributing circumstances." It is precisely because there is no inherently existing subjective consciousness in here that is illuminating and knowing appearances over there, that it can be said that appearances are self-appearing and self-knowing. The act of appearing occurs right where the appearance is, within the limitless space of awareness. So appearances do not really exist objectively out there, and consciousness does not really exist subjectively in here either. As we saw in his *Great Commentary to Mingyur Dorjé's Buddhahood in the Palm of Your Hand*, Karma Chakmé cites the *Vairocanābhisambodhi Tantra*:

> Whatever is of the nature of space is of the nature of the mind. Whatever is of the nature of the mind is of the nature of enlightenment. O Vajrapāṇi, thus, the mind and the domain of space and enlightenment are nondual.

When consciousness appropriates thoughts and images pertaining to the ten directions and the three times, it seems to move in conjunction with those roving concepts, but this is an illusion. The substrate consciousness, which pervades the substrate—the space in which all inner and outer appearances arise—illuminates all appearances, but it never merges with them and never really moves, not even from one lifetime to the next. It is in this dimension of consciousness that we seek to rest when taking consciousness as the path. As a preparation for this, the Lake-Born Vajra explains in phase 1 of *The Vajra Essence*, "Remaining still without thinking of anything is called *stillness in the domain of the essential nature*. The various thoughts that move and arise are called *movement*. Not letting any thoughts go by unnoticed, but recognizing them with mindfulness and introspection, is identified as *awareness*." This is exactly the practice of identifying "the triad of stillness, movement, and awareness" that Lama Naljorpa taught to Tsampa Karma before his sealed retreat.

So, the practice of taking the mind as the path, as a seamless route to taking consciousness as the path, is essentially very simple. When you remain still without thinking of anything, you are already resting in the domain of the obscurative essential nature of the mind, which is the substrate consciousness. Continuing in this practice until you are continuously, simultaneously, and effortlessly aware of the stillness of your awareness and the movements of the mind—called *manifest mindfulness*—brings you closer and closer to a direct, naked experience of your own substrate consciousness. When all outer appearances of your environment and all inner mental appearances subside into the substrate, you achieve the third kind of mindfulness, called *mindfulness devoid of mindfulness*. As Boundless Great Emptiness states in phase 1 of *The Vajra Essence*, "Once lucid, clear consciousness has entered the central channel—the domain of pervasive, empty space—when it is directed inward, all appearances and mindsets disappear as they completely dissolve into an ethically unspecified, pervasive vacuity." The final step on this path is inverting your consciousness in upon itself—*self-illuminating mindfulness*—and that is when you will have fully achieved śamatha. At that point, you are actually ready to take ever-present consciousness as the path until your realization of vipaśyanā has progressed to the point where you can establish the actual nature of the ground of being by way of the view. Then you can progress swiftly to the main practice of sustaining the view of the Great Perfection by way of meditation.

Especially for those of you who have been devoting a great deal of time and effort to spending many hours in meditation each day in full-time retreat, as the weeks and months go by, you may wonder how well you are progressing. While it is certainly important to examine whether your practice is authentic, ruminating over comparisons can be a waste of time. As Düdjom Rinpoché writes in his *Extracting the Vital Essence of Accomplishment* regarding the various stages on the path, "These demarcations of meditative experiences and realizations may occur in a normative sequence, without prescribed order, or all at once, according to the specific capacities of different individuals. But at the time of the fruition, there are no differences."[188]

While the "nine stages of mental stillness" of the developmental model may seem orderly and linear in their progression, in reality that may not turn out to be the case for each individual practitioner's experience along the road to śamatha. This unpredictability is all the more evident in terms of the discovery model, in which there are just these four kinds of mindfulness.

188. B. Alan Wallace, *The Vital Essence of Dzogchen*, 12.

Tertön Lerab Lingpa corroborates this point in *The Vital Essence of Primordial Consciousness*:[189]

> Do not contaminate [your practice] with many critical judgments. Do not be impatient with your meditation, and avoid great hopes and fears that your meditation will turn out in one way and not another. At the beginning you should have many daily sessions, each of them of brief duration, and focus well in each one. Whenever you meditate, bear in mind the words 'no distraction and no grasping,' and put this into practice.

It can be helpful during formal sessions and between them to ask yourself, "Am I right now practicing correctly and to the best of my ability?" If the answer is yes, then allow yourself to discard any evaluations of how fast or how well you are progressing. Be satisfied in the knowledge that you are practicing correctly in the present moment, without hope or fear regarding the future outcome of your practice.

The Lake-Born Vajra repeatedly emphasizes that simply taking consciousness as the path, even after having achieved śamatha, does not in itself bring one onto the authentic path of Dzokchen. In phase 6 of *The Vajra Essence* he comments:

> Insofar as this consciousness functions in a way that does not realize the view, outer appearances are reduced to an ethically unspecified state, and since these appearances are still taken to be real, reification is not counteracted. Inwardly, your own body appears to be ethically unspecified, so the fixation of reifying the body is not counteracted. And since both outer and inner appearances are taken to be ethically unspecified and autono-

189. Wallace, *Open Mind*, 32.

mous, you do not transcend the mind, so this is still called the *mind*.

So even if you abide in the culmination of taking consciousness as the path, without yet realizing saṃsāra and nirvāṇa as great emptiness, you still will not have identified pristine awareness or yet reached the Dzokchen path. But the purification of the mind that takes place through traversing the path to śamatha is the immediate prerequisite to first identifying unimpeded conscious awareness, then realizing the empty nature of the mind, and finally to making manifest, as the Lake-Born Vajra says, "the originally pure ground—self-emergent, lucid, clear, nondual primordial consciousness." Once you realize the great emptiness of all phenomena included within saṃsāra and nirvāṇa, then you can identify the "dharmakāya—primordial consciousness that is present as the ground" and this will constitute "the path wisdom and the creative power of primordial consciousness." These are the crucial realizations that enable you to enter and proceed along the authentic path of Dzokchen.

Nonetheless, we must begin where we are. As we have seen, Karma Chakmé concludes his presentation on śamatha with the words, "Once you have cultivated śamatha by itself, then the greater the śamatha, the greater the creative power and fine qualities of vipaśyanā. If śamatha is weak, the power of vipaśyanā will be weak, just as little rain falls from a small cloud, or a small flame burns from a small piece of wood. Therefore, I beg you now to dispense with recitations and other virtuous practices, and do your best to still your mind single-pointedly!" Thus, it is crucial to recognize that the inconceivable transformative power of vipaśyanā will only come once we have gained the stability of flawless śamatha by itself.

What is it that will turn your reading and study of all of these sublime teachings into an irreversible path within your mindstream? Clearly, it may require thousands of hours of practice, and eventually, an uninterrupted flow of single-pointed practice, which is what a "retreat" actually means.

But whether you are preparing for a short-term or a long-term retreat, it is of utmost importance not to allow an ordinary goal-setting state of mind—entangling you in a mesh of hope and fear—to infect your aspiration and intention to come to the culmination of the nine stages of śamatha or the four types of mindfulness, much less to achieve realizations of uncontrived bodhicitta and direct insight into emptiness. These stages of spiritual evolution must arise naturally out of an unshakable intention to emerge from the habitual patterns of saṃsāra and to transform your mindstream—no matter how long it takes—so that you may become a suitable vessel for all the realizations of the path to enlightenment, thus gaining the transcendent, omniscient capacity to be of ultimate service to all sentient beings. So, remain steady, study carefully, practice constantly, and never give up.

List of Oral Commentaries

"The Meaning of the Path of Dharma: A Four-Part Talk" by B. Alan Wallace, given at the Buddhist Society, London, June 2019.
Courtesy of the Buddhist Society and the Meridian Trust.

Commentary to Atiśa's "Blaming Everything on a Single Culprit" and "Cutting the Root of Suffering and Equalizing Excitation and Laxity" by B. Alan Wallace, given at the Vajrayana Institute, Sydney, December 2022.
Courtesy of the Vajrayana Institute, Sydney, Australia.

The full retreat, called "Ancient Wisdom for Modern Times," is available here:

"The Wisdom of Atisha and Knowing Our Minds" by B. Alan Wallace, given at the Center for Contemplative Research in Crestone, Colorado, September 13–20, 2021.
Courtesy of the Santa Barbara Institute for Consciousness Studies.

"Atisha's *Pith Instructions on the Middle Way* and Commentary by Prajñāmoksha" by B. Alan Wallace, given in Santa Barbara, California, September 19–20, 2020.
Courtesy of the Santa Barbara Institute for Consciousness Studies.

"Retreat on Atiśa's Pith Instructions on Theory and Practice" by B. Alan Wallace, given in Santa Barbara, California, November 7–8, 2020 (includes *A Guide to the Two Realities*).
Courtesy of the Santa Barbara Institute for Consciousness Studies.

H. H. the Dalai Lama's commentary to *The Eight-Verse Mind Training* given at the Institute for Higher Tibetan Studies, Mt. Pèlerin, Switzerland, July 1979. B. Alan Wallace is the interpreter.
Courtesy of the Library of Tibetan Works and Archives, Dharamsala, India.

H. H. the Dalai Lama's teaching on Geshé Langri Thangpa's *Eight-Verse Mind Training* given at the Ahoy Arena in Rotterdam, the Netherlands on September 17, 2018.

H. E. Jamyang Dagmo Sakya Dagmola's teaching on Drakpa Gyaltsen's commentary on *Parting from the Four Types of Clinging*, given in Santa Barbara, California, January 2012.
Courtesy of Tara Ling Santa Barbara.

H. H. the Dalai Lama's commentary to *A Shower of Siddhis: Guidance in the View of the Middle Way as a Song of the Four Recollections*, in Zollikon, Switzerland, 1979. B. Alan Wallace is the interpreter.
Courtesy of the Library of Tibetan Works and Archives, Dharamsala, India.

Gyatrul Rinpoche's talk on Karma Chakmé and Mingyur Dorjé, translated by Sangye Khandro, given at the Shambhala Meditation Center of Los Angeles, January 6, 1989.
Courtesy of Shambhala Meditation Center of Los Angeles.

An eight-week retreat on the *Sharp Vajra of Conscious Awareness Tantra* and Düdjom Lingpa's commentary, by B. Alan Wallace, given in Pomaia, Italy, April to May 2018 (from which "Taking the Aspect of the Mind as the Path" is excerpted).
Courtesy of the Santa Barbara Institute for Consciousness Studies.

This is also available from the Wisdom Experience:

Domang Yangthang Rinpoché's commentary on "Sayings of Master Atiśa," given in Sikkim, India, 2015.
Courtesy of Anika Mothersdale.

Lecture 1:

Lecture 2:

Commentary on Domang Yangthang Rinpoché's text *A Summary of the View, Meditation, and Conduct*, by B. Alan Wallace, given in London, 2017.
Courtesy of the Meridian Trust.

Session 1: Session 2:

Documentary on Yangthang Rinpoché:
Domang Yangthang.
Courtesy of Rayonner Films, 2022.

Drupön Lama Karma's "Experiential Instructions on Śamatha," given in Santa Barbara, California, October 19–20, 2019.
Courtesy of the Santa Barbara Institute for Consciousness Studies.

"The Way of Shamatha Retreat" with Alan Wallace given in Sydney, December 2019.
Courtesy of the Vajrayana Institute, Sydney, Australia.

"The Shamatha Trilogy" by B. Alan Wallace, given as part of the 2022 eight-week retreat on *The Vajra Essence* at the Center for Contemplative Research in Crestone, Colorado.
Courtesy of the Santa Barbara Institute for Consciousness Studies.

"Fathom the Mind. Heal the World." An in-person and virtual retreat given by B. Alan Wallace, Eva Natanya, and Anuradha Choudry in Crestone, Colorado, October 1–7, 2022. Days 3 and 4 are on Asaṅga's method for mindfulness of breathing.
Courtesy of the Santa Barbara Institute for Consciousness Studies.

Lama Alan's introduction to the Center for Contemplative Research.
Courtesy of the Center for Contemplative Research.

"Quintessential Shamatha Instructions" by B. Alan Wallace, given as guidance to retreatants at the Center for Contemplative Research in Crestone, Colorado, March 9, 2025.
Courtesy of the Center for Contemplative Research.

Bibliography

Source Texts, in Order of the Translations within This Volume

Atiśa Dīpaṃkara Srījñāna. "Blaming Everything on a Single Culprit" (*Le lan thams cad gcig la gda' ba'i le'u*) and "Cutting the Root of Suffering and Equalizing Excitation and Laxity" (*Sdug bsngal gyi rtsa ba bcad de bying rgod mnyam pa nyid du sgom pa'i le'u*). In *The Collected Works of the Glorious Lord Atiśa, Jo bo rje dpal ldan a ti sha'i gsung 'bum*, 28–32 and 94–100. Compiled and edited by the Paltsek Research Institute for Ancient Tibetan Manuscripts, Dpal brtsegs bod yig dpe rnying zhib 'jug khang. Beijing, China: Krung go'i bod rig pa dpe skrun khang, 2006. (Also consulted: *Bka' gdams glegs bam las btus pa'i chos skor*, 63–67 and 151–59. Specially compiled for The Library of Tibetan Classics. Delhi, India: Institute of Tibetan Classics, Bod kyi gtsug lag zhib dpyod khang, 2005.)

———. *A Guide to the Two Realities. Satyadvayāvatāra. Bden pa gnyis la 'jug pa*. In *Jo bo rje dpal ldan a ti shas mdzad pa'i bden pa gnyis la 'jug pa la sogs pa'i gzhung tshan bzhi, Satyadvayāvātārādigranthacatuṣṭa, Four Treatises—Entering into the Two Truths etc. of Ācārya Dīpaṁkaraśrījñāna*, 49–58. Sarnath, Varanasi: Central Institute of Higher Tibetan Studies, 2000.

———. *Pith Instructions on the Middle Way. Madhyamopadeśa. Dbu ma'i man ngag*. Toh 3929, *Bstan 'gyur* (*sde dge*), vol. 110, 190–91. Also consulted: Atīśa. *Dbu ma'i man ngag ces bya ba. Bstan 'gyur* (*dpe bsdur ma*), Par gzhi dang po, vol. 64, 283–84. Beijing, China: Krung go'i bod rig pa dpe skrun khang, 1994–2008.

Prajñāmokṣa. *Commentary to Pith Instructions on the Middle Way. Madhyamopadeśavṛtti. Dbu ma'i man ngag ces bya ba'i 'grel pa*. Toh 3931, *Bstan 'gyur* (*sde dge*), vol. 110, 232–46. Also consulted: Prajñāmokṣa. *Dbu ma'i man ngag ces bya ba'i 'grel ba. Bstan 'gyur* (*dpe bsdur ma*), Par gzhi dang po, vol. 64, 346–64. Beijing, China: Krung go'i bod rig pa dpe skrun khang, 1994–2008.

Langri Thangpa Dorjé Sengé. *The Eight-Verse Mind Training. Blo sbyong tshig brgyad ma*. Version accessed from https://www.lotsawahouse.org/bo/tibetan-masters/geshe-langri-thangpa/eight-verses-training-mind.

Khenchen Appey Rinpoché Ngakwang Yönten Zangpo. *Meditation Guidance on the Mahāyāna* Parting from the Four Types of Clinging. *Theg pa chen po zhen pa bzhi bral gyi sgom khrid*, 3–4. Kathmandu, Nepal: International Buddhist Academy, 2017.

Mañjuśrī and Sakyapa Masters. *Practical Instructions on Parting from the Four Types of Clinging: Teaching of the Noble Mañjughoṣa and a Succession of Sakya Scholars and Adepts. Zhen pa bzhi bral gyi gdams ngag: rje btsun 'jam dbyangs dang sa skya'i mkhas grub rim byon gyi gsung*, 5, 13–14. Dharamsala, India: Library of Tibetan Works and Archives, 2017.

Tsongkhapa Losang Drakpa. Root Verses from *Guidance in the View of the Middle Way*. Excerpted from *Dbu ma lta ba'i khrid yig*. In *The Collected Works of the Lord, Rje'i gsung 'bum*, vol. *ba*, 741–43, 788 (1–2a, 24b). Printed from the Tashi Lhünpo wood blocks. Dharamsala, India: Sherig Parkhang, c. 1997.

———. *The Synthesis of Practice Spoken by the Noble Mañjughoṣa. Rje btsun 'jam pa'i dbyangs kyis gsungs pa'i nyams len mdor bsdus*. In *The Collected Works of the Lord, Rje'i gsung 'bum*, vol. *kha*, 332–34 (*Bka' 'bum thor bu*, 59b–60b). Printed from the Tashi Lhünpo woodblocks. Dharamsala, India: Sherig Parkhang, c. 1997.

———. *On the Union of Śamatha and Vipaśyanā*. Excerpted from *The* [*Concise Presentation of the*] *Steps of the Path to Enlightenment*. *Byang chub lam gyi rim pa*, also known as *Lam rim chung ngu* or *Lam rim 'bring*. In *The Collected Works of the Lord, Rje'i gsung 'bum*, vol. *pha*, 421–34 (210a4–216b4). Printed from the Tashi Lhünpo woodblocks. Dharamsala, India: Sherig Parkhang, c. 1997.

———. *Garland of Supreme Medicinal Nectar: Questions and Answers. Zhu lan sman mchog bdud rtsi'i phreng ba*. In *The Collected Works of the Lord, Rje'i gsung 'bum*, vol. *ka*, 301–26 (1a–13b). Printed from the Tashi Lhünpo woodblocks. Dharamsala, India: Sherig Parkhang, c. 1997.

Lhodrak Drupchen Namkha Gyaltsen. *Garland of Supreme Medicinal Nectar: Questions and Answers. Zhu lan sman mchog bdud rtsi phreng ba*. In *The Collected Works of Lhodrak Namkha Gyaltsen, Lho brag nam mkha' rgyal mtshan gyi gsung 'bum*, vol. 1, 581–97. Reproduced from a rare manuscript preserved at Orgyan Chöling Monastery in Bumthang. Thimphu, Bhutan: Kunsang Tobgey, Druk Sherig Press, 1985. Also consulted: *Zhu lan sman mchog bdud rtsi phreng ba. Lho brag nam mkha' rgyal mtshan gyi gsung 'bum*, vol. 2, 899–921. Reproduced from a rare manuscript originally preserved in the temple of Thikchi in Lhodrak. Delhi, India: Tshering Dargye, 1972. Further consulted: *Zhu lan sman mchog bdud rtsi'i phreng ba. Lho brag nam mkha' rgyal mtshan gyi gsung 'bum*, vol. 2, 765–83. Lhasa, Tibet: Bod ljongs bod yig dpe rnying dpe skrun khang, 2004.

Longchen Rabjam Drimé Öser. *Golden Garland of Nectar: Questions and Answers. Zhu len bdud rtsi gser phreng*. In *Snying thig ya bzhi, Mkha' 'gro snying tig*, vol. (*waṃ*), 1–34. Reproduced from prints from the A 'dzom chos sgar par khang woodblocks. Delhi, India: Sherab Gyaltsen Lama, 1975.

Losang Kalsang Gyatso, the Seventh Dalai Lama. *A Shower of Siddhis: Guidance in the View of the Middle Way as a Song of the Four Recollections. Dbu ma'i lta khrid dran pa bzhi ldan gyi mgur dbyangs dngos grub char 'bebs.* Version accessed from https://www.lotsawahouse.org/bo/tibetan-masters/seventh-dalai-lama/song-of-four-mindfulnesses.

Karma Chakmé. *Great Commentary to Mingyur Dorjé's Buddhahood in the Palm of Your Hand: Guidance in the Cycle on the Avalokiteśvara Body Maṇḍala, in the Profound Aural Lineage of the Sky Dharma (Namchö) Mind Treasure. Gnam chos thugs kyi gter kha snyan brgyud zab mo thugs rje chen po lus dkyil gyi skor gyi khrid sangs rgyas lag 'chang gi 'grel chen.* In *The Collected Works of Karma Chakmé, Gnas mdo karma chags med gsung 'bum*, vol. 57, 415–69 (chapters 15–16). Nang chen rdzong: Gnas mdo gsang sngags chos 'phel gling gi dpe rnying nyams gso khang, 2010.

Mingyur Dorjé (1645–1667). The root text for Karma Chakmé's commentary is from *Guidance in the Great Perfection called Buddhahood in the Palm of Your Hand, from The Cycle on the Body Maṇḍala in the Profound Aural Lineage of the Sky Dharma (Namchö) Mind Treasure. Gnam chos thugs kyi gter kha snyan brgyud zab mo lus dkyil gyi skor las: rdzogs pa chen po'i khrid sangs rgyas lag 'chang (za). Gnam chos*, vol. 1, 207–209. Paro Kyichu, Bhutan: Dilgo Khyentsey Rinpoché, 1983.

Düdjom Lingpa. *The Essence of Clear Meaning: A Short Commentary on the "Sharp Vajra of Conscious Awareness Tantra." Shes rig rdo rje rnon po'i rgyud kyi 'grel chung don gsal snying po*. Edited by Pema Tashi. In *The Collected Works of the Emanated Great Treasures: The Secret, Profound Treasures of Düdjom Lingpa. Sprul pa'i gter chen bdud 'joms gling pa'i zab gter gsang ba'i chos sde*, vol. 21, 353–61. Thimphu, Bhutan: Lama Kuenzang Wangdue, 2004.

———. *The Essence of Profound Mysteries: Guidance for Revealing One's Own Face as the Nature of Reality, the Great Perfection. Rang bzhin rdzogs pa chen po'i rang zhal mngon du byed pa'i gdams pa zab gsang snying po*. In *The Collected Works of the Emanated Great Treasures: The Secret, Profound Treasures of Düdjom Lingpa*, vol. 16, 361–72. Thimphu, Bhutan: Lama Kuenzang Wangdue, 2004.

Sera Khandro, Kunsang Dekyong Wangmo. *Pith Instructions on Liberation as a Body of Light, The Glorious Guru's Oral Transmission, A Commentary on the Meaning of* Buddhahood Without Meditation: Guidance Along the Swift Path to the Great Transference, from the Dharma Cycle of Mahā-Ati Yoga, *which Upholds the Lineage of the Vital Essence of the Enlightened Mind of Samantabhadra, Set Forth as a Memorandum. Mahā ati yoga'i chos skor las myur lam 'pho ba chen po'i gdams pa ma bsgom sangs rgyas kyi don 'grel dpal ldan bla ma'i zhal lung kun tu bzang po'i thugs bcud brgyud 'dzin 'od skur grol ba'i man ngag brjed byang du bkod pa*. In *The Collected Works of the Emanated Great Treasures: The Secret, Profound Treasures of Düdjom Lingpa*, vol. 21, 476–88. Thimphu, Bhutan: Lama Kuenzang Wangdue, 2004. (The root text for Sera Khandro's commentary, by Düdjom Lingpa, is *Mahā ati yo ga'i zab chos dgongs pa klong rdol las zab gsang rdzogs pa chen po'i yang zab bcud kyi dwangs ma myur lam 'pho ba chen po'i gdams pa ma bsgom sangs rgyas* in *The*

Collected Works of the Emanated Great Treasures: The Secret, Profound Treasures of Düdjom Lingpa, vol. 12, 147–72.)

Domang Yangthang Rinpoché. *A Summary of the View, Meditation, and Conduct. Lta sgom spyod gsum mdor bsdus*, unpublished edition, 1–16.

English-Language References

Amipa, Sherab Gyaltsen. *Waterdrop from the Glorious Sea: A History of the Sakya Tradition of Tibetan Buddhism*. Translated by B. Alan Wallace. Rikon, Switzerland: Tibet Institute, 1976.

Apple, James B. *Jewels of the Middle Way: The Madhyamaka Legacy of Atiśa and His Early Tibetan Followers*. Somerville, MA: Wisdom Publications, 2018.

———. *Atiśa Dīpaṃkara: Illuminator of the Awakened Mind*. Boulder, CO: Shambhala Publications, 2019.

Dudjom Lingpa, Traktung. *A Clear Mirror: The Visionary Autobiography of a Tibetan Master*. Translated by Chönyi Drolma. Rangjung Yeshe Publications, 2011.

Düdjom Lingpa. *Düdjom Lingpa's Visions of the Great Perfection*. Translated by B. Alan Wallace and Eva Natanya. Revised Edition. 3 vols: *Heart of the Great Perfection*, *Buddhahood Without Meditation*, and *The Vajra Essence*. New York, NY: Wisdom Publications, forthcoming.

Gyatrul Rinpoche. *The Generation Stage in Buddhist Tantra*. Translated by Sangye Khandro. Ithaca, NY: Snow Lion Publications, 2005.

Hopkins, Jeffrey, and Kevin Vose. *Tsong-kha-pa's Final Exposition of Wisdom*. Ithaca, NY: Snow Lion Publications, 2008.

Jacoby, Sarah H. *Love and Liberation: Autobiographical Writings of the Tibetan Buddhist Visionary Sera Khandro*. New York, NY: Columbia University Press, 2014.

Jinpa, Thupten. *The Book of Kadam: The Core Texts*. Somerville, MA: Wisdom Publications, 2008.

———. *Essential Mind Training: Tibetan Wisdom for Daily Life*. Somerville, MA: Wisdom Publications, 2011.

———. *Tsongkhapa: A Buddha in the Land of Snows*. Boulder, CO: Shambhala Publications, 2019.

———. *Wisdom of the Kadam Masters*. Somerville, MA: Wisdom Publications, 2012.

Karma Chagmé. *Naked Awareness: Practical Teachings on the Union of Mahāmudrā and Dzogchen*. Commentary by Gyatrul Rinpoché. Translated by B. Alan Wallace. Ithaca, NY: Snow Lion Publications, 2000.

Padmasambhava. *Natural Liberation: Padmasambhava's Teachings on the Six Bardos*. Commentary by Gyatrul Rinpoché. Translated by B. Alan Wallace. Somerville, MA: Wisdom Publications, 2008.

Ricard, Matthieu. *The Life of Shabkar: Autobiography of a Tibetan Yogin*. Boston, MA: Shambhala Publications, 2001.

Sera Khandro Dewai Dorje. *A Dakini's Counsel: Sera Khandro's Spiritual Advice and*

Dzogchen Instructions. Translated by Christina Lee Monson. Boulder, CO: Shambhala Publications, 2024.

Tenzin Gyatso, the Fourteenth Dalai Lama. *Illuminating the Path to Enlightenment: A Commentary on Atisha Dipamkara Shrijnana's* Lamp for the Path to Enlightenment *and Lama Je Tsong Khapa's* Lines of Experience. Translated by Geshe Thupten Jinpa. Long Beach, CA: Thubten Dhargye Ling, 2002. https://www.lamayeshe.com/shop/illuminating-path-enlightenment-ebook.

Thurman, Robert A. F., translator and editor. *The Life and Teachings of Tsong Khapa*. Somerville, MA: Wisdom Publications, 2018.

Tsong kha pa blo bzang grags pa and Joshua W. C. Cutler, editor-in-chief, with the Lamrim Chenmo Translation Committee. *The Great Treatise on the Stages of the Path to Enlightenment*, 3 vols. Ithaca, NY: Snow Lion Publications, 2000, 2002, and 2004.

Wallace, B. Alan. *The Art of Transforming the Mind: A Meditator's Guide to the Tibetan Practice of Lojong*. Boulder, CO: Shambhala Publications, 2022.

———. *Minding Closely: The Four Applications of Mindfulness*. Boulder, CO: Shambhala Publications, 2021.

———. *Open Mind: View and Meditation in the Lineage of Lerab Lingpa*. Edited by Eva Natanya. Somerville, MA: Wisdom Publications, 2017.

———. *The Vital Essence of Dzogchen: A Commentary on Düdjom Rinpoché's Advice for a Mountain Retreat*. Boulder, CO: Shambhala Publications, 2025.

Wallace, B. Alan and Tsong kha pa blo bzang grags pa. *Balancing the Mind: A Tibetan Buddhist Approach to Refining Attention*. Ithaca, NY: Snow Lion Publications, 2005.

Yudron, Gaea. *Stories from the Early Life of Gyatrul Rinpoche*. Ashland, OR: Vimala Publishing, 2022.

Index

A

Abhidhānottara Tantra, 166, 185
Abhidharma, 286
abode
  meditation pitfalls and, 128, 129, 130–31
  mistaken views and, 125
absolute space of phenomena (dharmadhātu), 33n29
  as mind, 188, 191, 249
  never wavering from, 63
  no divisions in, 61–62
  transforming thoughts into, 33–37
  vipaśyanā and, 289
activity, nine kinds of, 251
actual nature of the mind (*cittatā*)
  as the actual continuum, 239n160
  as all buddhas, 186, 192
  as clear light, 120
  and delusion, 191
  as dharmakāya, 185
  indivisible from actual nature of the body, 292
  investigating, 195
  as liberative, 186
  as being like space, 100
  as pure, 166
  as radiant luminosity, 325
  as seed of everything, 193
  mental engagement with, or directed attention to, 162, 297–98
  realization of, encompassing other practices, 181
  realized by śamatha without a sign, 311
actual nature of reality (dharmatā), 12
  appearances arising as, 134
  defined, 33n29
  extinguishing appearances into, 236–37
  inconceivable, 63, 96
  neither one nor many, 41, 42
  necessity of familiarization, 152
  realized in what way, 43–44, 96, 113
  transforming thoughts into, 33
  transitional phase of, 255
Adhyāśayasaṃcodana Sūtra, 153
aggregates
  emptiness and, 94, 108, 109, 177
  reality of mind and, 186
  transcendent wisdom and, 164
Amitābha, 7, 146, 147
analytical meditation, 73–74, 81
  of learned paṇḍitas, 182
  nonconceptuality and, 117–18
  pliancy and, 114
  śamatha and, 103–4, 115, 116
  stillness and, 104
appearances
  asserted as mind, 128
  dependent emergence of, 229–31
  illusory nature of, 295–96
  as light of dharmakāya, 185
  as luminosity of the mind, 183
  luminosity of space and, 325–26
  mistaking pristine awareness for, 122
  primordial consciousness and, 59–60, 62

staring down the face of, 273, 277, 300
subduing the mind that reifies, 217
subsiding of the five physical fields of, 294
view of cutting through and, 234
apprehender and apprehended, freedom from, 58, 183, 234
Ārya Avalokiteśvara Padmajāla Tantra, 155
Ārya Brahmaviśeṣacintiparipṛcchā Sūtra, 180
Āryadeva, 190, 217
ārya, bodhisattva, 3, 11–13, 33n29, 48, 105, 106, 111
āryas, five abodes of, 171
Asaṅga, 116, 287, 290, 299
on mindfulness of breathing, 304–11
Aṣṭasāhasrikāprajñāpāramitā Sūtra, 164, 313
Atiśa, Dīpaṃkara Śrījñāna, xi–xii, xiv, xvi, xxii, 64, 69–70, 80, 89, 113, 149, 296, 313
brief biography of, 3–5
dialogues and, 5–8
Madhyamaka and, 8–11, 16–17
two realities and, 11–15, 41–44
attentional balance, as name of ninth stage of mental stillness, 116
Atyayajñāna Sūtra, 185
autonomy, flawless śamatha and, 169
Avadhūtipa, 3, 9, 33, 36
Avaivartacakra Sūtra, 162
Avalokiteśvara, xii, 7, 8, 45, 50n36, 70, 109, 139, 146, 147, 158, 194–95, 202
Avalokiteśvaravikrīḍita Sūtra, 193
awareness
of awareness, 293, 299, 300, 302
flow of nonconceptual, 290–91
resting in stillness of, 306–8, 309–10, 319
sambhogakāya and, 157
settling in its own nature, 278
stillness, movement and, 157, 205, 259, 269, 277, 326
See also pristine awareness

B

Bari Lotsāwa, 70
Bhadrakarātrī Sūtra, 161–62
Bhāviveka, 9n20, 13–14, 42, 58
blessings
of the actual continuum, 239–40
guru yoga and, 210, 211, 279
bliss
all-pervasive, great, 185
experience of, 116, 205, 216, 252, 318
flawless śamatha and, 169
going astray and, 127, 169, 216
Bodhibhadra, 3, 9
Bodhicaryāvatāra (Śāntideva), 149, 150, 154–55, 176
bodhicitta
generation of, 45, 79–80, 100, 209, 236, 241, 252, 277
importance of, 8, 135, 141, 180
uncontrived, xii, xix, xxii
Bodhipathapradīpa (Atiśa), xxii, 149, 177
Bodhisattvapiṭaka Sūtra, 190
bodhisattvas, path of, 49–50, 87, 285
bodily formations, 307, 322
body
emptiness of mind and, 292–93
involuntary movement of, 302–3, 309–10
mindfulness of, 303, 306, 310, 320, 322
settling in its natural state, 298–99, 302
as space, 292, 295
Book of Kadam, The (Atiśa), 5–6, 7, 10, 16
breath/breathing
cleansing stale winds, 278
counting, 261–64, 275, 304–5
harm to body and mind and, 304
practice of mindfulness of, 221n154, 290–91, 292–94, 295, 302–11, 322–23
prāṇa imbalances and, 302–4, 306, 308–11
riding downward and upward movements of, 290–91, 308–9
settling in its natural rhythm, 290, 297–311, 319–20, 322–23
Tsongkhapa on, 297
buddha nature, xvii, 210, 239n160
Buddha Śākyamuni, 303, 313

visualization of form of, 157–60, 266, 279
Buddhadharma, three aspects of, 79
Buddhahood Without Meditation (Düdjom Lingpa), 206, 209
buddhas
bodily signs and speech of, 38
nature of mind as, 185, 186, 192
paying homage to, 46, 48
Butön Rinchen Drup, 88

C

Candrakīrti, 9, 10, 15, 43, 84, 89, 110, 113, 141, 175
Center for Contemplative Research, xxiii
central channel, vital energies in, 156–57, 198n137, 327
Chögyal Phakpa, 73
circumstances, meditation pitfalls and, 131, 132
Cittamātrins, 59, 128, 182
clairvoyance, 282
clarity
body posture and, 156
resting in sheer, 291
vacuous, wide-open, 214
clear light
compassion of, 120, 122–23
dreams arising as, 273
essential nature of, 120–21
manifest nature of, 121–22
nature of mind as, 47, 55, 183–84, 313
as nature of reality, 96
Clear Mirror, A (Düdjom Lingpa), 201
cognizance
consciousness and, 300, 323–24
luminosity and, 292, 293, 319
Commentary on Bodhicitta, 106, 107
companions
meditation pitfalls and, 128–29
mistaken views and, 125
compassion
all-pervasive, 47, 250
arising of vipaśyanā and, 140
cultivating, 81, 95, 135
great, 49, 140–41, 150
going astray from, 122–23
immeasurable, 8, 25, 38
Mahāyāna path and, 49–50
nirmāṇakāya and, 250
śamatha and, 150
unimpeded, 123, 187
conceptual elaboration
freedom from, 12, 13, 205, 215, 215n149
refuting extremes of, 52
conceptualization
calming the scattering of, 168, 276–77
cutting off from within, 183
as enemy or thief, 58
going beyond, 163, 165–68
as indeterminate, 56–57
śamatha and increased awareness of, 268–70
settling in natural state of silence and, 298–311
transformation of, 32–37
vital energies and, 221
as wisdom of discernment, 104–7, 110–13
See also thoughts
Concise Presentation of the Stages on the Path to Enlightenment, The (Tsongkhapa), xiii, 87, 103–18, 314–15
conduct
in Dzokchen approach to śamatha, 295–96
performed at wrong time, 133–34
pitfalls regarding, 133–35
releasing thoughts and, 253–54
confidence, developing, 301
confined outlook, those with (non-āryas, ordinary people), 14, 42, 42n31, 44, 48, 51, 105, 127n89
consciousness
domain of boundless, 127, 171
eight configurations of, 169, 196, 273
peering into nature of, 324
profundity of, 164
space and, 286, 292
stages of dissolution and, 273–74
subtle continuum of, 287–88
taking, as the path, 313–30

two defining characteristics of, 323–24
corpse position, 298–99, 321
cutting through (trekchö), 149, 206, 289, 295
taking hold of the ground with view of, 233–35
Cycle on the Avalokiteśvara Body Maṇḍala, 146–47

D

Dalai Lama (Fourteenth), xii–xiii, xvii–xviii, 7
Dalai Lama (Seventh), Losang Kalsang Gyatso, xiii, 85–86
brief biography of, 91–92
dark near-attainment, 273–74
dedication prayers, 126, 199, 252, 278, 282
demonic views, 124
dependent relationships
appearing phenomena and, 229–31
emptiness and, 89
meditation upon, 93–94
depression, dispelling, 37–40
designation of names
seeking basis of, 226–31
view of cutting through and, 234
desire realm, 127, 286, 294
Devaputraparipṛcchā Sūtra, 181
Dharma practice
authentic, 135–36
devotion to, 235–36, 250
greatest obstacles to, 136
Dharmadhātustava (Nāgārjuna), 109–10, 193
dharmakāya
arising thoughts and, 123, 254
essential nature and, 248, 249
identifying the ground, 316–17
nature of mind as, 185, 186, 189, 289
space and, 63
stillness and, 157
substrate vs., 252
sustaining attention on, 161
Dharmakīrti, 162–63
Dharmasaṃgīti Sūtra, 150
dhyāna
birth in three realms and, 171
five, factors, xxi, 294, 318
four stages of, 151–52, 170–71
Dignāga, 167
direct crossing over (tögal), xv, 149, 202, 209
common preliminaries and, 235–36
prerequisites for practice of, 233–41
uncommon preliminaries and, 236–41
view of cutting through and, 233–35
direct perception, 59
of emptiness, 14–15, 42, 183
direct view, 124–25
dispersion, faults of, 129, 131–32
dissolution, stages of, 273–74
distractions
abandonment of, 153–54
fully pacifying, 160–61
divine eye, 282
Dorjé Dechen Lingpa, 243
Dorjé Drolö, 202
dreams
lucid, 13
seeing deity in, 143
substrate consciousness and, 273–74
Dromtönpa (Drom), xii, xiv, 5, 6–7, 7n15, 16
Drupön Lama Karma, xviii, xx
brief biography of, 257–60
dualistic appearances, 13
as illusory, 96
primordial consciousness and, 60, 62
See also appearances
Düdjom Lingpa, xv, 209, 298, 300, 308, 317, 327
brief biography of, 201–6
Düdjom Rinpoché Jikdral Yeshé Dorjé, 202, 203
Düdjom Tersar (*The New Treasure Teachings of Düdjom*), 202
Dzokchen (Great Perfection), xiv, xv, 4, 141, 174n126, 202, 280, 315
achieving śamatha in tradition of, 214–21, 285, 289–95
entering path of, 204, 206
guru yoga and, 210–11, 236–41

mode of being of, 235
posture in context of, 321–22
substrate consciousness and, 288–89
view of, 248–50
Dzongter Kunsang Nyima, 203

E

Eight-Verse Mind Training, The (Geshé Langri Thangpa), xii, 16, 67–68
empowerments, 137
receiving four, 236, 239, 252, 301
emptiness
appearances and, 93–94, 96, 229–31
benefits of cultivating wisdom of, 177–82
of body and mind, 292–93
dependent relationships and, 89, 93–94
direct realization of, 14–15, 43, 183
four compelling reasonings for, 52–53
guru yoga and, 210
indivisible with compassion, 49–50
indivisible with luminosity, 122, 123, 127, 249, 278, 279
Mañjuśrī's instructions on, 84–85, 88–89, 93–94, 100
mistaken views of, 121, 124
mistaking pristine awareness for, 122–23
not realized by conceptual or nonconceptual consciousness, 14–15, 42
sixteen kinds of, 14
transcendent wisdom that realizes, 174–77
ultimate reality and, 11–12, 13, 42–44
view of cutting through and, 234
wisdom of discerning analysis and, 106–13
see also actual nature of reality
enlightened representations, meditating on, 157–61
enlightenment
benefiting sentient beings and, 35
nature of mind and, 184, 326
realization of emptiness and, 43
realization of mind and, 189–90
roots of virtue and, 278
three main causes of, 141
total absence of conceptualization as, 164
vajra-like samādhi, 61–62
wisdom of emptiness and, 175
entertainment, abandonment of, 153
Essence of Clear Meaning, The (Düdjom Lingpa), 204
Essence of Profound Mysteries, The: Guidance for Revealing One's Own Face as the Nature of Reality, the Great Perfection (Düdjom Lingpa), 206
essential nature
dharmakāya and, 248, 249
emptiness and, 278
going astray from, 120–21
stillness in domain of, 326
of what is to be abandoned, 216–18
of your own mind, seeking out, 190–99
eternal kingdom, taking hold of, 271, 282
eternalism, 127, 182
ethical discipline, 37, 167–68
wisdom and, 176, 180–81
excitation, 58, 294
freedom from, 117
methods for dispelling fault of, 38–40, 58, 130–31, 159
existence and nonexistence, extremes of, 55, 60, 127
external objects
establishing emptiness of, 182
as mind, 183, 187
See also appearances
extrasensory perception, 149, 150, 170, 255

F

faults, acknowledging, 23–24, 25
five fields of knowledge, 47–48
five poisons, 125, 130, 132
five senses
in flawless śamatha, 169, 169n124
going astray by impeding, 127
mind devoid of, 21–23
subsiding of, 293, 294, 314–15
food and clothing, pitfalls and, 129, 138
form realm, 127, 286, 294
four immeasurables, 8, 25, 26

method for cultivating, 38–39
four revolutions in outlook, 209, 235
fruition, pitfalls regarding, 135

G

Ganden Aural Lineage, xiv
Garab Dorjé, 258, 281
Garland of Supreme Medicinal Nectar: Questions and Answers (Khenchen Lhodrakpa), xiii–xiv, 90, 119–44
gaze
for meditation, 131–32, 156, 266, 282
staring into space in front of you, 290, 296, 299–300, 322, 323, 324–25
generation, stage of, 202, 266, 269
Geshé Chekawa, 16
Geshé Langri Thangpa, xii, 16
Geshé Ngawang Dhargyey, xvi–xvii
Geshé Potowa, 112–13
Godan Khan, 72
good and bad experiences
equal taste of, 249
seeing as delusive appearances, 216–18
Great Commentary to Mingyur Dorje's Buddhahood in the Palm of Your Hand, The (Karma Chakmé), xv, 326
The Analytical Cultivation of Vipaśyanā, 173–99
The Cultivation of Śamatha, 149–72
Great Mother [*Sūtra*], 108–9
Great Presentation of Ati[yoga], The, 238
Great Treatise on the Stages of the Path to Enlightenment, The (Tsongkhapa), 86–87, 297
Guhyasamāja Tantra, 92
Guidance in the View of the Middle Way (Tsongkhapa), xiii, 85–86, 93–94
Guide to the Two Realities, A (Atiśa), 8, 10, 11–15, 17, 41–44, 113
guru
devotion to, 210, 219, 220, 236–37, 240
kindness of, 24–25
supplicating, 95, 278–79
Guru Rinpoché. *See* Padmasambhava
guru yoga, xv, 301
authentic practice of, 210–11, 236–41, 252–53
meditation for, 238–40
Gyatrul Rinpoché, xiv–xv, xviii, 203, 243, 245, 320–21

H

habitual propensities
appearances and, 187
delusion and, 191
sleep and, 273–74
hearing, learning through, 51, 53, 128, 140
Heart Essence of the Ḍākinīs, The, 207
Hevajra Tantra, 179, 237
Hīnayāna path, 49. *See also* Śrāvakayāna path
homage, explanation of elements of, 45–48
hope and fear, abandonment of, 216–17
human birth, precious, 198, 235, 247–48

I

identification, transcendence of, 280
identitylessness
dependent relationships and, 94
meditation on, 81, 182
of person, establishing, 223–26
of phenomena, establishing, 226–31
union of śamatha and vipaśyanā and, 118
vipaśyanā and view of, 103
wisdom of discerning analysis and, 107–10
illusory body, manifesting, 84, 229
impartiality, 25, 38
impermanence, 81, 235, 247
inference, emptiness and, 9n20, 14–15, 42
introspection
meaning of, 275–76
sentry of, 58
See also mindfulness and introspection
investigation and analysis, 169–70, 275. *See also* reasonings
isolation, samādhi and, 164, 167–68
Iyengar, B. K. S., 321

J

Jamyang Khyentsé Chökyi Lodrö, 73

Jetsun Drakpa Gyaltsen, 71
Jewel Garland of Dialogues, The (Atiśa), 5–6, 16
  Blaming Everything on a Single Culprit, 19–26
  Cutting the Root of Suffering and Equalizing Excitation and Laxity, 27–40
Jinpa, Thubten, 6, 16, 89
Jñānagarbha, 13, 14, 51–52, 52n40, 57
joy
  body posture and, 156
  first dhyāna and, 170
  immeasurable, 25, 38

K

Kadam tradition, xii, xiv, 5, 16–17, 89
Kālacakra Mūla Tantra, 162
Kālacakra Tantra, 286
Kamalaśīla, 9, 104, 113, 159
karma
  accumulation of, 125, 130
  laws of, 235–36
Karma Chakmé, xiv–xv, 204–5, 319, 326, 329
  brief biography of, 145–47
Karma Kagyü tradition, 146
Karmapa Karma Rakshi, 145
Karmavajra, 91, 119–44. *See also* Lhodrak Drupchen Namkha Gyaltsen
Kāyatrayastotra, 163
Khenchen Appey Rinpoché, xii, 73
Khenchen Nyima Gyaltsen, 6
Khön Könchok Gyalpo, 69
Khyeuchung Lotsāwa, 201
kindness, recognizing and repaying, 24–25
Kosala Sutta, 313
Kṣitigarbha Sūtra, 180
Kurukullā Tantra, 186
Kuśalamūlasaṃparigraha Sūtra, 152
Kusum Gongdü, 260

L

Lake-Born Vajra, 202, 229, 298, 314, 316, 317–18, 325, 326, 328, 329
Lama Naljorpa Sönam Druktop, 257–60, 269, 326
Lama Umapa Pawo Dorjé, xiii, 84, 85
lamdré tradition, 71, 73
Lamp for Dispelling the Five Obscurations, A, 285–96, 308, 311
Laṅkāvatāra Sūtra, 183
laxity, 58, 294
  freedom from, 117
  methods for dispelling fault of, 38–40, 58, 129–30, 159
Lerab Lingpa, 291, 302, 328
Lhodrak Drupchen Namkha Gyaltsen, xiv, 89–91
life, clinging to this, 75, 77, 78
Longchenpa, 90–91, 202, 243, 278
loving-kindness, 25, 38, 135
Lukdzi Repa, 267–68
luminosity
  appearances as, 183
  consciousness and, 323–24
  experience of, 205, 216, 252, 294, 318
  flawless śamatha and, 169
  indivisible with emptiness, 122, 123, 127, 249, 278, 279
  meditation pitfalls and, 127
  mind and appearance of, 194
  of space, 325
  substrate consciousness and, 214–15, 215n148, 293, 314–15, 318–19

M

Machik Labdrön, 290
Madhyamaka, 280
  Atiśa and, 8–11, 16–17
  compelling reasonings and, 52–53
  phenomenal world and, 286, 289
  Svātantrika and Prāsaṅgika distinctions, 9, 13–14, 84–85, 182
Madhyamakāvatāra (Candrakīrti), 84, 110, 175
Mahāmudrā, xiv, 146, 264, 270, 280
  four yogas of, 215n149, 264–65
mahāmudrā of withdrawal, 162
Mahāmudrātilaka Tantra, 186, 188
Mahāparinirvāṇa Sūtra, 184–85

Mahāprātihāryanirdeśa Sūtra, 153
Mahāsatipaṭṭhāna Sutta, 303, 320, 322
Mahāyāna path, 49–50
  of accumulation, xvi–xvii, xix, xxii, 8
  Middle Way and, 49–50
Mahāyānasūtrālaṃkāra (Maitreya), 48, 150, 163
Mahoṣṇīṣa Sūtra, 178–79
Maitreya, xvi, 47, 48, 80, 143
malevolent beings, nature of, 166–67
manifest mindfulness, 205, 214, 215, 292, 294, 301, 326
manifest nature
  going astray from, 121–22
  as luminous, 123, 278
  sambhogakāya and, 249
Mañjuśrī (Mañjughoṣa), xii, 6, 139, 202
  greatness of, 79–80
  Sakya lineage and, 70, 71, 75, 220
  Tsongkhapa and, xiii, 84–85, 86, 88–89, 93–94, 99–101
Mañjuśrīgarbha, 143
mantra recitation, 140, 165, 269
Mantrayāna, 49
  path of passion and, 136–37
  pitfalls and, 128, 140
  profound methods of, 182–83
Matibhadraśrī, 91, 120–44. *See also* Tsongkhapa, Losang Drakpa
meditation
  brief introduction to, 80–81
  faults of, 58, 129–32
  four pitfalls regarding, 126–33
  instructions on, 250–53
  many short sessions of, 131, 276
  mental afflictions and, 130–33
  mistaken extremes and, 126–28
  pith instructions in Dzokchen tradition, 289–95
  preparation for, 54, 277
  teaching on non-referential, 277–82
  transcendent, 87
meditative equipoise
  mudrā of, 156
  post-meditation and, 252–53, 280–81, 295
  resting in, 62, 117, 151, 167, 250–53, 280, 294–95
  undistracted, 161
  wisdom and, 57
meditative experiences
  classes of, 215–16
  five kinds of, 253
  not grasping at, 128, 252
  pranic imbalances and, 302–3
  of recognizing thoughts, 269–70
  sounds and, 264
memories
  absence of, in flawed śamatha, 169
  reawakening of, 265–66
mental afflictions
  calming of, 156–57
  isolation from, 167–68
  meditation pitfalls of, 125, 130–32
  self-grasping and, 32, 35
  taking, onto the path, 125–26, 131, 132–33
  turning away from, 67
mental engagement
  approximating vipaśyanā, 115
  directed, 274–75
  meditating without, 110–11
  relinquishing, 58, 87, 96
mental speech, settling in natural state of silence, 297–311
merit
  of cultivating transcendent wisdom, 174–75, 177–79
  dedication of, 64, 199, 278
Middle Way
  Atiśa and, 8–11
  freedom from extremes and, 49–50
  two realities and, 11–15, 50
  See also Madhyamaka
Milarepa, 265, 267–68, 271, 282
mind
  clear light nature of, 47, 55, 183–84, 313
  devoid of being any of the five senses, 21–23
  distinguishing qualities of, 275–76
  emptiness of body and, 292–93

enlightenment as full realization of, 189–90
as indeterminate, 55–61
as luminous emptiness, 279–80
malevolent beings and, 166–67
as root of everything, 23–24, 183–90, 193–94
seeking out essential nature of your own, 190–99
settling in its own nature, 278, 291, 319
taking, as the path, 204–5, 213–21, 293, 301, 302, 303–4, 314–19, 326–27
as treasury of mysteries, 192–93
mind training, 4, 16, 67–68
mindfulness, 100, 132
of body, 303, 306, 310, 320, 322
of breathing, 221n154, 263, 292–94, 295, 300, 302–11, 320, 322–23
essential nature of path and, 214–15
faults of stagnant, 219–20
four kinds of, 205, 214–15, 291–92, 293–94, 300–301, 326–28
guarding mind with, 154–55
nonconceptual flow of, 309–10
post-meditative states and, 281
rope of, 58
stages of dissolution and, 273–74
two meanings of, 274–75
mindfulness and introspection
as awareness, 326
important tools of, 58, 274–76, 318
sustaining without distractions, 272–73
third dhyāna and, 170
mindfulness devoid of mindfulness, 205, 214, 215, 293, 294, 327
Mingyur Dorjé, 146–47
miraculous deeds, 134
misconduct
as root of suffering, 27
sickness as broom for, 34–36
modern physics, phenomenal world and, 286–89
modernity, degeneration and, xviii–xix, xx, 285
Mongolia, 72
movement
distinguishing between stillness and, 213, 214, 291–92
experience of, 269–70
nirmāṇakāya and, 157
recognizing, 326
stillness, awareness and, 157, 205, 259, 269, 277, 326
Mūlamadhyamakakārikā (Nāgārjuna), 52

N

Nāgārjuna, 9, 10, 43, 44, 51, 52, 52n40, 60, 84, 89, 106, 107–8, 109–10, 113, 141, 150, 167, 193, 287
Naktso Lotsāwa, 5, 9, 10
Namchö (Sky Dharma) cycle of teachings, 146–47
Nandagarbhāvakrāntinirdeśa Sūtra, 152
Ngok Lekpé Sherab, 6, 10
nihilism, 121, 127, 182
ninefold cleansing of stale winds, 278
nirmāṇakāya
movement and, 157
pristine awareness as, 187, 250
sustaining attention on, 159–60
nirvāṇa
equality with saṃsāra, 234, 249
mind as root of, 189, 193
non-abiding, 49
nonconceptuality
analytical meditation and, 117–18
body posture and, 156
experience of, 205, 216, 252, 294, 318
going astray and, 127
mere, 205, 215
mindfulness and, 309–10
śamatha and, 87, 162, 290, 291, 295
wisdom of discerning analysis and, 105–6, 111–13
nonmeditation
in Dzokchen, 221, 252
among four yogas of Mahāmudrā, 215n149, 264
nonphysical entities, investigation of, 55–61
nothingness, domain of, 127, 171
Nubchen Sangyé Yeshé, 321–22

Nyingma tradition, 69, 146, 204

O

obscurations
  afflictive and cognitive, 13, 42
  five, xx–xxii, 294, 317
  purifying, 252
obscurative reality
  deconstruction and negation of, 53, 54–55
  nature of, 12–14, 41, 43–44
  as one of two realities, 48, 51–52
one taste, 215, 215n149, 218, 230, 249, 264
Orgyen Rinpoché, 194. *See also Padmasambhava*

P

Padmasambhava (Guru Rinpoché), xi, 4, 7, 90–91, 145, 146, 202, 323. *See also* Lake-Born Vajra
Padmavikrīḍita Sūtra, 187
Pancaviṃśatisāhasrikāprajñāpāramitā Sūtra, 177–78
Paṇchen Losang Chökyi Gyaltsen, 290
Paṇḍita Matibhadraśrī, 139. *See also* Matibhadraśrī
paranormal abilities, 151–52
Parting from the Four Types of Clinging (Sachen Kunga Nyingpo), xii, 70–71, 73–74, 75–81
partless particles, 54–55
passion, path of, 136–37
past lives, recalling events from, 265–66
Pegyal Lingpa, 260, 272
Pema Lungtok Gyatso, 206
Pema Tashi, 204
personal deity (yidam), 3, 3n7
  dwelling as, 96
  meditation on form of, 157–61, 274–75
  as nature of mind, 186
  seeing face of, 142–43
personal identity
  identitylessness of, 223–26
  investigating origins of, 224
  manner of clinging to, 223–24
  searching for essential nature of, 224–25
  teaching analogies for appearance of, 225–26
phenomena
  clinging to, 75, 78
  dependent relationships and, 94, 229–31
  emptiness that realizes all, 177
  identitylessness of, 183, 226–31
  investigating referents of, 226–29
  mind as root of all, 189
  two realities and, 51–53
phenomenal world
  eighteen elements of, 286
  in modern physics, view of, 286–89
  substrate consciousness and, 288–89
phowa, 244
Phuchungwa Shönnu Gyaltsen, 6
physical entities, investigation of, 54–61. *See also* external objects
Pitāputrasamāgama Sūtra, 152
pith instructions, 33, 43, 49–50, 79
Pith Instructions on Liberation as a Body of Light (Sera Khandro), 209, 233–41
Pith Instructions on the Middle Way (Atiśa), 8, 10, 15, 17, 113
  commentary to, 45–65
Pith Instructions on Transcendent Wisdom (Ratnākaraśānti), 115, 117, 297–98
pliancy
  respiration and, 305, 307
  śamatha and, 114–15, 281, 297–98
  vipaśyanā and, 114–15
pointing-out instructions, 128, 221
post-meditative states
  meditative equipoise and, 252–53, 280–81, 295
  practices for, 252, 291, 295–96
  transcending distinction between meditation sessions and, 62, 277
posture
  for atiyoga (Dzokchen), 321–22
  for cultivating śamatha, 155–57, 168, 278, 289–90, 320–21
  meditation pitfalls and, 129
  See also gaze
Pradarśanānumatoddeśaparīkṣā, 164–65
praising others, 24, 25

Prajñāmokṣa, xii, 10–11, 17, 64
Prajñāpāramitā Sūtra, 164
Prajñāpāramitāsaṃcayagāthā, 49, 150, 162, 175, 176, 177, 181–82
prāṇa system
  correct posture and, 156
  downward and upward movements in, 290–91, 308–9
  imbalances in, 302–4, 306, 308–11
  maintaining balance within, 221, 291
Prāsaṅgika Madhyamaka, 84–85, 182
pratyekabuddha, 128, 177
preliminaries, xv
  common, 235–36
  uncommon, 236–41
Presentation of Samayas, 237
pride, guru's instructions on, 28–29, 37, 40
primordial consciousness
  actualizing kāya of, 166, 289
  appearances and, 59–60, 62, 122
  creative displays, or creative power, of, 123, 289, 316, 329
  five facets of, 238, 239
  mastering ground and path of, 234–35, 316–17
  nature of mind and, 186, 249
  specific instances of, 61
primordial wisdom (of an ārya), 33n29
  nature of mind and, 184–85
  śamatha and, 152, 163
  ultimate reality found by, 11–12
  wisdom of discerning analysis and, 112
pristine awareness
  as all-pervasive compassion, 249–50
  all phenomena as displays of, 234
  cutting through to, 248–50, 289
  distinguishing between mind and, 252
  domain of, 213
  dream state and, 273–74
  empty essential nature of, 120–21, 248
  great nonmeditation of, 221
  manifest nature of, 121–22, 249
  mistaking, for appearances, 121–22
  mistaking, for emptiness, 122–23
  natural glow of, 121, 122
  path, 318
  referent of the tantras as, 186
  staring down the face of, 277
  thoughts ceasing in, 254
  of the three kāyas, 248–50
  vidyādharas and, 174n126
prostrations, 238

Q

quantum cosmology, 287–89

R

rainbow body, xv, 202, 203, 209
Rangjung Dorjé, 170
Ratnākaraśānti, 5, 10, 115, 117, 297–98
Ratnakūṭa Sūtra, 105, 190
reasonings
  compelling, 52–53
  discerning analysis, 105–13
  investigation of physical and nonphysical entitles, 54–61
  view of transcendences and, 182
Rechungpa, 279, 280
remembering, mindfulness as, 274
Rendawa Shönu Lodrö, 83
respiration. *See* breath/breathing
resurgent engagement, 275–76
rūpakāyas, 62, 63–64

S

Sachen Kunga Nyingpo, xii, 70–71, 75, 79–80
Sakya lineage, 69–74
Sakya Paṇḍita Kunga Gyaltsen, xii, 71–72, 182, 220
samādhi
  called "isolation," 164
  manifesting vajra-like, 61–62
  śamatha and, 150
  of supreme vehicle, 140–41
  thoroughly achieving, 116
Samādhirāja Sūtra, 109, 153–54, 157–58, 163, 266
Sāmaññaphala Sutta, xxi
Samantabhadra, 120, 146, 157, 158, 161
śamatha

analytical meditation and, 103–4, 115, 116
being stuck to nectar of, 271
benefits of cultivating, 80–81, 149–55, 172, 329
birth in three realms and, 127, 168, 169, 171, 216, 219–20
cultivating, by itself, 168–72
defined, xi
experiential instructions on (Drupön Lama Karma), 261–82
falling exclusively into, 127
five obscurations and, xx–xxi, 294, 317
fivefold sequence to achieve, 322
flawed, 168–69, 268n167
flawless, 169–72, 205, 319
importance of, xvii–xviii
increased awareness of thoughts and, 268–70
mindfulness and introspection and, 58, 274–76
mindfulness of breathing and, 261–64, 290–91, 292–94, 295, 302–11
nine stages of mental stillness (nine attentional states), 116, 160–61, 258–59, 268, 327, 330
nonconceptuality and, 87, 162, 290, 291, 295
pith instructions in Dzokchen tradition (B. Alan Wallace), 285, 289–95
pliancy and, 114–15, 281, 297–98, 305, 307
posture for cultivating, 155–57, 168, 278, 289–90, 320–22
reawakening of memories and, 265–66
settling mental speech by way of respiration and, 297–311
stagnant, 219–20, 267–68
substrate consciousness and, 169n124, 205, 214–15, 215n149, 220, 287–89, 326
suitable outer and inner conditions for, xxii–xxiii
sustaining without attachment, 170, 216–18
taking consciousness as the path and, 313–30
taking mind as the path, 204–5, 213–21, 293, 301, 302, 303–4, 314–19, 326–27
teaching on non-referential, 277–82
union with vipaśyanā, 87, 103–14, 115–18, 205–6, 218, 220–21, 329
with a sign, 157–61, 266–68
without a sign, 161–72, 319
samayas, guarding, 136, 137, 138, 241
sambhogakāya
awareness and, 157
manifest nature and, 249
pristine awareness as, 186
sustaining attention on, 160–61
Saṃdhinirmocana Sūtra, 51, 114–15, 162
Saṃdhivyākaraṇa Tantra, 187
Sampuṭa Tantra, 165, 183
saṃsāra
dispelling chronic disease of, 138
equality with nirvāṇa, 234, 249
mind as root of, 189, 193, 194
suffering of, 235
See also three realms
Saṃvarodaya Tantra, 63
Śāntarakṣita, 4, 9, 52n40, 54, 69
Śāntideva, 149, 167
Saptaśatikāprajñāpāramitā Sūtra, 177
Saraha, 167–68, 171–72, 181, 193, 202
Sarasvatī, 84, 138
Śāriputra, 109
Sarvabuddhasamayogaḍākinījālaśambara Nāma Uttara Tantra, 179–80
Sarvatathāgatatattvasaṃgraha Tantra, 178, 190
Śatasāhasrikāprajñāpāramitā Sūtra, 151–52, 163–64, 174, 175–76
Sautrāntikas, 182
season, meditation pitfalls and, 129
Secret Treasury of the Ḍākinīs of the Actual Nature of Reality, The, 207
sectarianism, pitfall of, 126
self-cognizing awareness, 272, 275
self-concerns, clinging to, 75, 77–78

self-emergent, spontaneous effulgence, 265–66
self-grasping
personal identity and, 223–24
relinquishing, 32–37
as root of bondage, 20–21, 32
as root of misconduct, 27–28
self-illuminating mindfulness, 205, 214, 215, 215n148, 293, 294, 327
senses. *See* five senses
sentient beings, benefiting
enlightenment and, 35
mind training and, 67–68
rūpakāyas and, 62, 63–64
Sera Khandro, xv
brief biography of, 206–11
Serlingpa, 9–10, 15, 80
Seven-Point Mind Training, The, 16, 313
Sharp Vajra of Conscious Awareness Tantra, 204, 221, 308
Sherab Gyaltsen Amipa, 71–72
Shower of Siddhis, A: Guidance in the View of the Middle Way as a Song of the Four Recollections (Seventh Dalai Lama), xiii, 85–86
sickness, as spiritual mentor, 34–36
siddhis
achievement of, 165, 285
common and supreme, 140–41
signs
abandonment of, 110–11
engaging with, 108
single-pointed mindfulness, 205, 214, 215, 291–92, 294, 300
single-pointedness, 118, 215n149, 264–65
discerning analysis and, 115
four dhyānas and, 170
śamatha and, 159, 160, 206
striving too hard in practice of, 219–20
six transcendences, wisdom of emptiness and, 87, 175, 176, 178, 179, 180, 182
six yogas, 141
sleep
flawed śamatha as being like deep, 168
stages of dissolution and, 273–74
solitude, remaining in, 100, 153–54, 251
Sonam Deutsen, 203
Song of the Four Recollections (Seventh Dalai Lama), xiii, 95–97
sounds, meditative experiences and, 264
space
consciousness and, 292
domain of boundless, 127
energy of, 287
meditative equipoise as being like, 280
modern view of, 286–88
nature of mind and, 184, 248, 325–26
space of phenomena (dharmadhātu), as one of eighteen elements of phenomenal world, 286
spiritual mentors, not straying from, 218–20
Śrāvakabhūmi (Asaṅga), 116, 304–7
Śrāvakayāna path, 58, 128, 169, 177
extreme of nirvāṇa and, 49
gaze and, 131
mindfulness of body and, 322
mindfulness of breath and, 305–6
Śrī Siṃha, 202
Śrīgupta, 55, 57
stabilizing meditation, 73–74, 81, 104, 182
Stages of Meditation (Kamalaśīla), 104, 105–6, 110–12, 117
stillness
analytical meditation and, 104
dharmakāya and, 157
distinguishing between movement and, 213, 214, 291–92
domain of essential nature and, 326
movement, awareness and, 157, 205, 259, 269, 277, 326
nine stages of mental, 116, 160–61, 258–59, 268, 327, 330
nonconceptuality and, 118
resting in, of awareness, 306–8, 309–10, 319
samādhi of mental, 163–64
settling mind in, 168
substrate
dharmakāya vs., 252

Dzokchen distinction, 288–89
space of, 288
two types of, 215, 215n148, 215n149
substrate consciousness, 169n124
Dzokchen distinction, 288–89
mere nonconceptuality and, 205
sleep and, 273–74
substrate vs., 288
as subtle continuum of mental consciousness, 287–88
taking mind as the path and, 214–15, 220, 293, 326–27
vacuity and luminosity of substrate and, 214–15, 293, 314–15, 318–19
suchness
meditation upon, 103, 104, 105, 111–12
merit of samādhi of, 178
siddhis and, 165
union of śamatha and vipaśyanā and, 117
suffering
cutting root of, 27–37, 165
of saṃsāra, 16, 49, 235
Sukhāvatī, 147
Summary of the View, Meditation, and Conduct, A (Yangthang Rinpoché), xvi, 246, 247–56
Sūtra in High Praise of Realizing the Mind, 189
Sūtra on Generating the Power of Faith, 179
Sūtra on the Complete Blossoming of Great Realization, 178
Synthesis of Practice, The (Tsongkhapa), xiii, 86, 99–101

T

"Taking the Aspect of Mind as the Path" (Düdjom Lingpa), 204, 213–21, 317
Tantra of Complete Non-Abiding, 181
Tantra of Inconceivable Coemergence, 185, 191
Tantra of the Great Perfection, the View that Thoroughly Dispels Ignorance, Primordial Consciousness Perfectly Complete from Its Depths, 188–89
Tantra of the Ocean of Secret Ambrosia, 180, 181
Tantra of the Synthesis of the Mysteries of the Great Compassionate One, 186–87
Tārā, 3, 5, 8, 32
Ten Wheels of Kṣitigarbha Sūtra, 179
thoughts
absence of, in flawed śamatha, 168–69
arising as dharmakāya, 123, 254
arresting and subduing, 299–300, 302, 320
dispelling, 131
experience of recognizing, 269–70
as luminosity, 163
merging many, into one, 262–63
natural lucidity of, 248
releasing, 253–54, 254n163, 280, 290
transforming into absolute space, 32–37
See also conceptualization
three realms
attachment to meditative experiences leading to birth in, 127, 168, 169, 216, 219–20
clinging to, 75, 77, 78
foolish meditation and, 127
four dhyānas and birth in, 171
perfect transcendence of, 175
Tibet (Land of Snows), Vajrapāṇi's predictions for, 139–40, 142
Tilopa, 193–94, 270
Treasury of Mysteries Tantra, 191–93
Trisong Detsen, 4, 69
Tsongkhapa, Losang Drakpa, xiii–xiv, 17, 205, 297, 298, 314
brief biography of, 83–91
Vajrapāṇi on life and legacy of, 139, 142, 143
See also Matibhadraśrī
Tsongkhapa: A Buddha in the Land of Snows (Thubten Jinpa), 89
Tulku Drimé Öser, xv, 207–8, 209
Tulku Natsok Rangdrol, 203
Tulku Pednam, 203
twelve links of independent origination, 19
two realities
Atiśa's explanations of, 41–44, 48
introduction to terminology for, 11–15

as neither one nor different, 50–51
phenomena and, 51–53

U

ultimate reality
nature of, 11–12, 13, 41–44
as one of two realities, 48, 52–53
as sublime authentic wisdom, 52, 52n38
Uttaratantra, 184

V

vacuity
body posture and, 156
experience of, 216
going astray and, 127
substrate/substrate consciousness and, 214–15, 215n148, 293, 314–15, 318–19
See also nonconceptuality
Vaibhāṣikas, 182
Vairocanābhisambodhi Tantra, 62, 165, 166, 183–84, 326
Vajra Essence, The (Düdjom Lingpa), xv, 202–3, 231, 298, 314, 320, 325, 326, 328–29. *See also* Lake-Born Vajra
Vajracatuḥpīṭha Tantra, 186, 188
Vajracchedikā Sūtra, 63
Vajradhara, 157, 161
Vajramālā Tantra, 155, 165–66
Vajrapāṇi (Lord of Mysteries), xiv, 70, 89, 90, 119–44, 202
homage to, 119–20
Vajrapañjara Tantra, 184, 185–86
Vajrapāṇyabhiṣeka Tantra, 166
Vajrasamādhi Sūtra, 180
Vajrasattva, 157, 158, 160, 186
Vajraśekhara Tantra, 166–67
Vajravārāhī, 145, 202, 207
valid cognition, 12–13, 42, 52, 59–61
vase breathing, 221n154, 278
Vasubandhu, 62
vidyādharas, 174, 174n126, 289
Vidyākokila, 3, 9
view
in Dzokchen tradition, 248–50, 286–89
false, of extremists, 189
five pitfalls regarding, 124–26
as primary, 250
that transcends identification, 280
as wisdom of emptiness, 174
Vikramaśīla, 4, 5, 10
Vimalamitra, 243, 253
vipaśyanā
absolute space of phenomena and, 289
achieving partial degree of, 271–72
cultivating transcendent wisdom, 174–82
defined, xi
discerning analysis and, 105–7, 110–13, 115
identitylessness and, 81, 103, 107–10
identitylessness of person and, 223–26
identitylessness of phenomena and, 226–31
mind as root of everything and, 183–90
nonconceptuality and, 87, 105–6, 111–13
pliancy and, 114–15
seeking out essential nature of your own mind and, 190–99
sustaining, as distinct from śamatha, 103
union with śamatha, 87, 103–14, 115–18, 205–6, 220–21, 329
Vajrapāṇi on experience of authentic, 140–41
view of Great Perfection and, 327
Virūpa, 71
visualization practice, 266–67
vital energies
in central channel, 156–57
conceptual mind and, 221
See also prāṇa system
Vital Essence of Dzogchen, The: A Commentary on Düdjom Rinpoché's Advice for a Mountain Retreat (Wallace), 210
Vital Essence of Primordial Consciousness, The (Lerab Lingpa), 302–3, 328

W

well-being, experience of, 170, 294
wisdom
cultivating transcendent, 87, 108–9, 164, 177–82
discerning, as itself indeterminate, 56–57

of discerning analysis, 105–7, 110–13, 114–15
of emptiness, realizing, 174–77
Mahāyāna and, 49–50
meditative equipoise and, 57
śamatha and, 104, 150
seeing with one eye of, 217–18
two divisions of, 173

Y

Yangthang Rinpoché, xvi, 299, 319
brief biography of, 243–46
Yeshé Tsogyal, 7n15, 90, 137n98, 202
Yogācāra, 10, 15

Z

Zangdok Palri, 202

About the Authors

B. Alan Wallace is president of the Santa Barbara Institute for Consciousness Studies as well as of the Center for Contemplative Research. He trained for many years as a monk in Buddhist monasteries in India and Switzerland. He has taught Buddhist theory and practice in Europe and America since 1976 and has served as interpreter for numerous Tibetan scholars and contemplatives, including His Holiness the Dalai Lama.

After graduating summa cum laude from Amherst College, where he studied physics and the philosophy of science, he earned his MA and PhD in Religious Studies at Stanford University. He has edited, translated, authored, and contributed to more than forty books on Tibetan Buddhism, medicine, language, and culture, and the interface between science and religion.

After teaching for four years in the Department of Religious Studies at the University of California, Santa Barbara, he founded the Santa Barbara Institute for Consciousness Studies and later the Center for Contemplative Research. Both organizations focus on the interface between contemplative and scientific ways of exploring the mind and its potentials, and the latter has created a conducive environment for dedicated practitioners to remain in long-term meditation retreat with the aspiration to reach the Mahāyāna path in this lifetime. See www.centerforcontemplativeresearch.org.

EVA NATANYA is a scholar of Indian and Tibetan Buddhism, Christian theology, and comparative religion, and has served in many capacities as a spiritual teacher, translator of Tibetan texts, author, and retreat leader.

Following a nine-year career as a professional ballet dancer with both the New York City Ballet and the Royal Ballet of England, she earned an MA in Christian Systematic Theology at the Graduate Theological Union, and a PhD in Religious Studies from the University of Virginia. Her dissertation examined the complex interactions of Madhyamaka, Yogācāra, and Abhidharma teachings as they underlie the Vajrayāna philosophy of Jé Tsongkhapa. She has spent more than four years in solitary meditation retreat, is the co-founder of the Center for Contemplative Research, and currently serves as a resident teacher at the CCR's Miyo Samten Ling Hermitage in Crestone, Colorado, while continuing her solitary retreat practice.

What to Read Next from Wisdom Publications

Dzokchen
A Commentary on Dudjom Rinpoché's "Illumination of Primordial Wisdom"
B. Alan Wallace

"I highly recommend that those with a connection to the Dzokchen teachings acquire this book and rely upon it to enhance their confidence and growth as they progress along the Dzokchen path." —Dzigar Kongtrul Rinpoche

The Attention Revolution
Unlocking the Power of the Focused Mind
B. Alan Wallace
Foreword by Daniel Goleman

"Indispensable for anyone wanting to understand the mind. A superb, clear set of exercises that will benefit everyone."—Paul Ekman, Professor Emeritus at University of California San Francisco, and author of *Telling Lies* and *Emotions Revealed*

Fathoming the Mind

Inquiry and Insight in Düdjom Lingpa's Vajra Essence

B. Alan Wallace

Fathoming the Mind continues the commentary to Düdjom Lingpa's *Vajra Essence* that appeared in *Stilling the Mind*, daringly contextualizing Buddhist teachings on the Great Perfection as a revolutionary challenge to many contemporary beliefs.

Open Mind

View and Meditation in the Lineage of Lerab Lingpa

B. Alan Wallace

"Tertön Sogyal is celebrated as one of the greatest Tibetan Buddhist teachers in the 20th century. This is a precious book that carries his profound wisdom. Thanks to Alan Wallace for doing such great job in translating it into English. *Open Mind* is a gift to those who have affinity with the way of Dzogchen."—Anam Thubten, author of *The Magic of Awareness*

Natural Liberation

Padmasambhava's Teachings on the Six Bardos

Commentary by Gyatrul Rinpoche

Translated by B. Alan Wallace

"Illuminates the most profound questions about who we are and provides a roadmap for the journey through life, death, and rebirth in great depth and simplicity."—Tulku Thondup

Transcending Time
An Explanation of the Kālacakra Six-Session Guru Yoga
Gen Lamrimpa
Translated by B. Alan Wallace

"With remarkable clarity, Gen Lamrimpa makes the practice accessible to all practitioners. Lama Alan Wallace has done a superb job of translating the text into English. Highly recommended."—*Midwest Book Review*

Stilling the Mind
Shamatha Teachings from Düdjom Lingpa's Vajra Essence
B. Alan Wallace

"A much needed, very welcome book."—Jetsun Khandro Rinpoche

Tibetan Buddhism from the Ground Up
A Practical Approach for Modern Life
B. Alan Wallace

"One of the most readable, accessible, and comprehensive introductions to Tibetan Buddhism."—*Mandala*

About Wisdom Publications

Wisdom Publications is the leading publisher of classic and contemporary Buddhist books and practical works on mindfulness. To learn more about us or to explore our other books, please visit our website at wisdom.org or contact us at the address below.

Wisdom Publications
132 Perry Street
New York, NY 10014 USA

We are a 501(c)(3) organization, and donations in support of our mission are tax deductible.

Wisdom Publications is affiliated with the Foundation for the Preservation of the Mahayana Tradition (FPMT).